FOUR MUSICAL ANGELS

Florentine painter, c.1340-50
Christ Church, Oxford

MODERN MUSICAL SCHOLARSHIP

edited by

EDWARD OLLESON

ORIEL PRESS

STOCKSFIELD

BOSTON   HENLEY   LONDON

working methods of their predecessors. They are by no means reactionary, however. Here too, no doubt as a result of the most recent tools and techniques of research, a new feature is discernible in the striving, more than ever before, for perfection and completeness. This trend is extremely welcome and gives opera research a scope never previously achieved. But it does give rise to a problem which for the older generation did not exist, at least to this degree. The early researchers, of whom those mentioned above represent only a few examples, were not only involved with fundamental investigations in specific subject areas; already, to a greater or lesser extent, there was an inclination towards synthesis. As many comments reveal, this involved making the best of their inevitably incomplete material. They had the courage to draw conclusions — if only because they often did not suspect how incomplete their knowledge really was. For .today's scholars, however, the craving for an obviously still far-off completeness in source-material has often raised questions as to the justification of synthesis, and that not only within the sphere of opera research. I am reminded of Friedrich Blume's warning words in his lecture on contemporary historical research in music delivered at the 1967 Congress in Ljubljana,[9] where he referred to the danger of forfeiting the power to synthesize.

For opera research, however, the danger is insignificant. In the first place, works such as Donald Grout's *Short History of Opera* and others provide examples to the contrary; secondly, as already mentioned above, it is only in the last 25 years that one has been able to speak of opera as an independent research area at all, and it therefore has much more to make up for than most other areas. Consequently, the accumulation of new facts is of primary importance at the moment. Furthermore, most of the pertinent works on special topics — and I do not wish to single out any in particular — show an endeavour towards classification in broader contexts. Recent writings on opera reveal an interweaving of independent yet interrelated specialized studies, among which the most distinguished work projects a sort of partial synthesis. This seems appropriate to present requirements.

Modern opera research, or that of the fourth generation, thus carries its very own stamp. It is a child of its time just as that of the first generation was, and as such it differs sharply from the latter. The historical position of the two generations, however, is comparable: when Kretzschmar writes in the introduction to his *Geschichte der*

Oper that interest in the subject had been hidden by over a century's 'deepest indifference' and had only revived within the last decades, then the same applies, more or less, today — except that in this case it is a question only of a few decades of flagging interest. But something of the feeling of excitement at a new beginning, evident in the words of Schiedermair quoted at the outset of this paper, is also found in the opera research of our own time, although, as has been shown, progress is often combined with tradition.

Translated by CARMEN DEBRYN

NOTES

1. 'Grundprobleme der Operngeschichte', *Bericht über den musikwissenschaftlichen Kongress in Basel 1924*, Leipzig, 1925, pp. 22–35.
2. 'Über den Stand der Operngeschichte', *Bericht über den 2. Kongress der internationalen Musikgesellschaft in Basel 1906*, Leipzig, 1907, pp. 212–16.
3. C. von Winterfeld, *Johannes Gabrieli und sein Zeitalter*, Berlin, 1834; E. Vogel, 'Claudio Monteverdi', *Vierteljahrsschrift für Musikwissenschaft*, iii (1887), 315–450; H. Goldschmidt, *Studien zur Geschichte der italienischen Oper im 17. Jahrhundert*, Leipzig, 1901–4.
4. *Histoire de l'opéra en Europe avant Lully et Scarlatti*, Paris, 1895, p. 23 note.
5. Bulthaupt, *Dramaturgie der Oper*, Leipzig, 1902; Bitter, *Die Reform der Oper durch Gluck und Wagner*, Braunschweig, 1884.
6. *Die Oper*, Berlin, 1913.
7. 'Aus Deutschlands italienischer Zeit', *Jahrbuch der Musikbibliothek Peters für 1901*, Leipzig, 1902, pp. 45–61.
8. *Vierteljahrsschrift für Musikwissenschaft*, viii (1892), 1–76.
9. 'Historische Musikforschung in der Gegenwart', *Report of the Tenth Congress Ljubljana 1967*, Kassel, 1970, pp. 13–25.

MODERN MUSICAL
SCHOLARSHIP

Series Editor Dr. P. W. Kent
© 1978 Board of Management of the Foster & Wills Scholarships
Oxford University, England
First published in 1980
by Oriel Press Ltd (Routledge & Kegan Paul Ltd)
Stocksfield, Northumberland, England NE43 7NA

Set in Plantin
Printed and bound in Great Britain by
Knight & Forster Limited, Leeds

ISBN 0 85362 169 1

IN THE SAME SERIES

FOREWORD

THE OXFORD INTERNATIONAL SYMPOSIA have been in being for five years, and characteristically the deliberations have alternated broadly between the humanities and the sciences year by year. For the first time, there has been an opportunity, happily, for musicology to form the focus of attention for one of the meetings. As on previous occasions, this was held in the inimitable surrounding of Christ Church and included some 30 scholars from different parts of the world. This Symposium, in 1977, was greatly helped by the support given by Professor Denis Arnold, Heather Professor of Music at Oxford and Plenary Chairman of the Symposium, and by Dr. Edward Olleson, who as Oxford Secretary of the proceedings did so much to facilitate the academic arrangements of the meetings.

This Symposium owes very much to the generous financial arrangements provided on this occasion by the Stifterverband für die deutsche Wissenschaft, and most particular thanks are extended for their interest and continued support. In addition, one also recognizes the contributions made to the project, culminating in the production of this volume, by the Kulturabteilung of the German Foreign Office and by the staff (especially Herr F. Eschbach) of the London office of the Deutscher Akademischer Austauschdienst (DAAD).

The year 1977 was one of special regard as it saw the commemoration of 25 years' work in the United Kingdom of the DAAD. In celebration, the Symposium members and their guests joined in a Beethoven recital played by the Allegri String Quartet on a late summer's evening in the exquisitely beautiful Upper Library at Christ Church. It was an altogether memorable occasion.

The Symposium series is held under the auspices of the Board of Management of the Foster and Wills Scholarships of Oxford University, and proceeds from this volume, like its predecessors, are devoted to these scholarships which exist for Anglo-German exchange.

P. W. Kent,
Van Mildert College,
Durham

v

PREFACE

FOR SEVERAL YEARS, thanks to the generosity of German sponsors, Oxford has been able to entertain small groups of distinguished scholars at the International Symposium held in Christ Church each autumn. In 1977 it was the turn of the Faculty of Music to play host to colleagues from Britain, Europe and America.

The aim of the conference was broad rather than narrow. Participants were given the all-embracing theme — too cumbersome to serve as the title of this volume — 'Modern Musicology and the Historical Tradition of Musical Scholarship', with a view to allowing each to talk within his own area of particular interest, and in the hope of encouraging perhaps some degree of cross-pollination between the many different branches of our discipline. And while no small gathering could reflect everything that is going on in musical scholarship today, the five days in Christ Church provided papers on a wide variety of subjects and lively discussion across boundary-lines.

All who took part are indebted to the Board of Management of the Foster and Wills Scholarships, under whose auspices the Symposium took place, and to the Stifterverband für die deutsche Wissenschaft, whose sponsorship made possible the rare luxury of a conference that was international without being impersonal. The Dean and Governing Body of Christ Church allowed us to meet in incomparable surroundings, and the Steward and his staff made everyone at home. All administrative arrangements were looked after by the London office of the German Academic Exchange Service under its Director, Mr. Franz Eschbach, to such effect that even the Oxford Secretary of the Symposium could enjoy the week as a participant, secure in the knowledge that in terms of running the proceedings he was superfluous. Mr. Bruce Allsopp, of the Oriel Press, has been endlessly helpful and patient with his contributors and editor. Finally, acknowledgement must be made of our great debt to Dr. Paul Kent, who has provided so much of the propulsion to the inauguration and continuation of the Symposium series.

Edward Olleson

CONTENTS

Chapter 1

THE PROFESSION OF MUSICAL SCHOLARSHIP

Denis Arnold

AFTER a certain time, academic disciplines begin to feed off themselves. If views have been formed, they can be controverted. If archives have been explored, they can be proved incomplete. Teachers will influence groups of pupils who form so-called schools; and it is probable that there will be opposing schools of thought and technique. Since scholarly activity is to some extent solitary, it encourages introspection, and nothing becomes more fascinating than examining one's own motives and those of one's fellow professionals. Such philosophising and historiography can be sterile. After all, scholars do not usually influence events; they are, rather, observers; and to observe only the onlookers of history is at best an antiquarian pursuit, and at worst the collection of trivia. It is not necessary to follow nineteenth-century attitudes of hero-worship to believe that history is formed by the activist, be he king or revolutionary, or, in our case, the composer or performer. So, for the musicologist to regard musicology should be a passing occupation, something done between the investigation of music and musicians. Nevertheless, kept in its place, thought about the basis of our discipline has its uses, especially for the teacher, whose attitudes — some would say prejudices — affect his disciples who usually have neither the experience nor the capacity to understand them completely. And our profession is by now so flourishing and widely spread that we affect, in one way or another, a large number of people.

The implications of the word 'profession' are, to English ears, ambiguous. One meaning suggests the high calling beyond the simple concept of trade or business, with the practitioner disinterested in the rewards of his calling. But there is another implication: that the professional makes his living by practising his *métier*. In this he is

1

contrasted with the amateur or dilettante, who may have as great an interest but will inevitably lack the skill — and, more important, the necessity to follow the matter to the end, whatever the cost in time and energy. Such distinctions are, of course, artificial, as we know from the sports-field. After all, there is payment in time as well as money; and in musicology, a man of independent income may be just as professional as those who earn their stipend in university or college. Even so, when professional men become organized, when hierarchies have developed, inevitably attitudes change, for better or for worse, and it is in this sense that the profession of musical scholarship has changed during this century — maybe even in the last 50 years.

It may seem strange that the development of such professional attitudes could be for the worse. No one would accept an unorganised medical profession, where it was impossible to discover who was skilful at treating various diseases. Most of us, indeed, prefer to go to an acknowledged 'top man', whose enormous fees and senior hospital post denote his surgical skill. Moreover, none of us would return to nineteenth-century conditions in medicine. Yet in our own discipline this pattern does not necessarily apply. Although we know more than our forbears, although we are, on the whole, better trained in our profession, we may not be able to do any better than they did. We may even do much worse. My own field provides one example. The classic study of Giovanni Gabrieli was written by Karl von Winterfeld in the early 1830s. It is an astonishing piece of work which has not been supplanted by another even after 143 years; and this in what is nowadays a fashionable area of study. If Winterfeld had been professor of musicology at some great university it would still have remained a considerable achievement. But he was far from that. Born in 1784 of a noble family, he studied law at Berlin University and eventually became a civil servant — and a distinguished one. As far as we can discover, his musical training was that of an amateur, and indeed the main influence on his life from this point of view was his membership of the Berlin Singakademie then conducted by Zelter. This was certainly an 'antiquarian' organisation interested in the revival of Bach and Handel, and this no doubt accounts for the fact that when Winterfeld had the opportunity in his late twenties to go on the customary Grand Tour of Italy, he collected music rather than archeological pieces — or rather, he made copies of 'old' music. We possess his notes taken on this tour and they show in some detail what music he looked at. He was both industrious and possessed of flair. He looked at much of the best music of the sixteenth and seventeenth centuries, and although there is little sign in his later writings that he

2

had seen, say, Caccini's *Le nuove musiche,* the breadth of his self-education was to serve him well.

When he settled to his professional life in Breslau, he was fortunate in being able to develop his tastes because of the library of the Klosterbibliothek and the existence of the Königliche Akademische Institut für Kirchenmusik. It was a long time before he produced his Gabrieli study, and how he first came to this subject is not quite clear, since Gabrieli can hardly have seemed at that time the major figure that we now know him to be. Still, it was a fortunate choice. The source material is comparatively restricted. One man can transcribe all the church music, at least (the madrigalian and instrumental works are somewhat more scattered), and Winterfeld did so. Naturally he looked at surrounding material and transcribed some Monteverdi and Schütz. He read papers on the basso continuo and the beginnings of the oratorio to the academy of his own foundation, the Schlesische Gesellschaft für Vaterländische Kultur — and also one on Gabrieli himself. Then came the three-volume study published in 1834.

Much of this story is not really surprising. The tour discovering old music must have seemed the logical thing for a member of Zelter's choir. The transcription of Gabrieli's music does not really present insuperable problems to anyone used to singing sixteenth-century church music, even if actually editing the later music is sometimes difficult because of the bad quality of the sources. It is not surprising that Winterfeld investigated Gabrieli's best pupil, given the central role of Schütz in German music; or Monteverdi, given that composer's notoriety even then, via the views of Martini and Burney. Nor is it surprising that Winterfeld investigated the Venetian historical background in view of the new knowledge of the Italian archives, exemplified by the work of Leopold von Ranke in another field and the situation of Venice in the Austro-German world.

All this was possible for the amateur. What is amazing is the balance of the study, the way it shows the origins of Gabrieli's style in the sixteenth century and the way it leads into the seventeenth; the unerring flair in the choice of the examples in the third volume; and the links between the needs of Venetian society and Gabrieli's music. New investigations in the Venetian archives have revealed fresh facts. A better knowledge of the madrigals and the instrumental music helps to round off the picture. A more detailed understanding of Venetian history and music in general refines the view of Gabrieli's development. Nevertheless, the essentials remain as Winterfeld stated them. When it is considered that there were few editions of any sixteenth-century composer's music, and none of them anything like complete;

only a single study of a great sixteenth-century composer — and that Baini's book on Palestrina, a classic of another kind, no doubt, but no guide to what Winterfeld was attempting; and histories such as Burney's also written on a very different basis, then Winterfeld's work seems a minor miracle.

Single cases make bad law. The remarkable fact about Winterfeld is that he was not alone. Since there were no courses of musicological study, musical scholarship was perforce the province of amateurs. Or rather people who started as amateurs; for frequently they became professionals, at least in the first sense of the word, as I have defined it. At university they generally studied law, like Ambros, or Classics, like Spitta; and it is interesting to see that the German teaching of their disciplines provided a solid basis for work in another field. If one compares the work of these Germans with that of the Italians who by this time were trying to emulate them, it is clear that while north of the Alps serious attempts at music history were being made, in Italy it was antiquarianism that prevailed. The obvious comparison to make is between Winterfeld and Francesco Caffi, also a lawyer and civil servant, whose history of the music at St. Mark's in Venice has also remained a standard work. Caffi's industry in investigating the archives is attested to not only by his book but by the overflowing boxes of his notes now in the Biblioteca Marciana; but when it comes to historical and stylistic method, he is simply not in the same class as his German counterpart. And the same must be said of the similar archival work of Davari, Bertolotti and later Solerti, all of it useful, none of it amounting to the true historical writing of Ambros's *Geschichte der Musik* of the 1860s or the critical analysis shown in Spitta's Bach biography of the following decade.

It is interesting that at this stage true musicians hardly ever enter the scholarly field. Whereas in the late eighteenth and early nineteenth centuries men such as Burney and Forkel were at least moderately skilled performers and in daily touch with music making, for much of the later nineteenth century, scholar and musician were separate human beings. It was in fact only at the end of the century that this changed, with, perhaps surprisingly, Robert Eitner, for bibliography and music do not often go together, and, less surprisingly, Hugo Riemann. Perhaps it should not come as a shock to learn that by the time of his 60th birthday, Riemann's *Festschrift* could list compositions up to Op. 68; but it is amazing to see that these were not by any means trivia, for large symphonic works are included amongst them. His activities as a pianist and piano teacher continued to occupy a large part of his energies until he was well into his 40s, even though in his latter years he was a university professor.

Perhaps the most astonishing thing about Riemann was his fecundity and diligence. In 1909 the list of his works filled 25 pages of small type, some of them brief articles and editions, some enormous enterprises. If much of Riemann's writing proved ephemeral, there remain the solid achievements of the *Musiklexicon* and the *Handbuch der Musikgeschichte;* to which we may add also the foundation of the first university Collegium Musicum at Leipzig in 1908. It all seems to prove that a musicologist's ideal foundation is that of the musician, although Riemann had studied philosophy and Classical languages in his teens at Berlin and Tübingen. Nonetheless, reading those works which express his theories on phrasing, and using the editions with copious additions, it is difficult not to have doubts. The very equipment of the modern musician to some extent defeats the scholarly imagination; for the essence of historical scholarship must be the power to imagine what different human beings, living in different conditions, thought and felt.

Yet whatever objections we may have to particular aspects of these men's work, the latter part of the nineteenth century was a good era for musical scholarship. The journals, the editions, the new organisations founded at the time prove this. As for the men themselves, they were splendidly individual, as is shown not only by the vagaries of Riemann's career but also by the steadfastness of Chrysander's, as he proceeded virtually single-handed with the production of the Handel Edition, regardless of financial difficulties. The institutionalising of musicology was perhaps the inevitable result of their work. For if they gained their education in diverse ways, they had a tendency to end as university professors. Ambros in Vienna, Spitta and Eitner in Berlin, Riemann in Leipzig; all these gained the coveted title and, naturally, pupils to match. The results of this can be seen in the number of theses completed in German universities towards the end of the century. Schaal's list shows the process at work. Until the 1890s there is no discernible trend; rather are there isolated forays into scholarship in 1855, in the 1870s and in the mid 1880s and so on. Then came the rush. First in the 1890s comes a regular stream of theses which continues to strengthen in the first decade of the present century. By 1914, the discipline is clearly well established; and with the exception of the war years there has been a steady growth until the present day. By the 1930s, some 70 to 80 theses were being presented each year in German universities; and by 1965 it becomes the daunting thought that in the three major countries where statistics are readily available, a total of some 200 theses were successfully completed.

The scholar who, in a sense, benefited most from this rush was Guido Adler. I say 'benefited' because he was not really its cause, though he did have a major part in shaping it. Rather he saw what needs it caused. He was typically nineteenth-century in education, gaining some musical training at the Vienna Conservatoire with Bruckner then, like so many others, being trained in law, presumably because that is what bourgeois families expected, and then in 1880 taking his doctorate in musical history, followed by a *Habilitationsschrift* two years later. This second is significant because it surely shows the intent to be a university teacher, and sure enough he became professor at Prague in 1885, then succeeded Hanslick at Vienna in 1898. There in the year he arrived he founded the Musikhistorisches Institut which was to be the model for so many others. His achievement was, to quote the admirable obituary by Rudolf von Ficker, no less than to make musicology into a 'selbständige Disziplin'. It would be an impertinence for me to even attempt to summarize his achievement when my German colleagues know so much better than any Englishman could the precise significance of his work. Nevertheless something must be said about the consequences of this achievement. I do not know whether it was Adler's deliberate intention to make musicology into an independent academic study, or whether this came about because the strength of his commitment to his pupils demanded it. Either way, there are two consequences of this process. The first is, quite simply, that there has to be systematization in teaching methods. The evolution of a mode of thinking cannot be left to the individual, if only because there are weaker, less penetrating members of the group who will not arrive at the answers by their own efforts. The second, which follows from the first, is that in an academic environment this organizing of curriculum and method of study will almost certainly simulate those in other disciplines. Von Ficker's assessment that Adler found musicology still in the late Romantic stage of biographical and aesthetic study and gave it an 'objektive kritisch-wissenschaftliche Methode' is undoubtedly just; and we have been living in its wake ever since.

I deliberately did not translate von Ficker's term because the temptation would have been to use the word 'scientific', and that causes as many problems as it solves. Much depends on the definition of the word. It may be possible to define it as does Egon Wellesz, a pupil of Adler, as a 'humane science concerned with individual facts rather than general laws'. But even with this mild usage of the word, it is not difficult to feel that scepticism so well expressed by Jacques Handschin in his address to the International Congress in Basle in

1949. For once the word 'science' has been accepted, it is tempting to expect qualities in the discipline which are essentially similar to those in the older scientific studies. These do not just deal in facts: they deal in certainties. And as they deal with the ascertained, they also deal with the predictive. If the theory cannot be tested by performing the experiment once again, it is as yet unproven.

There have been and still are some people who think that history is similarly predictive; but there must now be more who believe that 'the only thing we learn from history is that we do not learn from history'. It would not be too strong to say that Adler lived at a time when the concept of the scientific was more revered than it is today. There is indeed a useful parallel with another discipline. Adler was born within a year of Freud; and when one reads the history of psycho-analysis, one realises how strongly not just Freud but also his principal followers wanted their study to be scientific. Their quarrels — and seldom have a body of like-minded men been so frequently divided — came from their desire for certainty. Any branch of medicine is, of course, predictive — which is why comparatively few practitioners of psychological medicine today would grant psycho-analysis the status of a science, although they will agree that Freud's work in the classification of mental states was germinal. And we might also agree that Freud's artistic insights have been of great value in modern thought. Perhaps it is a case of setting out for the Indies and discovering America.

I draw this analogy with psycho-analysis, not merely because the two methods of study arose about the same time, rather because the nature of the subject matter is not dissimilar. One cannot study a mental state, only its manifestations. Similarly one cannot study the historical phenomenon of music, only its residue. The sound has gone, the notational residue remains. We can arrive at some approximation via the study of performing practice and additional techniques; but it will remain an approximation. Even this assumes some composer's 'ideal performance' instead of one possibility out of many, which is what music has been until very recent times. If we are now discovering the limitations of so-called 'Urtexts', our actual detailed lack of knowledge of performing methods should make us even more humble. What did Cuzzoni sing on the first night of *Ottone*? Did Handel approve? And what indeed did she sing on the second night? These are not only insoluble problems: they are problems which if they could be solved would be unending.

Even more intractable are the problems concerning the significance of music. Adler's main interest being in style, it was natural for him to explore the style rather than the surroundings of the work of art, to use again von Ficker's distinction. Nevertheless the insistence that it is impossible to divorce these aspects is one of the contributions that ethnomusicologists have to offer to music historians. Yet it is not difficult to see why we are reluctant to acknowledge this. The ethnomusicologist still has much of the information at his disposal. If he thinks of some new question, he can ask the participants in the act of music, whether composer, performer or audience. For the historian, the participants are dead. They may have left clues. Some gauge of the interaction between them can be found in economic factors. Presumably the willingness to pay to attend, or perhaps to keep up a musical establishment, is some measure of the success of the musician in conveying his thought — and also of the value of that thought. Here one has only to think of Wagner's appalled reaction to the first Bayreuth Festival just over a century ago, an event which, if we did not know otherwise, would have seemed an example of true success in the attempt to achieve a rapport between the different parties to the musical experience. If Wagner's intentions were not plain when he had the opportunity to direct affairs, what chance have we, deprived of his determination and experience, to understand his meaning? Yet we might assume from exterior evidence that, being successful, the effects on the various commentators of those performances — and that evidence is much fuller than for most musical events — represents Wagner's intended effects.

To approach the matter from another viewpoint, the difficulties of interpreting the 'theory of the affections' are well known. Leaving aside the complexities of late Baroque figuration, even when the matter seems fairly straightforward the very lack of information is frustrating. For example, the Venetian organist and teacher Girolamo Diruta gives in his *Il Transilvano* a list of moods corresponding to the various modes, and the organ registrations which must be used for each. The group of organists to which he belongs was comparatively small, and one might assume that his proposals represent a concensus of their opinions. Yet when one begins to apply these suggestions our problems begin. The 'seventh tone' is said to be 'allegra e soave' and on an organ should be given a bright registration. These are useful pieces of information for the performer; but is the result what was desired? To take a specific example, Diruta's Venetian contemporary Gabrieli wrote a canzona for instruments on the seventh tone. Agreed that it is both *allegra* and *soave*; but that is a very inadequate description of a piece full of subtle pastel shades.

The beginnings of any communications study lie surely in establishing the significance of the means of communication. In any literary discipline this leads immediately to finding out not only what the words mean, but the emotional and intellectual imagery inherent in them. It is obvious that words change their meaning, and that their overtones differ from one man to another. There is thus an immense area for not only research but also disagreement, even when the facts have been established. How much more does this apply to musicological study, where the information available is more inexact, and in which there is an additional cause of inexactitude. If one writes about music in the ordinary ways of prose, one is transferring from one inexact medium to another. If, on the other hand, statistical methods are brought into play, one is automatically falsifying the results by pretending that an imprecise medium can be represented by a precise one. We all know examples of the first; the romantic prose paraphrase of music is still a common phenomenon. The essential failing of the second is less easy to see; but if one thinks that counting the incidence of, say, the $^6_4$ chord in sixteenth-century music is a more exact kind of information, we must remember that it is so only in isolation. It can only be done by ignoring the amplitude and the exact duration of the sound, both matters surely of major importance in considering any music. No doubt the computer will aid us to make many factual correlations; but it will be as well to remember that it cannot supply information which does not in the nature of things exist.

This may seem as if musicological writing is doomed to failure. This is, of course, a proposition that I, as an editor of *Music & Letters*, must deny; and I do deny it out of conviction. Nor do I wish to decry precision in writing and research, although we must understand clearly what the term implies in the context of our discipline. But in understanding the limitations of musicological activity, we must also understand their implications for the study of the subject. Before musicology became Adler's 'selbstständige Disziplin', all musical scholars had trained in other fields — predominantly law, Classical languages and philosophy or theology. A few had a professional training in music, but even Riemann, the practical musician par excellence, had passed some time studying law. It was a situation compounded in England where at the Universities of Oxford and Cambridge it was possible to take a music degree only as a part-time subject. First the undergraduate had to devote his main energies to Classics, philosophy or cognate subjects. These were in the main intellectual disciplines. Law, Classics as it was then studied, theology all demand the detailed scrutiny of texts, the elucidation of their meanings. They train the mind systematically, they imply logical thought. Given the university environment for musicology, it is not surprising that it also has followed these paths. The establishment of texts and the study of notation have formed a large part of modern musicology. Although much still remains to be done, it is true that the greater part of the essential literature of music is available in one form or another in texts which though not perfect are at least quite coherent. The cognate questions concerning the production of sound, by the study of acoustical laws and by the measuring of musical instruments, have been another preoccupation. Thirdly, stylistic analysis, varying from superficial description to intense quasi-mathematical methods, has, especially in recent years, taken up much of the student's energies. Fourthly, because musicians have become musicolog ists, performance practice has recently emerged as a substantial subject.

As developers of the intellect, how do these compare with the old extra-musical studies? As far as *Aufführungspraxis* is concerned, this is mainly a matter for musical experiment and imagination. The interpretation of texts is sometimes needed, the ability to understand precisely what a writer on music means — and this can be difficult, as readers of such a source as Praetorius's *Syntagma musicum* will know. But by and large it is experience that is the most necessary ingredient for the scholar; that and integrity, that is the determination to obey the rules implied by the basic texts, and to reject those ideas which merely seem attractive to the modern ear. The study of acoustical phenomena and instruments is clearly a scientific study capable of predictions and experiment, of measurement and classification. It is in the fields of notation, textural criticism and analysis that some difficulties of balance and method begin.

At first sight textual criticism might appear exactly analagous with Classical studies; and so it may be. Yet, for the greater part of the music of historical eras, the establishment of a text is comparatively easy. Although revisions of Berlioz confront problems, these can hardly compare with the establishment of an Ancient Greek text. Nor, to move back to an earlier era, can the transcription of most sixteenth-century music, even if that surviving only in manuscript sources can prove exacting. There are, however, areas in which textual criticism does become a serious intellectual pursuit: music of the ancient and associated civilisations, a certain amount of medieval music and some later music in which there is a multiplicity of sources and no clear order of authenticity. It is in precisely these fields that so much distinguished musicological work has been done. Most of the really distinguished men in our discipline have at some time explored these areas, and many of its best graduate students like cutting their eye-teeth on their problems. Yet this immediately causes its own difficulties. Very often the music that presents such challenges is not of great importance; it will almost certainly not be the kind of music that lends itself to performance, and this in its turn leads to the divorce of the musicologist and musician.

Much the same applies to a great deal of analytical work. No one would deny that the capacity to analyse the constituent parts of concepts is a necessary part of any philosophic, legal or literary study. Equally, no musician is fully equipped without being able to break down a composition into its essential procedures. To examine a piece of music in considerable detail is a skill which any musicologist must possess. But we must be clear what we are doing. What we are examining is not music, but music as embodied in notation. Now it is clear that there are areas in music in which composers thought, as it were, 'notationally'. Beethoven's sketch books prove that he was concerned with pattern of the kind which reveals itself on paper. The same may be said to be true of writers of fugues and canons, of isorhythm, of a good deal of twentieth-century music, as well as the staple forms derived from the Viennese classics. But there is a great deal of music to which it does not apply, and especially two differing types of genre. One is simply where the quality of sound is an important feature, as in any richly orchestrated music or, to quote from my own field, music for *cori spezzati*. Notation may reveal the skill in writing counterpoint or grouping the instruments, yet it is very weak in conveying the actual sound — and this applies even to those who are skilled score-readers. We may be preserved — though we shall probably not be — from statistical surveys of the use of crescendo and sforzandi in the Mannheim School; but it may well be that these elements are more important than thematic development or considerations of tonality in many of their compositions. The other type of genre in which notation is inadequate is any in which there is a union of music with something else: words, stage, dancing. It is not very useful to apply musical analysis to areas in which the drama is paramount; and how rarely do we attempt to consider say, Tchaikovsky's ballets as anything more than not very interesting music, simply because we are too concerned with a single element. Key-schemes are not very relevant in the consideration of opera, when even so supposedly symphonic a composer as Wagner was at times content to make changes to suit different singers; while the deep-laid thematic analyses of Lorenz seem today to ignore the issues of dramatic music in the interests of making Wagner part of the more respectable tradition of pure music. It is a common fault also in literary studies; how often are Shakespeare's thoughts interpreted as quasi philosophic concepts, rather than as part of a dramatic framework natural to a man of the theatre?

I repeat that provided we are conscious of the place of these intellectual skills among the broader aspects of historical musicology, no great harm will be done. The difficulty comes because means are often mistaken for ends; and it is especially easy to make this mistake when the acquisition of techniques comes at the very time when a student is making his first attempt at writing an extended work: his doctoral thesis. In this, the tendency to attempt intellectual dexterity rather than musical understanding is natural with the clever; while the less gifted will be tempted to show necessary industry by transcribing some text, listing variants and writing a descriptive preface to some usually minor composer who assumes a far too prominent position in the candidate's mind. So does a just perspective disappear.

There is no ready solution to this problem. The happiest antidote to false intellectualism and narrow horizons would be to revert from the state of being the professional to that of being professor — in the best sense of that word. The intellectual stretching so necessary for the musicologist would then be done in another discipline — languages, Classical studies, law or philosophy. By which I do not mean just that smattering of subjects given for the primary degrees of some English and American universities, in particular, but a real investigation of one of these subjects in depth. After this, the student could turn his newly developed skills to musicology where he could follow some broader topic which intrigued both his mind and spirit. This is a council of perfection. The days when universities were filled with the well-off are gone, and the ample time for mental development no longer exists for the student who must soon turn professional. So the best we can do is to keep encouraging our pupils to widen their horizons; and also to study a subject which is not merely a challenge to their intelligence but engages their emotions and musicality. If the pre-Adler days will not come back, at least we can learn a lesson from the great musicologists of those times: they all loved music.

I should like to conclude, by quoting two illustrious musicologists who worked in the ancient universities of England, both of whom had links with Guido Adler. The first is Edward Dent, who contributed not merely a chapter to Adler's *Handbuch der Musikgeschichte* but also to the *Festschrift* for his 75th birthday. In an essay characteristically called 'The Universal Aspect of Musical History' he did a quite remarkable thing: he attacked the *Handbuch*, which to him assumed, 'if I may say so, that its readers are all well on their way to become professors at German universities. They are preparing dissertations and Habilitationsschriften'. What would he have thought of later developments, one wonders! For Dent, an ideal history 'must be a book for the general reader and it must be planned and executed as a work of literature'. In an age of turgid prose and dull cataloguing, most of us might applaud that. But I cannot do better than leave the final word with that pupil of Adler and revered member of the University of Oxford, Egon Wellesz. Describing the techniques of paleography, textual and stylistic criticism and much else, he finishes the article on 'Musicology' for the fifth edition of *Grove's Dictionary* thus:

> However, once this task is achieved, the musicologist must operate as an historian. It will depend upon the greatness of his own experience of them how far he will succeed in presenting as living things the works which he studies.

Chapter 2

THE PURPOSES AND DESIRABLE CHARACTERISTICS OF TEXT-CRITICAL EDITIONS

Arthur Mendel

SOME 25 years ago, as a callow choral conductor without musicological training, I was working on a projected book on Bach performance. Eager to support my conclusions with copious quotations from seventeenth- and eighteenth-century writers, I soon realized that this would result in a very big book. And since I had observed how often original sources are inaccurately quoted or mistranslated, even in the writings of the most eminent scholars, I had the idea of publishing a separate collection of these excerpts, reproduced in facsimile, as a companion to the book I was writing.

Such a collection would have presented difficult questions of design and format and been expensive to produce. Besides, since its contents would have been polyglot, the demand for it (around 1950) would have been limited. As luck would have it, a leading university press, not knowing that I had already made a contract for my projected book with a commercial publisher, inquired whether I might be interested in publishing it with them. My reply was to suggest that while doubtless the commercial publisher expected to make a modest profit on my book, the collection of source-excerpts seemed a highly appropriate project for a non-profit institution. The suggestion for a division of labour on this basis appealed to the university press perhaps less strongly than I had hoped. But that was not the reason they gave for turning it down. They had brought in for consultation the chairman of the exceptionally distinguished music faculty at their university, and he explained that 'people do not want to do their own research by reading the sources; they want you to tell them what to do'.

It is a cliché frequently repeated in the policy statements of text-critical editions that they are intended not only for the scholar but also

14

for the practical musician. The scholarly editors of such editions seem to feel called upon to justify them, and to prove that they themselves are in favour of performance.[1] The picture these editors form of the practical musician seems sometimes to be not a very good likeness. That this practical musician is not as often unwilling to do some thinking of his own as editors frequently imagine, I will illustrate by another anecdote.

In 1960 there was held at the Fondazione Cini the first of a number of meetings to discuss the possible issuance of a new complete Monteverdi edition. In the wide-ranging discussions of the committee, which consisted mainly of musicologists, such questions were raised as whether markings for tempo, dynamics, articulation and so on should be added for the guidance of the practical musician, who was presumed to need them in dealing with music of a style unfamiliar to him. The view was expressed that just as the nineteenth century had issued its interpretations of earlier music in print, we should not hesitate to do likewise. The chairman of the meeting was the eminently practical musician, Renato Fasano, conductor of the Virtuosi di Roma. At this point he lost patience with the discussion, and exclaimed in effect: 'Don't clutter up your scores with performance markings or continuo realizations; we performers will only have to disregard the markings and substitute our own realizations!'

In this he was agreeing, doubtless unconsciously, with the position taken more than 100 years earlier by another practical musician — Moritz Hauptmann. Hauptmann had played the violin for twenty years in Spohr's orchestra, had taught theory and composition to Ferdinand David, Joseph Joachim and Hans von Bülow, among others, and in 1842, on the recommendation of Mendelssohn, had been named Cantor of St. Thomas's, Leipzig. He was one of the organizers of the Bach-Gesellschaft, and was from its beginning until his death eighteen years later the chairman of its *Directorium*. The original constitution of the Gesellschaft had provided that 'for vocal works a piano reduction be placed at the bottom of the score'. During the work of preparing for publication the B minor Mass, which was to have been the first volume to appear, Hauptmann became increasingly convinced that the inclusion of a piano reduction would be a serious mistake. He thereupon circulated a memorandum among the directors and organizers of the edition explaining his reasons for thinking so:[2]

> A score edition with a piano reduction at the bottom is like a book in a
> foreign language with the translation of each word printed under the

text, for the benefit of those not knowing that language — such a book as is sometimes used for language-instruction in elementary schools. There can be no objection to such editions used for such purposes. But where the aim is to set forth the pure text of a classic author, not for translation and language-instruction but to further the understanding and enjoyment of the author in his own language, a knowledge of the meaning of each word and more than that must be assumed.

In an original edition of the works of Bach the addition of a piano reduction would be completely unworthy . . . . It would be unworthy in many-voiced movements because the polyphonic web . . . cannot be reproduced in a piano reduction . . . . [It would be] even more serious in those movements in which what is required is not a compression of the many-voiced score, but on the contrary the many-voiced elaboration of what Bach only suggested [at most] in outline [i.e. movements having only continuo accompaniment, figured or unfigured] . . . . No two editors would carry out this task in the same way . . . . Who would trust himself in a composition by Sebastian Bach to realize the ideas barely suggested by Bach as Bach himself would have done? It would perhaps be least of all to anyone exhibiting such self-confidence that those responsible for the promised 'critical and authentic' edition would be justified in entrusting such a task.

In some ways Hauptmann's reasoning may seem exaggerated. He appeared to assume that in Bach's compositions with only figured-bass accompaniment it was always Bach himself who improvised that accompaniment at the keyboard. But Bach must at times have participated in or even heard the performance of a work of his of this sort with someone else at the keyboard, whose realizations were certainly different from what his would have been.

This puts squarely before us the difference between the function of the performer and that of the editor of a critical edition. The performer is invited — indeed compelled — by the incompleteness of even the most explicit notation, to put the stamp of his personality on a performance. The conscientious performer tries not to compete for attention with the composer. But the older the work, the less explicit was its original notation, and the more the composer expected the performer to complete its details. If today no two performances even of works notated in such minute detail as, say, those of Schoenberg are the same, how much more widely must performances have varied when the continuo-realization was improvised; when the very media of performance were not specified; when accidentals had to be added and text-syllables distributed by the performers; or, still earlier, when not even the relative durations of the notes were unambiguously notated! It was a function of the performer to make the necessary

16

choices. The editor of a critical edition should leave the modern performer as free as possible to fulfill the same function.

But how free is that? There were, after all, conventions that performers of the period had grown up with, limiting their freedom and guiding their choices. There were primers, too: on *musica ficta*, on mensuration, on text-placement, on diminution (i.e. ornamentation) and so forth, and as time went on writings on these subjects became more explicit and detailed, less limited to some elementary rules for the beginner and addressed more to the accomplished musician. Unfortunately for us, it was not until nearly the end of the development of a genre or a style, when the notation of these things had become fairly explicit in the manuscripts and prints of the music itself, that the manuals became similarly explicit.

The earliest rules for text-placement in vocal music — those given by Giovanni Maria Lanfranco in 1533[3] — appeared just at the time when composers, copyists and publishers had begun to relieve the performer of his duties in this regard by placing the syllables carefully themselves. The more explicit rules of Zarlino and Stocker were promulgated when they were hardly needed any more. Pietro Aron's *Aggiunta* to his *Toscanello in Musica,* one of the most detailed expositions of some of the principles of *musica ficta,* was published only in 1529,[4] well after the deaths of Ockeghem, Obrecht, Isaac, Pierre de la Rue and Josquin. We can only guess whether and to what extent these rules and principles reflected — as it would be convenient to think they did — what performers had been doing for a long time. (How long?) But even if we knew this, we should have no sure guide, since even the later rules are not unambiguous and allow for many exceptions.

What is clear is that the choice of accidentals and the placement of text-syllables in music dating from before about 1520 — along with the choice of performing media, ornamentation, articulation and (to an extent that is still uncertain) tempo — belonged to the realm of performance practice, in some degree governed by conventions that we only partly understand.

Editors of critical editions should not give the appearance of knowing more than they do know. Nor is it only in the matters mentioned that they should not usurp the performer's functions. And here I must apologize for returning to what may seem a worn-out controversy. I mean the matter of bar-lines in music from before 1600 (and in some music considerably later). Quite apart from the more general considerations that I believe argue against the use of bar-lines, or even *Mensurstriche,* let me point to an exceptional but not unique piece: the

17

third Agnus dei of Josquin's *Missa Ave maris stella*.[5] This movement opens with a melody paraphrasing the beginning of the hymn 'Ave maris stella', imitated at the time-interval of three semibreves. In this it is like the Kyrie, 'Et in terra', and 'Patrem'. This imitation between Bassus and Altus continues canonically for the space of sixteen semibreves. The third entrance follows three semibreves after the second, and begins a canon between the Tenor and Superius, also at the distance of three semibreves. The precedent has been set in the first three sections of the Mass for paraphrasing the beginning of the hymn-melody in imitation at the time-interval of three semibreves, and the Tenor–Superius canon quotes almost literally the first three *tempora* of Kyrie I. This canon continues at the same time-interval right up to the coda of the movement.

Thus the rhythmic organization of the Agnus III has an unmistakable three-semibreve regularity. This is reinforced by the Bassus near the end of the movement (Ex. 1). The Kyrie, 'Et in terra' and 'Patrem' all begin in *tempus perfectum*. But in all sources and in all voices this Agnus has the sign ₵. The Bassus and Altus after their canonic beginning go their separate ways, and for the most part show no clear grouping in either two or three semibreves — nothing as clear, for example, as the two-semibreve regularity of a long passage in the opening duet of the 'Et in terra', despite the *tempus perfectum* mensuration of that section.

Ex. 1

Why should a piece in which such regularities as there are group three semibreves much more often than two be notated in ₵ rather than in O or ⊕? Two possibilities suggest themselves. On the one hand, the sign ₵ may have indicated a tempo different from O or ⊕. This is what it should have indicated if (as some later fifteenth-century writers state) two semibreves in *integer valor (tempus imperfectum* or *perfectum)* equalled three semibreves in ⊕ and four semibreves in ₵, or, to put it the other way, a semibreve in ₵ was only half as long as in C or O, and only three-quarters as long as in ⊕. But it seems questionable whether by the time of this Mass (which is presumably not one of Josquin's early works) these precise theoretical tempo-distinctions prevailed in practice — if, indeed, they ever had. An alternative, simpler explanation is that the lost manuscript from which all the extant sources directly or indirectly descend had a mensuration-sign that was meant to be ⊕ but was defective (through an accident in the writing or subsequent to it) and was mistaken for ₵.[6] While this hypothetical explanation is more attractive, in that it would resolve the problem of how the editor is to treat this piece, can he disregard the unanimous testimony of the extant sources in favour of ₵?

How shall the piece be barred in a critical edition? In reduced notation, to bar it in two minims to the bar, as in the Smijers edition, makes it appear as if the whole piece were in a cross-rhythm against a norm that is never established in the music, and of which the only traces are the mensuration-sign and the form of the rests. To bar it in three minims will puzzle the reader if the original mensuration sign is indicated, as of course it should be. Can one be so sure that the ₵ in all the sources is simply a mistake as to feel justified in barring the piece in three minims, and explaining why in a footnote or in the critical report? All these problems disappear if bar-lines are omitted and if only every sixth semibreve (in the original note-values) is numbered:

Ex. 2

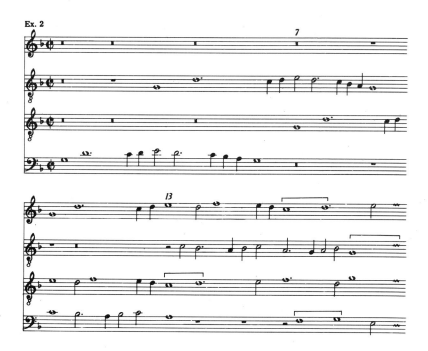

19

Is this a forbiddingly unpractical way of presenting the piece? Certainly it would have seemed so years ago. But practical musicians interested in performing a Josquin Mass are not completely new to such music. They do not imagine any more that everything notated in semibreves (or, as in this case, in semibreves, minims and crotchets) goes at a snail's pace. Indeed there is a growing interest among performers concerned with such music in performing it direct from photocopies of the original choir-books or part-books. Konrad Ruhland has done this regularly for years with his Munich Capella Antiqua, whose singers and players are not musicologists. Bernard Bailly de Surcy has demonstrated it repeatedly with his group, which includes amateurs, at meetings of the American Musicological Society.

Of course, one of the difficulties (as well as one of the advantages) is that without bar-numbers or rehearsal-letters performers must listen closely to each other as well as count carefully, like string-quartet players, if they are not to lose their place. And sources often have mistakes — in pitch, usually fairly obvious and easily corrected, and in rhythm, often more disconcerting. Even from these difficulties, performers can learn much; but they do not always have time for such experience in preparing a piece. Putting the originally separate parts into score, correcting their undoubted mistakes, and providing rehearsal numbers, or periodic tempus-numbers (or, in reduced notation, bar-numbers) undoubtedly can make for the convenience of performers. But it should do so without limiting their choices by over-interpretive editing.

Who are the performers that must be kept in mind when one is editing such music? A few of them are specialists, who will perhaps arrive at their own understanding of the music no matter how it is presented. Some, on the other hand, are doubtless complete strangers to any music earlier than Bach, but their number surely is far smaller than it used to be. In between are the conductors of those amateur choirs mostly associated with universities, colleges, and secondary schools, who are increasingly aware that the notation of earlier music is unlike modern notation, and who wish to know 'just what the composer wrote'. While we cannot quite satisfy this desire, what we ought to give them instead is not a fusion of the music (or of the skeleton of it which the surviving sources represent) with our individual ideas about how it should go, but whatever information the sources provide, separate from our suggestions as to what this information means.

So far, I have been concerned mainly to show that performers do not need spoon-feeding by editors. But there is another aspect of this question. A recent book by Leo Steinberg[7] on Michelangelo's frescoes in the Pauline Chapel abounds in symbolisms attributed to the paintings. The author explains:

> ... there are, after all, two ways to inflict injustice on a great work of art: by overinterpreting it, or by underestimating its meaning. If unverifiable interpretations are rightly regarded as dangerous, there is as much danger of misrepresentation in restrictive assertions that feel safe only because they say little.

Steinberg thinks interpretations should 'make visible what had not previously been apparent' and, once stated, 'so penetrate the mind that the picture seems to confess itself and the interpreter disappears'. E. H. Gombrich, in a review of Steinberg's book,[8] pays tribute to his gifts of sensibility and imagination. But he rejects the equating of under-interpretation with over-interpretation: he points out that 'once we have "fused" such meanings and forms it becomes difficult to separate them again, and before we know where we are we have imposed on a great work of art a reading which is hard to get rid of .... [Under-interpretation leaves] the work intact, though it may fail to exhaust the inexhaustible; [over-interpretation] lodges itself in the mind and distorts our experience for ever after, even if we refuse it credence'.

There is much truth in Gombrich's criticism, even as applied to a book that exists, after all, quite separately from the painting it interprets, and that is openly the expression of one man's opinions. In this it corresponds, say, to the writings on music by such men as Riemann, Schenker, Schering, Tovey, Smend, and Lowinsky. From them we have all learned, without always having their interpretations lodge in the mind or distort our experience even in instances when we have refused them credence. But writings are different from editions, and even editions openly embodying personal opinions — in which the work of art and its interpretation are presented together, if not always 'fused' (as they are in Riemann's, or in some of Schering's) — are different from critical editions of collected works or series of monuments, with the quasi-scriptural authority that performers and musicology students tend to attribute to them.

In all the three aspects of editing that I have briefly discussed — text-underlay, accidentals, and barring — there exists the danger of imposing the editor's choices on performers, score-readers at the keyboard, and even those who in reading the scores silently are hearing imaginary performances in the mind's ear. In text-underlay modern editors tend to impose modern German and English habits of placing the accented syllables at metric strong points — habits quite foreign to composers whose native language was French, by no means universally applied by those of other background, and probably inappropriate to much music before about 1520. Differentiation between original and editorial text-underlay through typographical expedients is probably unnoticed or ignored by most users, who thus tend to take the text-setting in an edition as characteristic of the composer.

It is usually easier to distinguish editorial accidentals from those existing in the source(s) on which the edition is based. But they tend to suggest both too much and — what is generally overlooked — too little. Too much in that even the informed reader, when his attention is on some other aspect of the music (text-distribution, rhythmic questions and so on), is apt to read the accidentals along with the notes, and lodge in the mind a single version of the piece where other versions would be equally well or poorly grounded. (Today, when few users of critical editions are unaware that accidentals were added by performers, there is little danger that an edition without suggested accidentals in or above the staves will lodge an equally false impression.) Too little in that the suggested accidentals misleadingly imply that they have more justification than others that might have been included. If editors feel that they must include suggestions for accidentals, then footnotes, introductions, or critical reports would be a better place for them than in or above the staves of the score itself.

The problematic nature of bar-lines in polyphonic music has been discussed above. Regular bar-lines are doubtless partly related to the connection too often made between accented syllables and metric strong points. They are too often taken to imply that mensuration-signs are equivalent to modern time-signatures. They tend to obscure micro-rhythms, the flesh that clothes the rhythmic skeleton. Irregular bar-lines create the impression that there is no such skeleton.

Semi-finally, a few words that should be unnecessary about critical reports. No critical edition is complete without one. It is understandable, but lamentable, that the *Neue Schubert-Ausgabe,* for example, has given up publishing critical reports in favour of filing them in a few libraries. The inference that will be drawn by the majority of users is that only a few pedants will be interested to know what in the edition comes from Schubert, what is the product of the editor, and why. It is shameful that all issues of the new Beethoven Edition thus far and a number of the editions of the American Institute of Musicology should have been published with only a promise that some time in the future there will be a critical report. Unless the editor has done the essential work of preparing that report, his edition is unreliable. Until the report appears, there is bound to be a suspicion that the work has not been done. If he has in fact done it, there is no excuse for not publishing it at the same time as the score.

If editors really want to help the performer, what they should do is not provide him with ready-made answers to questions that have no definitive answers, but encourage him in every way possible (including frequent references in the score to the critical report) to think out answers for himself.

Finally, the work of preparing both the score and the critical report can now be greatly expedited by the use of electronic data-processing techniques. For music of the mensural period, these techniques now exist and are being used. They employ the computer — a device whose name is misleading in this connection, since what it mainly does is store, sort, and list information, not compute. The original sources are coded, one part at a time, at the rate of five or six minutes to the equivalent of a score page. The computer is programmed to put the parts into score for proof-reading, and, after correction, to compare the sources and list the variants — in addition to melodic and rhythmic variants in musical notation, all the other categories listed below:[9]

1. Location and layout in source
2. Lacunae in the sources
3. Ascription of composer and spelling of title
4. Designation of voices
5. Opening clefs
6. Clef-changes
7. Opening signature-flats
8. Changes in signature-flats
9. Opening mensuration-signs
10. Changes in mensuration
11. Mensurally altered notes
12. Line-endings
13. Page-turns
14. Note-repetitions after line-endings or page-turns
15. F-flats (*extra manum*)
16. Ligatures
17. Coloration
18. Accidentals
19. Placement of accidentals elsewhere than immediately before affected note
20. *Punctus divisionis*

21. Signs of congruence
22. Fermatas
23. Corrections
24. Rhythmic errors
25. Special notes
26. Categories for which no information was found
27. Percentage of variant-agreement of each source with each other

The only actual computing involved consists of tables showing the percentage of agreement of variants between every pair of sources. (Of course, other statistical information could easily be compiled if desired.)

The advantages of using the computer are great. It is easier to be accurate in coding an individual source than in comparing the sources and making notes of the variants by hand. If there are mistakes in coding which survive the proof-reading of the score produced from it, most of them will show up in the variant lists, and can be corrected. Once the coded material is correct, everything that the computer-programmes produce will match it in detail. (Computers do not make small mistakes.) The processes that have hitherto been normal in preparing the physical material for publication — compiling lists of variants by hand, copying them and all other such material and proof-reading of the typescript, setting them in type and reading the proofs, making the musical manuscript model for engraving, auto-graphy or some substitute process, and reading these proofs — all these are done automatically except the proof-reading, which is elimi-nated. (Of course the editor will wish to spot-check the computer output, to satisfy himself of its accuracy, but from that point on all he will need to look for is gross omissions or misplacings of material.) Indeed the computer automatically produces an excellent substitute for engraving.

The most sensational advantage of the use of the computer is economy — economy of time, of human patience and of money — in the performance of all the clerical, mechanical and repetitive tasks that have to precede the truly editorial process. It takes less time to code, proof-read and correct the coding than it does to find, sort and list the variants by hand. It takes almost no time to sort the variants in any desired way, and to produce lists or tables of them. From the discussion of the advantages for accuracy, above, it will be seen that the greatest economy lies in eliminating the most tedious and numer-ous man-hours, with consequent savings of expense. Even the computer's production of the finished musical score, camera-ready for the offset printer, is less expensive than other methods of comparable quality.

Another gain is in completeness. Experience has shown that computer-comparison of the sources turns up many variants that have been missed in painstaking comparison 'by hand' (for a work having many sources, hundreds). If it is desired to prune the lists and tables produced by the computer, this is easily done. Ludwig Finscher writes about past editions, prepared of course 'by hand': 'All too often philological principles . . . have given way to the appearance of philology and the mere pretense of scholarly work — the "intuitive" choice of sources and the mechanical [!] heaping up of inconsequential readings in critical reports that even in professional circles were the less read the more swollen they became'.[10] The 'intuitive' choice of sources has in the past often resulted from the near impossibility of assembling, sorting and weighing the great mass of data needed to make a rational choice, based on all the evidence. One of the faults of what Professor Finscher refers to as the 'mechanical' heaping up of variant-readings is that it was mechanical only in a figurative sense: literally, it was not mechanical enough. The computer renders this heaping-up process almost completely mechanical (or rather electronic-plus-mechanical), and thus at least accurate. Any winnowing must still be based on the judgement of the editor, of which intuition is a part.

But is the fact that even professional musicologists do not actually read long lists of variants really an argument against completeness? Doubtless 99 per cent of the details heaped up in the telephone directory are inconsequential to each one of us; but no two of us make the same selection of those we hold consequential. The analogy is striking, but of course it is not complete: in any variant-list, most of us would agree about most of the variants, as to whether they are consequential or not. But the trouble with any selective list is that it is under suspicion of having been selected with a view to supporting the editor's ideas about the relative importance of the variants and their sources. The significance of a variant may very well escape me and be apparent to you, but it cannot be apparent to anyone if it is not in the list. We all have biases, and they must affect our conclusions. But their place is in those conclusions and in our explanation of them — not in the presentation of the evidence.

Complete need not mean prolix. The computer output will deliver much information that need not go into the critical report. For example, if two sources have strikingly similar layouts, this fact

25

suggests that they may be closely related. For this reason, the end of each line is noted in the coding. But such striking resemblances are rare, so tables of the line-endings and page-turns will frequently show few or even no correspondences. A critical report based on computer-recension should list all the categories of information for which a computer-search has been made and indicate all those in which no pertinent information has been found. The recension lists all places where a longer note has been divided into two shorter ones at a line-ending. So in cases where there are few or no correspondences between line-endings the critical report need state only the maximum percentage of such correspondences between any two sources, and similar space-saving expedients may be applied to some other categories. The computer makes it possible to state in the critical report that *all* variants have been noted, and if they are presented in tables or other concise and logical form they are as easily found (and can be as easily ignored) as Arthur Mendel in the Princeton telephone directory.

NOTES

1.   'Musicologists often feel called upon to claim an "intrinsic" value in music whose chief interest for them actually, and quite legitimately, lies in its historical, not its aesthetic importance. To make such a claim is a mistake . . . . It should be recognized that to understand the history of music the musicologist must study and publish much music that he would not, if he is a sensible man, recommend to the practical musician as material for public performance' (A. Mendel, 'The Services of Musicology to the Practical Musician', in Arthur Mendel, Curt Sachs & Carroll C. Pratt, *Some Aspects of Musicology*, New York, 1957, pp. 17 f.).
2.   Moscheles, who according to Jahn had wished to be the editor of the piano reductions, apparently felt himself insulted by Hauptmann's memorandum, and resigned from the *Directorium* in consequence. Hauptmann's entire memorandum and Moscheles's reply are printed in Kretzschmar's account of the history of the Bach-Gesellschaft, which appeared in its 46th volume.
3.   *Scintille di musica*, Bressanone.
4.   Venice.
5.   Ed. A. Smijers ('Werken van Josquin des Prés', xv), Amsterdam, 1935.
6.   What is apparently the reverse situation (a hand-written $\mathbb{C}$ being mistaken for $\mathbb{O}$ by the engraver) seems to have occurred in the Gigue of Bach's Sixth Partita, BWV 830.
7.   *Michelangelo's Last Paintings*, London, 1975.
8.   *New York Review of Books*, 20 January 1977.
9.   Samples of computer-listings of variants are reproduced in Thomas Hall, 'Some Computer Aids for the Preparation of Critical Editions of Renaissance Music', *Tijdschrift van de Vereniging voor Nederlandse Musiekgeschiedenis*, xxv/1 (1975), 38–53. (Mr. Hall is the author of the programmes to put the parts into score and to make the recension of the sources by computer.)
   The work on which the material about computer recension in the present article is based was made possible by research grants from the Rockefeller Foundation, the National Endowment for the Humanities and Princeton University. The conclusions

presented here do not necessarily represent the views of any of these institutions.
10.   'Musikalische Denkmäler und Gesamtausgaben', *Musikalisches Erbe und Gegenwart*, ed. H. Bennwitz, G. Feder, L. Finscher & W. Rehm, Kassel, 1975, pp. 1–13.

POSTSCRIPT

Since this chapter was written, Don Harrán has presented 'The Earliest Writing on Text Underlay', *Acta musicologica*, 1 (1978), 217–40. It helps us little. Harrán translates scrupulously the opening sentence of this earliest writing: 'É da saper como no(n) / e / reson nessuna in dever assetar le parolle a nullo canto / altro che lintelecto de coluy che la [= l'ha] a notare' as: 'It should be recognized that there is no logic in how to adjust words to a melody beyond [that in] the mind of him who has to write it in notes'. But later he sums up the instructions given in six numbered remarks, three 'of concern to the singers' and three 'of concern to the composers'. That is, he now identifies 'him who has to write it in notes' with the composer. This is a big leap. How often did singers read from the composer's manuscript or an accurate copy of it? It is just because we have no assurance that the whole question arises. From here on, Harrán speaks repeatedly of 'the intentions of the composer', 'the composer's ideas', 'the composer's reasons'. He claims that instructions to 'make his intentions crystal clear' and 'never [to] write a syllable on any other note of a ligature than the first' were addressed to the composer. But if the composer had 'had specific ideas on how the text was to be set', as Harrán thinks his author believed, would he have needed such instructions? Are they not rather directed at scribes, and for the very reason that scribes (including the copyist of the folio containing the writing under discussion which Harrán reproduces in facsimile) were careless in these regards?

27

Chapter 3

FABURDEN — NEW SOURCES, NEW EVIDENCE:
A PRELIMINARY SURVEY

Brian Trowell

THE still unresolved controversy over the origins of faburden and fauxbourdon nicely illuminates two dangers in musical scholarship. First, that one must be sure, when making comparisons, that one is comparing like with like; and second, that in our romantic preoccupation with the music of great masters we keep our eyes too firmly fixed on very high-class polyphonic manuscripts which contain the music of the rich and powerful, so that we tend to neglect, perhaps, what more humdrum musical sources contain, and what can be built up around them from extra-musical sources, such as archives, literature and ritual. Faburden certainly does not offer great masterpieces, but this unassuming kind of popular music-making has a fascination of its own. The investigation of such a topic can take one interestingly and usefully into a surprising variety of different fields and across a surprisingly wide span of musical history.

Since I last wrote about faburden, almost twenty years ago, the ground has shifted a good deal, so that much of our old hypothesising has simply become irrelevant. I cannot hope to list, let alone summarize here, the literature that has contrived to multiply around the subjects of faburden and fauxbourdon, but a few contributions must be mentioned. The first (and so far the only) volume of Ernest Trumble's valuable *Fauxbourdon: an Historical Survey*,[1] the first comprehensive study of its subject, appeared, unknown to me at the time, in the same year (1959) as my own foray into the area,[2] which in turn provoked an attack on my views from Trumble.[3] Frank Harrison has provided, in particular, valuable studies of Pepys MS 1236 and of faburden in practice.[4] Sylvia Kenney finally laid Bukofzer's 'English Discant' to rest.[5] Ernest Sanders has greatly advanced our understanding of English music of the thirteenth and fourteenth

28

centuries.[6] Mary Berry, in her study of late plainsong sources, has discovered no less than 57 faburden tenors.[7] Dagmar Hoffmann-Axthelm's articles in Eggebrecht's *Handwörterbuch* contain much useful material.[8] John Caldwell has inventoried all the Tudor keyboard compositions built on faburdens and published most of them.[9] Paul Doe is doing the same for the early Tudor Magnificats, most of which are based on faburdens.[10] Finally I must mention Roger Bowers, musician, historian and archivist, whose researches among the records of our late medieval musical institutions have revealed much about the real roots of the culture.[11] I should perhaps add that there have been two further short contributions since 1959 on the philological/etymological side,[12] but that the authoritative *Middle English Dictionary*[13] finds the late Hermann Flasdieck's view convincing, that the word 'fauxbourdon' could have derived from 'faburden', but not *vice versa*.

'Quhat is faburden?', asked Scottish Anonymous. By way of answer, a very simple example, without any of the ornament at cadences frequently found, is a verse of the hymn 'Salvator mundi',[14] with a faburden bass jotted down in Tudor times (Ex. 1). This strongly resembles the nine other surviving 'Salvator mundi' faburdens; and indeed the room for variation in faburden is slight — one could choose for the bass only the fifth or third beneath the chant, and perhaps add a simple flourish or two to make suspensions at the cadences. The faburden, with the chant in the treble, doubled at the Fourth above, is pretty close to the directions of Wylde's Anonymous, or 'Pseudo-Chilston', who wrote the short tract that affords our only theoretical

Ex. 1

knowledge of early faburden.[15] The slight divergences are of a kind common enough in most surviving faburdens. Not all words end with an $\frac{8}{5}$ harmony; on the other hand, not all phrases begin with an $\frac{8}{5}$ (the exceptions all occur on unimportant words). The faburden, or bottom voice, does not proceed mechanically, but has evolved with the cumulative wisdom of many decades so that the bass line flows on without awkward contours, and so that the $\frac{8}{5}$ chords are sometimes points of repose, as in the first line, and sometimes points of stress, as in the second. The absence of $\frac{8}{5}$s from 'protege' onwards is noteworthy: the stream of $\frac{6}{3}$s seems to make the petition more urgent.

The technique of faburden, as described in Wylde's Anonymous, is familiar enough. The faburden proper, or lowest voice, is derived by singing fifths and thirds beneath the plainsong, which is the Mean, or middle voice. In order to be able to visualise these intervals from his book of chant, and within the four lines of the plainsong staff, the faburdener is told to imagine the notes a fifth higher than he sings them: that is to say, as unisons with and thirds above the plainsong. (This device of transposition or 'Sight' is borrowed from English discant.) The result is that the faburdener can never sing a B natural, but always sings B flats, as the imagined note for a B will always be the F-fa a fifth above. I have suggested that this alone would suffice to explain the name 'Fa-burden' as a composite of the English word burden, meaning a bass-part, and the solmisation syllable Fa : burden with B-Fa.[16] Trumble objected, and others have followed him,[17] that this would also apply to the Discant sight of Counter, which also keeps beneath the plainsong and also transposes down a fifth. On the face of it the Counter too will always visualise F-fa in sight and consequently always sing B flats; therefore, Trumble argues, a Counter might equally well be called a 'Fa-burden'. But this is not the case. If anyone were singing a Counter and wished to harmonize a plainsong B natural with the octave beneath, his ears and commonsense would tell him that he must not visualise an F-fa and sing a B flat. And of course, a frequently stated rule of Discant tells him that 'when he setteth a perfite corde ageynes a fa [in the chant], he most sing that perfite acorde a fa[;] and when [he] setteth a corde agayns a mi, he most sing that perfite corde a mi'.[18] Faburden, therefore, remains unique in this respect, and was given its name, I maintain, because of a solid technical characteristic.

Practical experience of faburden reveals another curious feature. Starting and ending one's faburden a fifth beneath the plainsong will of course shift the choice of hexachords to the flat side, at least for the outside listener, who is not mentally transposing. But with many plainsongs, if the faburdener observes the recommendations of Wylde's Anonymous and frequently sings a fifth 'at the last end of a word', his perpetual B flats will also involve him in E flats. Ex. 2, showing the Sarum version of the communion 'Vos qui secuti estis me' harmonized strictly according to the instructions of the faburden tract, makes this clear.[19] The top stave shows the plainsong in the Mean, doubled at the upper fourth by the Treble. The bottom stave shows the faburdener's 'sight' in small void notes and the actual line he derives from it, sounding a fifth lower. Wylde's Anonymous tells him to sing a fifth beneath the chant at the beginning and also whenever possible at the ends of words. Elsewhere he sings thirds. But he is not to sing a fifth under an E or a B in the plainsong; and no one has ever explained why not. Two of the E's come at the ends of words, where otherwise one should sing a fifth – at 'estis' and 'iudicantes'. An examination of the surrounding harmony makes it plain why the fifth A–E is unacceptable (there are no B's in this chant, and therefore the other forbidden fifth, E–B does not arise here, though the same objection would hold). The faburdener's perpetual B flats involve him in a number of inescapable E flats, and these in turn force him to sing every other E as an E flat. In order to sing these E flats he has to imagine B flats in sight at the fifth above, even though the chant itself has no B flats. In this case (and the same would hold for many other chants) his burden is characterised by B-fa in sight as well as B-fa in voice. All this explains why the fifths A–E and E–B are forbidden: they would quarrel far too fiercely with the perpetual B flats and frequent E flats, and the rule of Wylde's Anonymous is a simple precept for avoiding them. Many of the written monophonic faburdens have such notes expressly marked with a flat.

Ex. 2

31

I would still maintain that my former explanation accounts in the simplest possible way for the meaning and derivation of the term 'faburden'. Hoffmann-Axthelm, who accepted Trumble's objections to it, has proposed a derivation from the Scottish and Northern English word 'fa', a variant spelling of 'foe' (enemy): but in order to call the bottom voice a 'foe-burden', a bass-part in some mysterious way inimical to the burden, she has to maintain that the middle part is the burden, and that a burden was originally a bass-part bearing a cantus firmus. This is plainly not the case, or it would have been called a tenor in the normal way; and Wylde's Anonymous expressly talks about the middle voice as the 'mene' of the plainsong.

Dr. Hoffmann-Axthelm's careful listing of references to the Middle English noun 'burdoun' nevertheless repays serious study. Among the known English and Welsh references to three-part singing or Treble-song down to 1450,[20] there are some passages (referred to in note 21 below) in which it is impossible to know whether anything more precise is meant than the sort of three-part singing normal everywhere in Europe. But the well-known diatribe against excessive music in church, written by St. Aelred of Rievaulx between 1134 and 1143, seems to describe not three interweaving voices, but three layered or stratified voices whose lines do not cross and tangle with each other. One 'sings beneath' *(succinit)*, one 'discants' (above, it must follow) and the other 'divides and cuts into certain notes in between' *(medias notas)*.[21]

> . . . unde in Ecclesia tot organa, tot cymbala? Ad quid, rogo, terribilis ille follium flatus . . .? Ad quid illa vocis contractio et infractio? *hic succinit, ille discinit, alter medias quasdam notas dividit et incidit.* Nunc vox stringitur, nunc frangitur, nunc impingitur, nunc diffusiori sonitu dilatatur. Aliquando . . . in equinos hinnitus cogitur; aliquando . . . in femineae voci gracilitates acuitur, nonnumquam artificiosa quadam circumvolutione torquetur et retorquetur. Videas aliquando hominem aperto ore quasi intercluso halitu exspirare, non cantare, ac ridiculosa quadam vocis interceptione quasi imitari silentium . . . ut (vulgus) . . . non ad oratorium, sed ad theatrum . . . aestimes convenisse . . . si ad memoriam nugarum theatricarum prurientibus auribus immane fastidium gravitas honesta intulerit . . .

The Term 'Medius' or 'Mene' does not enter musical theory, so far as I know, until Cutell's discant treatise, probably of the 1390s;[22] it first appears in a musical manuscript a little later. It emerges in literature considerably earlier, however, perhaps as early as 1275, in the description of the Earthly Paradise in *St. Patrick's Purgatorium*:[23]

Oþer ioies he sieȝe anouȝ:
heiȝe tres wiþ mani a bouȝ,
þer on sat foules of heuen,
and breke her notes wiþ miri gle,
Bourdoun and mene gret plente,
and *hautain* wiþ heiȝe steuen.

Here we have the first of a series of no less than ten references to a regular complex of three voices: Hautain or Treble, Mene (= Mean) and Bordoun (Bourdoun, Burdoun, Burdon, Burdowne = Burden), which eventually becomes Tenor. The next, dateable 1300–1325, occurs at the end of *Cayphas*, a Palm Sunday play probably connected with Wells Cathedral.[24]

No gawe hom hit is fordays
Lengere ne tyd ȝou here no pays
Þe belle wol sone rynge
Doþ so þt ich cunne ȝou þonkes
Wyþ *bordoun hauteyn men* amonkes [read: 'mene, monkes']
lat me hure ȝou synge,

Robert Mannyng's *Story of England* (c. 1315?–1338), in a legendary account of the coronation of King Arthur and Queen Guinevere, has the following.[25] The section is headed '*De Cantu ad Missam*', and we note that organs are also playing:

When þe Procession was gon,
Þe Messe bygan sone anon:
Þer myghte men se fair samninge
Of þo clerkes þat best couþe synge,
Wyþ *treble, mene, & burdoun,*
Of mani on was ful swete soun
Of þo þat songe heye & low,
& þo þat couþe orgnes blowe.

The next appearance of our three terms add a fourth, Quatreble, and is in Welsh. It comes in a *Clwydd* writen by Iolo Goch ac Eraill around 1397,[26] praising Ieuan Trefor, Bishop of St. Asaph (in Flintshire, a secular cathedral). 'Awch' is a punning substitution for 'mên', needed for the alliteration; 'awch' really means edge, or fine blade, for which another word is 'min' (= mean):

Offeren fawr, hoff, eirian,
A gawn, a hynny ar gân;
Treble, chwatreble, awch atreg,
A *byrdwn* cyson, ton teg.

(A great and praiseworthy High Mass
do we have, and that in song;
Treble, quatreble, supporting mean
and the harmonious burden, a beautiful sound.)

The Visions of Tundale (1390–1410)[27] Brings the next reference, again in a description of the Earthly Paradise. 'Freres, monkes, nonnes and chanownes' are present.

On þo cordes wer instrumentis sere
Of musike, þat hadde swete sown and clere,
Organes, symbales and tympanes
And harpes, þat range all at ones.
Þai gaf a delectabull sowne,
Boþe *trebull and mene, and burdowne*.

By 1425–1450, Lydgate[28] has replaced 'Burdoun' with 'tenor'. Again we have a Mass, though a burlesque one, since the 'organys' are Jack Hare's nose, snoring in his sleep.

But woo is he that nyht shal be thi mate,
Thyn *orgons* so hihe begynne to syng thir messe,
With *treble mene & tenor* discordyng, as I gesse,
That al the hoggis that ben aboute liggyng,
To sing with the thei gynne hem thidir dresse,
. . . Yet wassayl N. and thyne be thi thrift, [N = Nomen, Jack]
with al thyn organys and thi melodye.

Another Welsh reference occurs in a poem by Dafydd Nanmor. 'Trwy blwm', 'through lead' (= *plwm*), presumably means 'through organ pipes', and may be a pun on 'triplum'.

Teg yw sŵn *by[r]dwn* lle bo
Trebl a mên trwy blwm yno.

(Fair is the sound of the burden, wherever
treble and mean are found through lead.)

Our last two references come from the popular level of the mystery cycles, the first from the Towneley Plays[30] and the second from the Macro Plays[31] (both *c.*1460):

Primus pastor: Lett me syng the *tenory*.
ijus pastor: And I the *tryble* so hye.
iijus pastor: Then the *meyne* falls to me . . .

. . . Now let us synge.
MYNDE: A *tenowur* to yow bothe I brynge.
WNDYRSTONDYNGE: And I a *mene*, for ony kynge.
WYLL: And, but a *trebull* I out wrynge,
The deuell hym spede, þat myrthe exyled!

Two references to Treble and Mean alone presumably (since a Mean is a middle voice) imply a third voice beneath. The first, from 1360–1370, comes in a poem to the nightingale formerly attributed to the great Dafydd ap Gwilym,[32] but thought by Dr. Thomas Parry to be the work of Madoc Benfras:

Main y can brif organ brudd,
mên a threble mwyn ei thrabludd

(Keenly he sings, solemn as the great organ,
mean and treble, a lovely sound.)

The next is again from the Towneley Plays (*c*.1460):[33]

The *meyn* shall ye nebyll,
and I shall syng the *trebill*.

By the same reasoning, a reference to Burden and Mean in the *Laud Troy Book* (1400–1425) must imply a Treble above (Diomedes is taunting Aeneas):[34]

I schal the teche for to chaunte,
I schal the teche bothe *burdone and mene*,
Ne be thow neuere so wroth ne wrene!

Chaucer twice uses 'Burdo(u)n' in *The Canterbury Tales* to mean a bottom voice. In the General Prologue (*c*. 1387) the Summoner sings a bass line beneath the Pardoner:[35]

Ful louude he soong 'com hider, loue, to me!'
This Somonour bar to hym a stif *burdoun*,
Was neuere trompe of half so greet a soun.

35

In 'The Reeve's Tale' (c. 1388) the Miller's wife is amusingly imagined as snoring (or worse) at an even deeper pitch than her drunken husband:[36]

> This miller hath so wisely bibbed ale,
> That as an hors he snorteth in his sleep,
> Ne of his tayl bihinde he took no keep.
> His wyf bar hym a *burdon*, a ful strong,
> Men mighte hir routing here two furlong.

'Burdoun', well attested in English only as meaning a bottom voice, was formed from French 'bordon', meaning a low note, humming or drone; the term may perhaps have attracted a flavouring from Middle English 'byrðen' (cf. the 'gravior vox' or 'heavier voice' of Pseudo-Tunstede and earlier theorists); and there may also be a link with medieval Latin 'burdo' in its meaning of shawm or brass instrument, attested in England since c. 1255.[37] What, though, is the significance of the whole recurring triad of voices, Hautain (Treble), Mene and Burdoun? I suggest that they refer to a kind of singing hinted at in the English discant treatises of the late thirteenth and the fourteenth centuries but contrary to the strict classical theory of discant, namely parallel singing by three voices. I suspect that it was popular in origin, which is why the terms are vernacular and not Latin. Such parallel singing, whether it grew from organum or from the popular singing in thirds mentioned as a northern speciality by Giraldus Cambrensis, took a prominent place in the duets and trios of late thirteenth century English music, some of it to English words; and this style, related to the conductus, continued in force in the great majority of the pieces preserved in score notation in English sources of the fourteenth century; but it had little or no place in the music of the Continental Ars Nova.

A freely composed setting in modal rhythm of 'Beata viscera' (not the communion),[38] dating from the late thirteenth century, shows parallel movement in $\frac{6}{3}$s (Ex. 3). But other parallel intervals occur in this insular repertory. There are $\frac{5}{3}$s, and as the range of voices expands $\frac{10}{5}$s become common and $\frac{10}{6}$s are also known. Sanders has surveyed the material in some detail; he points out that within a longer piece no one set of intervals is normally permitted to predominate for too long: $\frac{6}{3}$s will give place to $\frac{10}{5}$s, or the composer will vary the sonority with some contrary motion.[39] In an apparently free setting of what looks like a sequence text from the Leeds Manuscript (the 'Second Fountains Fragment'), a Cistercian source,[40] there is alternation between $\frac{6}{3}$s and $\frac{10}{5}$s, and the pace changes rapidly too (Ex. 4). As in faburden, the style

involves frequent contradictions between flats in the Burden and naturals in the Mean.

Sanders has also shown that only very few fourteenth-century English pieces in parallel style appear to be based on liturgical cantus firmi. He comments on the surprising opening of a 'Christi messis', also from the Leeds Manuscript.[41] But it seems likely that this is a sequence, in which the polyphony begins with the double versicle at verses 2 and 3: the missing first verse, sung in monophony, would have established the tonality and lessened the shock of the first bars. Later in the same piece there is a series of no less than nineteen consecutive $\frac{10}{5}$s (Ex. 5).

This kind of music, most of it no doubt freely composed, was distinguished by its extreme floridity — often simultaneous floridity in all parts at once — underlined by fixed parallelisms. The voices might be used for long stretches like the reduplicating mixtures of an organ; and several references to Hautain (Treble), Mene and Bordoun, as we have seen, associate our triad of voices with the organ. The fourteenth-century English theorist Anonymous V describes parallel singing in sixths, with octaves at the cadences. It would be easy to add a Mean to Ex. 6, in fifths and thirds above the Burden.[42]

Ex. 6

* : ♮ three notes too early in MS
+ : a note too high in MS

The parallel style removes all feeling for a stable tenor foundation and, as Sanders emphasises, profiles the top voice very strongly; the consecutive fourths and fifths between the upper voices would mirror any cantus firmus placed in the Mean at two levels simultaneously. Sanders is very probably right in looking to secular music as a source for the refrain forms, the sonorities and some of the underlying melodies of such music. The howls of outrage over elaborate church music uttered by John Wyclif and his followers in the last three decades of the fourteenth-century were doubtless directed in part against music of this sort: they attack the 'new song' (i.e. music not based on traditional chant) 'of their own finding-up', in which the sense of the words is destroyed by florid knacking or breaking. The expensive chapels of the magnates and bishops are its main habitat, but monks, friars and even parish priests are not immune.

Also prelatis disceyeun lordis & alle cristene men bi veyn preieris of
mouþ, & veyn *knackyng of newe song* & costy . . . foule ben oure lordis
blent to meyntenen open traitours of god, bi gret cost . . . for here
stynkynge & abhomynable *blastis & lowd criynge*; for bi þer *grete criyng*
of song, as *deschaunt, countre note & orgene,* þei ben lettid fro studynge
& prechynge of þe gospel; & *here owene fyndynge vp,* þat
crist & apostlis spoken not of, as is *þis newe song* . . .

. . . for þei don not her sacrifices bi mekenesse of herte & mornynge &
compunccion for here synnes & þe peplis, but wiþ *knackynge of newe
song, as orgen or deschant & motetis* of holouris [lechers] . . .[43]

Þan were matynys & masse & euen song, placebo & dirige & commen-
dacion & matynes of our lady ordeyned of synful men, to be songen wiþ
heize criynge . . . & of schort tyme þanne were more veyn iapis found;
deschaunt, countre note & orgon & small brekynge, þat stiriþ veyn men to
daunsynge more þan to mornynge . . . for whanne þer ben fourty of
fyfty in a queer þre of foure proude & lecherous lorellis schullen *knacke*
þe most deuout seruyce þat noman schal here þe sentence . . .[44]

The musical sources of fourteenth-century England are indeed
stuffed with new song, not based on chant and often composed to
otherwise unknown texts which are presumably also new. The great
bulk of this material is written in score notation and takes the form of
parallel discant on an apparently freely invented tenor. Its sonorities,
stratified movement and constant parallelisms seem to relate intimately to the development of faburden: the character and sheer
quantity of such pieces, as Sanders has said, have been seriously
underestimated by Besseler and Trumble.

What happened when such techniques were applied to normal
liturgical music? On the one hand we get many free settings, particularly of the Gloria, in which the refrain-forms and variation-
techniques of the chantless cantilena are used to endow the repetitive
clauses with a dance-like quality (Ex. 7).[45] When a plainsong is used,

Ex. 7

* MS : *e'd'e'*
† MS : *a b c'*

particularly as in Ex. 8, from a unique setting of the repetitive chant of the Credo,[46] the sonority is similar, but the simple sobriety of the chant now provides the continuity, and the style is more restrained.

The end of a fragmentary Te Deum from Gonville and Caius College MS 727/334[47] shows how the progressions familiar from later faburden were initially valued for their sonority alone, regardless of the position of the cantus firmus (Ex. 9). In our opening section, the Te Deum melody should probably be considered to be in the top

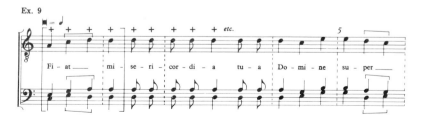

voice, transposed to the upper fourth, rather than in the Mean — the migration of the chant then seems much less surprising in bar 11. Then, for the low final section, the bottom voice has the chant; but almost exactly the same sonorous image is still preserved.

A setting of 'O lux beata Trinitas', once more from the Sloane manuscript,[48] again shows the chant in the Mean, transposed to the upper fifth (Ex. 10) — by far the commonest proceeding in the English fourteenth-century cantus-firmus pieces in score notation. The perhaps corrupt passage in the Mean in bar 8 of the first verse is presented in a simpler form, and one that is nearer the chant, on its repeat and at the end. Apart from that, and of course the consecutive fifths, the lower two voices and much of the Treble are virtually in

Ex. 10

highly rhythmicized faburden; the bass is the ancestor of a family of no less than fourteen strict faburdens on this chant.

The beginning of a setting of the hymn 'Conditor alme siderum' [49] shows how important the stratified layering of the parallel style was (Ex. 11): the notes of the hymn melody are distributed almost mechanically to the appropriate voice, simply in order to avoid crossing the parts. This was the main motive behind the purely English technique of migrant cantus firmus, and demonstrates again that the sonorous image of parallel layered movement was more important to the composer than the integrity of the chant.

Ex. 11

This selection of examples from a mass of similar pieces leaves little doubt that strict faburden must have crystallized out of this tradition and grown up on English soil. The date at which the technique of strict faburden solidified as an extempore practice seems to depend on two things: the absence of any mention of faburden in the earliest English vernacular discant treatises of *c.*1390–1410 (though most of these are fragmentary); and the prohibition of consecutive fifths in faburden. These two factors point to a date between the early and later layers of the Old Hall Manuscipt, namely *c.*1410. Here we should note Cecily Sweeney's belief, on grounds both of repertory and of paleography, that Wylde's Anonymous (Lansdowne MS 763) could be as early as 1430:[50] she offers a persuasive explanation of Hawkins's original misdating, which was followed by Hughes-Hughes, Bukofzer, Besseler and Trumble. Wooldridge, Ferand and now Charles Warren also place the manuscript at *c.*1430,[51] and S. B. Meech's analysis of the language and dialect led him to date the English discant tracts in the first half of the fifteenth century.[52] Two further concordances, unknown to Sweeney, link the source with earlier manuscripts, one of the fourteenth century,[53] the second of *c.*1425.[54] But she noted that the cryptic early paragraph in Latin on 'Cantus coronatus . . . scilicet ffaburdon' together with its surrounding material, also appears in Oxford, Bodleian Library, MS Bodley 515, dated by Madan in the first half of the fifteenth century.[55] Amongst the surrounding material, immediately before the faburden reference, and linked to it, is a description in Latin of the concordances belonging to the three degrees of discant which relates to the remarks of Anonymous IV, and may therefore be of considerable antiquity. The discant is in similar motion, parallel with the chant.

The first degree of discant, corresponding to the Mean in the vernacular treatises, may only sing the third and fifth; the second degree (Treble) has only the fifth and octave; the third degree (Quatreble) has more, the fifth (*recte* octave, no doubt), tenth, thirteenth and fifteenth. 'And all are to rise and fall with the plain-song.'[56]

De tribus gradibus discantus

Tres sunt gradus discantus. Primus diapente cum ditono. secundus diapason cum diapente [.] Tercius cum diapente [MS 'candiapente'] decima [,] id est diapason cum ditono[,] xiij[ma] cum xv[ma] qui secundum planum cantum debent ascendere et descendere naturaliter cum tenore plani cantus. Alius est cantus qui vocatur antiphona & Alius Vniuolus.

De cantu coronato

Cantus coronatus cantus fractus dicitur quia ad nullum gradum alligatur sed potest ascendere et descendere in consonacijs perfectis siue imperfectis indifferenter et cantus naturalis coronari potest s[c]ilicet faburdonij [*recte* faburdoun?]

Roger Bowers's archival research, too, reinforces an earlier dating for English faburden. He has discovered the earliest known English organist's indenture, a document of 1430. It is still in the archives of Durham abbey, where it originated, and is an earlier form of the well-known indenture for John Stele of 1447.[57] In 1430, it was expected of Stele that he should teach the monks and eight secular boys both to play the organs and to sing organ-song, namely 'Pryketonote Ffaburden deschaunte and counter'. It is unlikely that fauxbourdon, a technique first known to us as written polyphony from an Italian manuscript of high art-music dating from the late 1420s, could have been transmuted with quite such speed into a very different-sounding technique of formulaic harmonisation of chant *super librum*, to be taught as part of his routine duties by a north-country English organist to boys and Benedictine monks (not specialist musicians). We should recall, too, the reference to 'treble-song' at Durham, mentioned earlier (in footnote 21): in the 1390s, the monks complained of the absence of clerks, singers of 'organum', who had helped them sing 'the song which is called treble' in choir.

Dufay's early fauxbourdons are very different from faburden and could hardly have suggested the technique, They contain elements of late Ars Nova sonority that seem actually to militate against the logic of the style. They appear to be written for two solo upper voices with an instrument playing the textless tenor; the outer lines are made as different as possible within the rules of the game. The chant in the upper voices is embroidered somewhat with ornamental notes and given real rhythmic tension; and the tenor part moves about much more independently than was possible in faburden. The use of an instrumental timbre on the bottom line must have thrown the parallel fourths in the upper voices into startling relief; and the ornamental upper line was exactly duplicated by the contratenor altus (see Ex. 12).[58] The English examples of written-out three-voiced faburden sometimes present a slightly ornamental upper line, but the Mean tends to be much simpler and to keep to 'the old way of faburden', to use a phrase from the Scottish Anonymous. Ex. 12 comes from a quite different world from that of Ex. 2.

The early fauxbourdons of Binchois and Lymburgia, however, present a simpler, more homogeneous style; Lymburgia's *Magnificat secundi toni*[59] has text in the tenor as well and is probably choral. I suspect that all three composers were reacting to the sound of English faburden in two different ways, Dufay transmuting it in terms of the linearity of late Ars Nova music, and the other two reproducing it more directly.

Looking beyond France and Burgundy, no one has yet gone into the curious fact that the early Germanic and Iberian spellings of the term appear to derive from 'faburden', not from 'fauxbourdon'.[60] The earliest German reference is to Paumann playing 'faberdon' on the organ, in a poem published in 1447 by the Nuremberg poet Hanns Rosenplüt:[61]

er trug wol auf von golt in kron
mit Contra-tenor und mit *faberdon*
mit primitonus tenorirt er,
auf ela my so synkopirt er . . .

It is at least possible that one of the favourite cadential clichés in a *Fundamentum* ascribed to Paumann (M.C.P.C.) in the Buxheim Organ Book (Ex. 13)[62] derives from the fifths and thirds of faburden: I have noted over 30 instances of this descent to the cadence. The arrangement of 'Mit ganczem willen' in Paumann's earlier *Fundamentum* in the Lochaim Song-book (Ex. 14)[63] relies exclusively on the use of fifths and thirds in the lowest two parts until the last five bars, when the Mean drops out. The English spelling, or spellings like it, persisted in Germanic manuscripts and is mentioned along with 'faulxbordon' in a Regensburg treatise dated 1476.[64]

Ex. 13

Ex. 14

There are no mid-fifteenth-century examples of Spanish 'fabordón' known to me, but the first literary reference is very remarkable, and has not hitherto been discussed. It appears in the *Libro de vida beata* of Juan de Lucena, which was probably written in 1452–3, and put into final form by 1463. (It is not present in Lucena's model, a dialogue by Faccio). Lucena refers to *fabordón* as a crude, inharmonious and outmoded way of singing 'por uso' (which seems to mean a traditional rule-of-thumb), and he contrasts it with singing 'por razon, como músicos' — with science, like [learned] musicians. He plainly understands the technique and notation involved: he refers to the contradictory B♮s and B♭s (between the inner voice and the outer ones), and to the fact that [if two voices are a fourth apart] 'one is on a line and the other in a space' — which he uses as an image of disharmony:[65]

[El Marqués:] La música, sciencia enamorada, despierta el espiritu, y la persona recrea. No es cosa tan suaue como oyr diuersidat de voces sonoras entonadas sin discordia. Sy todos cantásemos, señor Obispo, en ésta nuestra Castilla por razon, como músicos, seríemos mejor acordados; mas cantando por uso, sy el uno en bemol, el otro en bequadro, el uno va en regla, sy el otro en espacio. El cantar fabordon, y sonar al destempre, denuncia lo qu'esperamos. Quiera Dios mentirir los augurios! Tornando à la música, segun los philósophos, los alegres más alegra, y contrista más los tristes . . .

The passage seems to invoke extemporised *fabordón* rather than a written form. There were almost certainly English choir-men both in Iberia and in South Germany in the 1440s. Alfonso V, King of Portugal, is said to have sent musicians to London in order to recruit singers for his chapel;[66] and in 1442 the Emperor Frederick III requested the Privy Council of England to send him singers: the composer Nicholas Sturgeon was deputed to find suitable candidates.[67] In neither case is it known who went, if anyone, but it is striking that it is precisely in the Iberian peninsula and in Germanic sources that the English-derived spellings are found. It is curious too, that the triumph of a simpler, apparently choral style of fauxbourdon in the Ferrarese manuscript *Mod B* in the 1440s coincides with the presence there of one or two English musicians.[68]

It is not yet possible to explain the name 'fauxbourdon' in a manner agreeable to all, and probably never will be. My own feeling is that it was a deliberately punning transliteration of the English word by Dufay. Such a vernacular term would otherwise scarcely have found its way into manuscripts of high art-music: if it had its origins in a musical characteristic, it would surely have been expressed in Latin, as is the canon attached to Dufay's communion. 'Faux-bourdon' seems likely enough to refer to St. James's pilgrim's staff or 'bourdon', and possibly even to Dufay's friend and patron Robert Auclou as well, since 'bourdon' could mean a flat-headed nail (*clou*). Less fancifully, Busnois's use of the technique of fauxbourdon in his chanson 'Terrible dame' deliberately makes play with the *lack* of a contratenor altus in the opening duet. The two lower voices, in empty and unsatisfied gymel, represent the lover who complains that he is dying 'par deffaut'; his lady, characterised by the top two voices, plus a third in fauxbourdon, asks 'Que vous *fault*?' – 'What do you *lack*?'. Eventually the two pairs of voices mesh contentedly together for four beats in four-voiced fauxbourdon.[69] The 'faux' of fauxbourdon may well refer to the lack of a written contratenor altus, and perhaps also to the feigning, 'feinte', perhaps, in Martin le Franc's phrase,[70] or 'fictus visus', the Sight, by which the contratenor is to transpose his part from the discantus. This is supported by the first literary reference to fauxbourdon, in a rondeau (*c*.1460) by Charles d'Orléans. He speaks of

> Musique *notée par Fainte*
> Avec faulxbourdon de Malheur!
> Qui est il ce nouveau chanteur,
> Qui si mal vient a son actainte?

And the Fauxbourdonneur replies: 'Je ne tiens contre ne teneur'.[71] In addition, a 'bourde' meant a lie, in old French, sometimes an amusing one, or an error; and the term 'bourdon', supposed to derive from it, surfaced into lexicography late in the seventeenth century as printer's jargon for a passage omitted in error — precisely the kind of trade slang that might not quickly find its way into high-class literature. It is an extraordinary coincidence that St. James's other symbol, the cockle shell or 'coquille', also came to be used as printers' jargon, to mean a transposition of letters. Was it an accident that the printers' predecessors in Paris, the copyists and illuminators, had their work-shops all along the Rue des Ecrivains, which is named after them, and which runs along the south side of St. Jacques de la Boucherie? Was St. James the patron saint of their trade guild?

England offers firmer ground, however. As an appendix to this paper I present a preliminary list of all the faburdens known to me, built up largely from the work of Harrison, Caldwell, Doe and Berry,[72] together with an inventory and analysis of their sources. Magnificat faburdens are not yet included. As Harrison has pointed out, many of the English polyphonic settings of Magnificat from c. 1460 to 1500 and even beyond are based, not on the chant, but on its faburden.[73] At least 40 settings survive (two are for organ), though ten are seriously incomplete. At least 25, and probably many more, are based on the faburdens that appear as monophonies in the following British Library sources: MS Lansdowne 462 (f. 2); MS Royal App. 56 (ff. 22^V ff.); printed book C.52 b. 51 (ff. 191–7); Add. MS 4911 (ff. 98^V–102, 103). These tenors, however, are not always true faburdens, especially those for Tones I and VI, though there is an earlier version for Tone I that is stricter. This finding would lead one to exclude five of the 25 faburden settings, placing them rather in the category of 'squares'. Including the monophonic sources, we have a minimum of 49 separate copies of faburdens to Magnificat, of which eleven would be more properly classed as 'squares'. The field is a vast one, however, and needs much more thorough and extensive investigation. It will be sensible to await Paul Doe's promised study. Also excluded from the list are the many fourteenth- and fifteenth-century English composi-tions whose bottom part proceeds largely or exclusively in fifths and thirds beneath a plainsong Mean, where there is no evidence that such a part also leads an independent life as a faburden.

Excluding Magnificat settings, there are 155 faburdens in 175 copies, scattered among 32 sources (see Appendix I). (The inclusion of Magnificat faburdens would bring the total to over 200.) The establishment of further close concordances will doubtless reduce this number, but there is no doubt that here we have a body of material comparable in number and liturgical scope with the repertory of fauxbourdon, though the written musical evidence of faburden comes later in time.

Appendix I is arranged by liturgical category; the analytical table of sources (Appendix II) is classified by notations, showing the various liturgical categories represented in each. Two thirds of surviving faburdens are hymns. There are 111 different copies of faburdens, reduced by concordances to 103, for 46 hymns (some, of course have the same tune in common). Of these hymns 25 have only one known faburden apiece. Ten have two, three have three and six have four. It is not surprising that two hymns used on many liturgical occasions, 'Salvator mundi' and 'O lux beata Trinitas', should have attracted ten and twenty faburden settings respectively. The faburden to 'O lux', uniquely amongst this repertory, was especially favoured as a cantus firmus for pedagogical purposes: fourteen canons, proportional exercises and so on survive, based on the whole or part of the faburden.

The processional hymn 'Salve festa dies' has many different sets of words for varying liturgical occasions. Most of the settings are not strict faburden (the commonest one begins with a unison), which is why they appear in parentheses in column 2 of the analytical table. This traditional counterpoint, like the so-called faburden to the Magnificat Tone I, can be traced back into the fourteenth century, apparently before strict faburden had evolved. Such a tune is more properly called a 'square' — but then all faburdens are also potential 'squares'.

Faburden was a useful technique for processions. Five settings have come down to us of the Easter Psalms 'Laudate pueri' and 'In exitu Israel', with their 'Alleluia' refrains. Only one Psalm faburden survives, though responsorial psalmody must have been a natural home for faburden.

There are eight settings of Te Deum, a single offertory and seven antiphons, one of them, the important 'Asperges' for Candlemas, with three faburdens. There may be a specimen of a Communion. Four of the nine Sarum Processional Rogationtide Litanies have faburdens, with roughly four related settings each. There are two unidentified items.

In the list of sources of faburden (Appendix III below) the first and second groups are closely related, but I have thought it worthwhile to make the distinction between them. Group (a) consists of four sources where 43 faburdens are copied with their plainsongs, usually on the same stave. Group (b) contains fourteen sources in which 34 faburdens are copied on their own as (normally) mensural monophonies. The interesting features of notation that both groups present will be discussed later. Group (c) has six manuscripts of sacred polyphonic vocal music in which 32 faburdens, usually without their plainsongs, have been employed as the basis for polyphony as cantus firmi in their own right. Twenty-four similar compositions appear in the five sources of group (d), listed separately here because their use for didactic purposes sets them at one remove from the practical sources. In group (e) appear six keyboard manuscripts containing 43 faburdens in polyphonic arrangement.

Groups (a) and (b) are the most unusual. They contain between them 77 faburdens — half the total repertory, in fact, together with the unlisted faburdens to Magnificat. Nearly all are plainsong books of the fourteenth, fifteenth and sixteenth centuries — most of them sources which went almost unregarded until Dr. Berry decided to study fifteenth- and sixteenth-century plainsong for its own sake. One is a Sarum gradual; no less than ten are Sarum processionals — one can hardly open one it seems, without finding polyphony — and two are Sarum Hymnals. Two odd men out are interesting. In MS Digby 167 is a leaf with two secular pieces and a faburden employing 'stroke' notation which could be read by an unlearned musician, since it avoids problems of perfection and alteration. The other case is Ryman's Manuscript — the work of a Franciscan poet who translated many Latin hymns into singable English versions and also wrote a great number of carols. These examples imply that faburden had its vernacular, even secular uses, as I have suggested elsewhere.[74] Indeed, I believe that the term 'burden', meaning 'refrain', which is not attested before the late sixteenth century in English, may owe its origin to the habit of singing a refrain in faburden.

The bulk of the faburdens in groups (a) and (b) were discovered by Dr. Mary Berry.[75] Her work has revealed the existence in plainsong books not only of monophonic faburden-parts, but also of a large number of faburdens indicated on the same staves as the plainsongs. Almost all are hymns. The faburdens are written in essentially three related notations: (*i*) some give dots or plainsong symbols over every note, either in unison with it or at the third above; (*ii*) others indicate only the thirds, so that unmarked notes in the chant are to be taken as unisons; (*iii*) the most economical notation of all indicates simply the rare unisons by means of dots or strokes through them. It is possible to prove that the third of these notations does indeed indicate faburden, though Dr. Berry leaves the matter undecided: in the hymn 'Deus Creator omnium' (No. 33 in Appendix I) a fuller and more explicit notation has been superimposed on the original stroked unisons, and this later version does indeed show them to be the only unisons in the piece. There are also occasional mensural notes amongst these notations, nearly always to show a simple cadential ornament.

Dr. Berry interprets the dots and plainsong symbols as actual notes, implying the transposition of the chant to form the Treble at the octave above (and to form the Mean at the fifth above). While this is certainly a possible way of handling a chant that lies low, I believe that these are all in fact notations that show the faburden 'Sight' and are intended to be sung a fifth lower. The dots resemble those used to show sighted notes in the discant treatise in London, British Library, Add. MS 21455; and a fortunate concordance between the first verse of a hymn in sight notation and its second verse as a monophony, presumably at its proper pitch, on a blank leaf in the same book, lends support to this hypothesis: for although the hymn, 'Deus Creator omnium' (Nos. 33 and 34), lies unusually low, the monphonic faburden runs in fifths and thirds beneath it.

I do not, of course, suggest that there was any absolute standard of pitch, though the frequent use of organ arrangements of faburden, no doubt in alternation with a choir singing the faburden with its plainsong, must have affected the issue of transposition. This whole matter must depend on a general study of transposition, of the kind that Sanders has begun. It is interesting, nevertheless, to note that an early sixteenth-century parish clerk of Faversham (Kent) was expected to 'sett the quyer not after his own brest but as every man beying a synger may synge convenyently his part and wher playn songe fayleth one of theym [the clerks] shall leve faburden and kepe the playn songe unto the tyme the quyer be sett agayne'.[76]

By far the commonest interval of transposition, when a chant was placed in the Mean in written fourteenth-century English music, was the upper fifth. This would bring the Treble of faburden to the upper octave, since it is a fourth above the Mean. In the notes to Appendix I I have indicated the transposition of the chant, in one voice or the other relative to the faburden, though in many cases this may have little significance; I have, however, noted cases where the presence of otherwise unexpected flats in the faburden suggests that the chant was imagined as being at its normal pitch in the Mean.

These insular sources, here collated for the first time, present a quite different picture from the sources of fauxbourdon. Fauxbourdon was doubtless extemporised *super librum* like faburden,[77] and we should now seek early traces of this; but it has left its main mark in history as sophisticated music, specially composed for professional performance, transmitted, even at its simplest, in learned notation in manuscripts which usually also contain the finest high-culture music of their time. The canonic instructions describing how to perform fauxbourdon are written in Latin, which is also the language used by musical theorists in discussing it. Faburden, though it came to leave its traces in polyphonic manuscripts, was essentially a means of formulaic improvisation which did not normally need to be written down; it was certainly used by sophisticated performers, but its chief advantage was that it could be sung by unlearned monks and musically unsophisticated canons and vicars-choral, many of whom were in any case not permitted to sing elaborate polyphony. The two insular treatises on faburden are in English, not Latin. Its essentially oral tradition helps to explain why there is such a gap between the first archival and theoretical references to faburden and the earliest concrete examples that we find in later manuscripts. Certain preferred forms of a faburden, 'fixing' the choices of fifth or third, no doubt came to be handed on orally, and from the 1460s we are able to trace such traditional faburdens where they were written down as a basis for composed polyphony, or perhaps for more elaborate organ extemporisations or simply in order to secure agreement where there were several singers, even several choirs, to a part,[78] or to establish 'composed' faburdens which depart from Wylde's specifications for extemporised faburden. The most cogent reason for 'fixing' faburden on paper, though, was undoubtedly that in time the faburden itself came to be used as a *cantus prius factus* for four-part harmonisation or other group improvisation. Guilielmus Monachus and Scottish Anonymous both describe such practices.[79] In such a case it would be essential to know the exact pitch of each note in the faburden. Monophonic faburdens, when they survive, are almost exclusively to be found in liturgical plainsong books. (Only one such single-line fauxbourdon tenor is known, the anonymous hymn 'Cultor Dei': perhaps significantly it is found in a source which is nearer to English influence and example than the Italian manuscripts, namely Cambrai, Bibliothèque Municipale, MS 29 (*olim* 32), f. 159.)

It is mainly because scholars have not been comparing like with like — on the one hand a mainly written tradition, and on the other a mainly oral one — that the question of the origins of faburden and fauxbourdon is proving so difficult to resolve. I hope that this preliminary study will have at least set the discussion on a proper footing.

NOTES

1. 'Musicological Studies', iii, New York, 1959; partly based on the same author's *Early Renaissance Harmony* (unpublished dissertation), University of Indiana, 1954.

2. 'Faburden and Fauxbourdon', *Musica disciplina*, xiii (1959), 44–78.

3. 'Authentic and Spurious Faburden', *Revue belge de musicologie*, xiv (1960), 3–29.

4. 'Music for the Sarum Rite', *Annales musicologiques*, vi (1958–63), 99–144; 'Faburden in Practice', *Musica disciplina*, xvi (1962), 11–34; see also *Music in Medieval Britain*, London, 1958.

5. ' "English Discant" and Discant in England', *The Musical Quarterly*, xlv (1959), 26–48.

6. See especially 'Cantilena and Discant in 14th-century England', *Musica disciplina*, xix (1965), 7–52; also his communication to the *Journal of the American Musicological Society*, xxxi (1978), 168–73.

7. Mother Thomas More [Dr. Mary Berry], *The Performance of Plainsong in the later Middle Ages* (unpublished dissertation), Cambridge University, 1970. I am most grateful to Dr. Berry for allowing me to put her remarkable discoveries into general circulation.

8. 'Bourdon' and 'Faburdon/fauxbourdon/falso bordone' in *Handwörterbuch der musikalischen Terminologie*, ed. H. H. Eggebrecht, Wiesbaden, 1972 ff. Her unpublished dissertation is *Tenor/Contratenor und Bourdon/Fauxbourdon*, University of Freiburg im Breisgau, 1970. Other articles in musical reference-works are R. Brinkmann, 'Faburden and Fauxbourdon' in *Riemann Musik-Lexikon*, 12th edn., ed. W. Gurlitt and H. H. Eggebrecht, Mainz, 1959–67; and my forthcoming 'Faburden and Fauxbourdon' in *The New Grove's Dictionary*.

9. 'Keyboard Plainsong Settings in England, 1500–1660', *Musica disciplina*, xix (1965), 129–53; the music is in *Early Tudor Organ Music I: The Office* ('Early English Church Music', vi), London, 1965.

10. See his *Early Tudor Magnificats I* ('Early English Church Music', iv), London, 1962, especially pp. x and 136 f.

11. *Choral Institutions within the English Church: their Constitution and Development 1340—1500* (unpublished dissertation), University of East Anglia, 1975.

12. M. Vogel, 'Musica falsa und falso bordone', *Festschrift Walter Wiora*, ed. L. Finscher and C.-H. Mahling, Kassel, 1967, pp. 170–76 (a brilliant and wide-ranging fantasia with, however, little application to the immediate problem); and R. A. Hall jun., 'L'etimologia di "falsobordone" ', *Archivio glottologico italiano*, liii (1968), 141–7, suggesting that the 'faux' of 'fauxbourdon' comes from 'fors' = 'hors', Latin 'foris', as in 'faubourg'.

13. Ed. H. Kurath, with S. M. Kuhn, Ann Arbor, 1956 ff., s.v. 'burdoun'.

14. No. 78 in Appendix I below.

15. In British Library, Lansdowne MS 763, ff. 116–116^V; for the most recent transcription see Trowell, 'Faburden and Fauxbourdon', pp. 47 f.

16. Op. cit., pp. 53 f.

17. 'Authentic and Spurious Faburden', pp. 28 f.; cf. Hoffmann-Axthelm, 'Faburdon', p. 2.

18. From Corpus Christi College, Cambridge, MS 410; see M. F. Bukofzer, *Geschichte des englischen Diskants und des Fauxbourdons nach den theoretischen Quellen*, Strasbourg, 1936, p. 146 (for other statements of the rule also pp. 143, 149).

19. Chant from *Graduale Sarisburiense*, ed. W. H. Frere, London, 1894, ii.203 and Pl. z.

20. Datings follow H. H. Carter, *A Dictionary of Middle English Musical Terms*, ed.

G. B. Gerhard, Bloomington, 1961, and the *Middle English Dictionary*.

21.   From the *Speculum caritatis*, written when Aelred was novice-master at the Cistercian abbey of Rievaulx: *Patrologiae cursus completus . . . , series secunda*, ed. J.-P. Migne, cxcv (1855), 571 f. (Here and in subsequent quotations I have italicized the significant terms.) There was also singing 'triparti vel quadriparti voce' at the Cistercian abbeys of Dore and Tintern in 1217 (see A. A. King, *Liturgies of the Religious Orders*, London, 1955, p. 95, citing J. M. Canivez, *Statuta Capitulorum Generalium Ordinis Cisterciensis ab anno 1116 ad annum 1786*, Louvain, 1933–9, i.472). For Benedictines singing 'triplici cantu' at Norwich Cathedral Priory *c*. 1260(?), 'in triplum/in triplis' at Westminster Abbey *c*. 1270, 'cantantes organum' with lay-clerks 'in cantu qui dicitur trebill' at Durham Abbey in the 1390s, and for five brethren 'aut certe organiste, si sint' singing 'triplici melodia' at St. Mary's, York, *c*. 1400, see references in Harrison, *Music in Medieval Britain*, pp. 113–15.

22.   For Cutell see Bukofzer, op. cit. 'Medium' as a voice-name appears in British Library, Harl. MS 2942, f. 121ᵛ: see Appendix I below, notes to section II. The 'Mean' fits the 'square' on f. 121 and contains some of the notes of the (migrant) chant: the remainder were presumably in the now missing treble.

23.   *c*. 1330 (*c*. 1300?); ed. E. Kölbing in 'Zwei mittelenglische Bearbeitungen der Sage von St. Patriks Purgatorium', *Englische Studien*, i (1877), 108. Not in Carter, *Dictionary of Middle English Musical Terms*; nor in Kurath, *Middle English Dictionary*, under 'Burdoun', or 'Hautein'.

24.   Ed. Carleton Brown, *Anniversary Papers by Colleagues and Pupils of G. L. Kittredge*, Boston, 1913, p. 110.

25.   Ed. F. J. Furnivall (Rolls Series: 'Rerum Britannicarum medii aevi scriptores', lxxxvii), London, 1887, i.393 f. Variant: 'burdowne'. The dialect is northern; Mannyng was associated with the Gilbertines of Sempringham.

26.   *Cywyddau Iolo Goch ac Eraill, 1350—1450*, ed. H. Lewis, T. Roberts & I. Williams, Cardiff, 1925 (2nd edn. 1937), p. 83; see also p. 245. I am most grateful to Mr. Osian Ellis for bringing this and the Nanmor quotation to my attention, and for his help with the medieval Welsh.

27.   Ed. W. B. D. D. Turnbull, Edinburgh, 1843, p. 61. Variants: 'trebulles', 'meyne', 'burdown'; I have replaced 'th' by the Middle English thorn. Again the dialect is northern.

28.   *Minor Poems*, Part II (secular), ed. H. N. MacCracken (Early English Text Society, original series, cxcii), London, 1934, p. 448.

29   *The poetical Works of Dafydd Nanmor*, ed. T. Roberts & I. Williams, Cardiff, 1923, p. 73. Variant: 'bwrdwn. Nanmor was active 1450–80.

30.   *Shepherds' Play, II*, ed. G. England & W. W. Pollard (E.E.T.S., extra series, lxxi), London, 1897, p. 122.

31.   *A Morality of Wisdom, Who is Christ*, ed. F. J. Furnivall & A. W. Pollard (E.E.T.S., e.s., cxci), London, 1904, p. 55. It is in the area of the mystery plays that we first come across the term 'three-man's song', which may probably be related to our triad of voices: 'In my lyf louely I lede, / Þat had leuere syttyn at þe ale, / iij mens songys to syngyn lowde, / þanne to-ward þe chyrche for to crowde' (*c*. 1425, Macro Plays, *The Castell of Perseverance*, ibid., p. 147). Carter omits 'Three mannys songe, tricinnium' (*c*. 1440, *Promptorium parvulorum*, ed. A. Way (Camden society Publications), iii (London, 1853), 492). *The Tournament of Tottenham*, a northern dialect poem written *c*. 1400–1440, ends with a mention of 'vi menys sang' which must surely be a mis-copying, 'vj' for 'iij': 'Mekyl myrth was þem amang: / in euery corner of þe hous / Was melody delycyous, / For to here precyus, / Of vi menys sang' (*Middle English Metrical Romances*, ed. W. Hoyt French & C. Brockway, New York, 1930, p. 988).

32. See *Geiriadur cenhedlaethol: a National Dictionary of the Welsh Language*, ed. W. Owen Pughe, 3rd edn., rev. R. J. Pryse, Denbigh, 1891–3, s.v. 'trebl'; *Barddoniaeth Dafydd ab Gwilym*, ed. O. Jones, W. Owen & E. Williams, Liverpool, 1873, p. 113. I am grateful to Mr. Osian Ellis for passing on to me Dr. Parry's opinion. Variant for 'organ brudd': 'acen prudd', meaning 'chief accent', a poetic term.

33. *The Judgment*, ed. cit. (see note 30 above), p.384

34. Ed. J. E. Wülfing (E.E.T.S., o.s., cxxi), London, 1902, p. 195.

35. *The Poetical Works of Chaucer*, ed. F. N. Robinson, Cambridge, 1933, lines 672–4. Variants: 'burdon', 'Bordoun'.

36. Ibid., lines 4162–6. Not in Carter.

37. See J. H. Baxter & C. Johnson, *Medieval Latin Word-list, from British and Irish Sources*, London, 1934, s.v. 'Burdo'. Also Harrison, *Music in Medieval Britain*, pp. 206, 249: 'sonantibus chalamis (quos "burdones" apellamus)' during the induction ceremonies of the Abbots of St. Alban's, quoting the *Gesta Abbatum* — perhaps the same source as the above? To this we may relate Ulrich von Richental's account of the ceremony when the English bishops arrived at the Council of Constance in 1414: 'die pusauner pusaunoten über einannder mit dreyen stimmen, als man sunst gewonlichen singet' (quoted by J. Handschin in *Schweizerische Musikzeitung*, lxxiv (1934), 459, along with an unverifiable reference given by Chrysander to singers performing 'Widerstreits' on the same occasion).

38. From Sanders, 'Cantilena and Discant', p. 51; Worcester Fragment No. 91.

39. Ibid., pp. 9–17.

40. Leeds Central Library, Archives Department, MS VR 6120, ff. 2–2ᵛ; beginning only.

41. Ibid., f. 4.

42. British Library, Sloane MS 1210, ff. 139ᵛ–40.

43. John Wyclif, 'Of Prelates', *The English Works*, ed. F. D. Matthew (E.E.T.S., o.s., lxxiv), London, 1880, p. 76.

44. 'Of Feigned Contemplative Life', ibid., p. 192. I have gathered fifteen further such references between 1350 and 1440. Other passages complain of dance-like music, of instruments played by friars (too literally the *joculatores Dei*), and of the use in church of 'swete notis of spectaclis or taverne songis' (*c*. 1389); a passage in Wyclif's *Prologue to the Psalms* may refer to some kind of burden (undersinging) performed by a large number of singers: 'EiꝪty and eiꝪte forsothe seiden the salmys, and two hundrid the vndersinging' (1382–4: John Wyclif, *The Old Testament*, ed. J. Forshall & Sir F. Madden, Oxford, 1850, p. 738).

45. Sloane MS 1210, f. 138. Note the B flats in the outer voices, as in faburden; the narrow-stepping Mean on its four-line stave looks very like a dance tune.

46. Ibid., f. 1: a fragmentary Credo apparently designed for Carthusian use, since the text contains the variant 'et vitam *futuri* seculi'. The lowest part is almost a pure faburden throughout the movement.

47. f. II.

48. f. 140.

49. Oxford, Bodleian Library, MS Laud. lat. 95, f. 133ᵛ.

50. 'John Wylde and the Musica Guidonis', *Musica disciplina*, xxix (1977), 46–48. She likens the handwriting to that of a scribe who was a Fellow of Merton College, Oxford, from 1429 to 1440, reproduced as Plate 17 of M. B. Parkes, *English Cursive Book Hands, 1250–1500*, Oxford, 1969.

51. H. E. Wooldridge in *The Oxford History of Music*, i (Oxford, 1905), 125; E. Ferand, *Die Improvisation in der Musik*, Zurich, 1938, p.171, suggests 'first half of the fifteenth century'; Warren, 'Punctus Organi and Cantus Coronatus in the Music of

Dufay', *Papers read at the Dufay Quincentenary Conference*, ed. A. Atlas, New York, 1976, p. 137, suggests 'early fifteenth century'.

52. 'Three Musical Treatises in English from a fifteenth-century MS', *Speculum*, x (1935), 235.

53. The passage in the *Speculum cantancium* (f. 59) listing the various musical sinners whose peccadillos the demon Tutivillus collects, is paralleled in the late fourteenth-century Doom Play (see M. D. Anderson, *Drama and Imagery in English Medieval Churches*, Cambridge, 1963, pp. 173 ff.).

54. See C. F. Bühler, 'A New Manuscript of the Middle English Tract on Proportions (sometimes attributed to Chilston)', *Speculum*, xxi (1946), 229–33; both versions of the tract descend ultimately from the fourteenth-century mathematician Bradwardine.

55. F. Madan & H. H. E. Craster, *A Summary Catalogue of Western Manuscripts in the Bodleian Library at Oxford*, Oxford, 1922, ii/1. 249 f.

56. I give the Bodley 515 readings (f. 90) of both passages, as they are better than those of the Lansdowne manuscript. The sources are connected, for Lansdowne 763 also had trouble with 'cum diapente' (lines 2–3), placing it later in the margin; 'quia' (line 8) for Lansdowne's 'et' suggests a new derivation of the term 'cantus fractus'. Both sources read 'xiij^{ma}', perhaps for 'xij^{ma}'? 'Univolus' (line 6) perhaps relates to Carter, op. cit., pp. 319 and 367, citing Bartholomaeus Anglicus' translation (1398) of John de Trevisa's *De Proprietatibus rerum*, 'Voys uniuolenta is nesshe and plyaunt'. See Postscript below.

57. Private communication from Dr. Bowers, whose generosity in these matters is already legendary; for the 1447 version see Harrison, *Music in Medieval Britain*, p. 187.

58. Communion from the *Missa Sancti Jacobi*: after Dufay, *Opera omnia*, ed. H. Besseler ('Corpus mensurabilis musicae', i) ii (Rome, 1960), 44. In the above example chant notes omitted are given in brackets.

59. Bologna, Conservatorio di musica G. B. Martini, MS Q 15 (*olim* 37), No. 319.

60. See H. Flasdieck, 'Elisab. *Faburden* "Fauxbourdon" und NE. *Burden* "refrain"', *Anglia*, lxxv (1956), 206; Brinkmann ('Fauxbourdon', p. 278b) finds this evidence 'noteworthy', presumably thinking it unlikely, as I do, that the English transmuted the term 'fauxbourdon' into 'faburden' and then exported it back to the Continent by 1447.

61. Cited in G. Adler, 'Studie zur Geschichte der Harmonie', *Sitzungsberichte der Wiener Akademie der Wissenschaften, philosophisch-historische Klasse*, xcviii/3 (1881), 788.

62. After *Das Buxheimer Orgelbuch*, ii, ed. B. A. Wallner ('Das Erbe deutscher Musik', xxxviii), Kassel, 1958, p. 239.

63. After *Locheimer Liederbuch und Fundamentum organisandi des Conrad Paumann*, facsimile ed. K. Ameln, Berlin, 1925 (reprinted Kassel, 1972), p. 72.

64. Cited in Hoffmann-Axthelm, 'Faburdon', p. 3b.

65. *Opúsculos literarios de los siglos XIV. á XVI.* (Sociedad de Bibliófilos Españoles, publications, xxix), Madrid, 1892, p. 157.

66. See L. de Freitas Branco, *Elementos de Sciencias Musicais*, Lisbon, 1931, ii.38.

67. See Sir H. Nicolas, *Proceedings and Ordinances of the Privy Council of England*, [London], 1834–5, v.218.

68. See N. Pirrotta, 'Ricercare e variazioni su "O Rosa Bella" ', *Studi Musicali*, i (1972), 67–72 (Galfridus de Anglia); and L. Lockwood, 'Dufay and Ferrara', *Dufay Quincentenary Conference*, pp. 7 f. (Robertus de Anglia, Johannes de Anglia, Johannes ab arpa de Anglia).

69. The opening of the chanson is quoted in A. Pirro, *Histoire de la musique de la fin du XIVe siècle à la fin du XVIe*, Paris, 1940, p. 120.

70. In *Le Champion des dames* (1441–2); cited in G. Reese, *Music in the Renaissance*, New York, 1954, pp. 12 f.

71. *Poésies*, ed. P. Champion ('Les Classiques français du moyen âge', xxxiv & lvi), Paris, 1923 &1927, ii.525 (italics mine).

72. I must express my gratitude to Dr. John Caldwell and Professor Paul Doe for their great kindness in sending me corrections and drawing my attention to further faburdens and to concordances I had missed. Professor Doe has also pointed out that faburden techniques continued for a while in music composed for the vernacular Anglican liturgy (cf. the Wanley manuscripts), but this material is not included here. See Paul Doe, pp. 81 f. below.

73. 'Faburden in Practice', pp. 20–22.

74. 'Faburden and Fauxbourdon', pp. 57 ff.

75. See the long and fascinating analysis of the repertory and its notation in her dissertation, pp. 246–84.

76. Ibid., p. 281, citing H. C. Baillie, *London Churches, their Music and Musicians, 1485–1560* (unpublished dissertation), Cambridge University, 1957–8, p. 57.

77. There are hints of this in the later fifteenth-century theorists; and the regulations of Charles V's chapel are suggestive: see E. van der Straeten, *La Musique aux Pays-Bas avant le XIXe siècle*, vii (Brussels, 1885), 181–6.

78. At a procession in London in 1531, '. . . next came ye blake fryars with their cross and every friar a cope, singinge the litany with faburden . . . after them came Paul's choir, every priest and clerck had a cope with all their residentiaries in copes, singing the litany with faburden . . .' (cited in D. Stevens, 'La Musique d'orgue en Angleterre avant la Réforme', *Revue de musicologie;* xxxii (1953), 147).

79. See the excellent analysis of various methods of formulaic harmonisation developed from fauxbourdon in Trumble, *Fauxbourdon*, pp. 46–67. Various references have been cited by C. A. Miller from the writings of Erasmus, and some of these support the notion that faburden had sprouted further techniques beyond simple three-part harmonisation by the time of Erasmus's visits to England: 'Jam qui crassiores sunt quam ut artem musicam queant perdiscere, non putant satisfieri festo diei, nisi depravatum quoddam cantus genus adhibeant, quod illi Fauburdum appellant. *Id nec thema praescripta reddit*, nec artis harmonias observat' (italics mine)(Erasmus, *Opera omnia*, ed. J. Clericus, Leiden, 1703–6, vi.713c–732c); 'Nam est hujus modi musices genus apud Britannos, ut multi inter se concinant, *quorum nullus eas sonat voces quas habent codicum notulae* (ibid., i.930a). Miller quotes these in English translation: 'Erasmus on Music', *The Musical Quarterly*, lii (1966), 339, 341.

POSTSCRIPT

Since the completion of this paper, John Aplin has discussed aspects of faburden in the reformed Anglican liturgy in 'A Group of English Magnificats "upon the Faburden" ', *Soundings*, vii (1978), 85–100. I have also discovered the explanation of the curious term 'Univolus' (see note 56 above). Both forms of the word must be mis-readings of 'Vinnola' or 'Vinnolus'. Bartholomaeus is quoting Isidore of Seville: 'Vinnola vox est mollis atque flexibilis. Et vinnola dicta a vinno, hoc est cincinno molliter flexo' (Migne, *Patrologia latina*, lxxxii. 166). This curious reference to crisped hair may connect with the term 'cantus crispus', which surfaces in 1505–6 and 1538 in connection with 'squares' (see Harrison, *Music in Medieval Britain*, pp. 165 & 181).

APPENDIX I

CHECKLIST OF SURVIVING FABURDENS (EXCLUDING MAGNIFICAT)

The columns are arranged as follows:

No: A separate number is allotted to each individual faburden, save in the case of close concordances, which are gathered under the same number.

Title: The complete liturgical incipit is used, even where the faburden omits the beginner's words or starts with the second verse of a hymn

Source: The sigla employed are given in Appendix III. Folio numbers follow, or 'p.' for page.

Type: Classified according to the categories in Appendix III and, where there are several settings of the same chant, presented in that order:

   (a)   copied with chant
   (b)   mensural monophony
   (c)   used as the basis for vocal polyphony
   (d)   used by a musical theorist or as a c.f. for canonic writing
   (e)   used in a keyboard piece

Notes: This column gives the liturgical occasion (for the first piece only, where there are two or more settings of the same chant); the number of voices, where the faburden is set in vocal polyphony; comments on the type of notation; any other points of interest, such as the presence of B flats and/or E flats that suggest the early form of faburden with the c. f. untransposed in the Mean.

60

Chant: Where possible, this column identifies whether the c.f. is to be thought of as the Mean (m) or Treble (t). Transposition upwards is shown by a figure giving the interval; the rarer downward transposition is indicated by a minus sign before the figure: thus 't8' means 'c.f. in Treble an octave above the original pitch', and 't-2' means 'c.f. in Treble, a tone beneath its original pitch'. It is assumed that the notation of, e.g. *H2951* indicates the 'sight' and implies transposition a fifth downward.

I: HYMNS

No.	Title	Source	Type	Notes	Chant
1	Ad cenam agni providi (i)	*H2951*, 46–47	a	2nd Vespers, Low Sunday. 5s dotted	m
2	Ad cenam agni providi (i)	*Pepys*, 52	c	2vv.	t8
3	A solis ortus cardine	*H2951*, 6^v–7	a	Lauds, Christmas Day. 5s dotted	m
4	A solis ortus cardine	*29996*, 163^v	e		t8
5	Aeterne rerum conditor	*H2951*, 12^v–14	a	Lauds, 1st Sunday after Octave of Epiphany and Sundays until Lent. 5s dotted	m
6	Aeterne rerum conditor	*29996*, 172^v	e		t8
7	Aeterne rerum conditor	*29996*, 11^v & 18	e	By Redford	t
8	Aeterne rex altissime	*H2951*, 47–48	a	Vespers, Vigil of Ascension. 5s dotted	m
9	Aeterne rex altissime	*Digby*, 31^v	b	Secular MS. Stroke notation	t8
10	Aeterne rex altissime	*CS2b21*, 188	b	Plainsong symbols, mensural cadences. B flat key-signature, with E flats	m
11	Aeterne rex altissime	*Pepys*, 70^v–71	c	3vv. Chant in discantus, free at times. B flats in top and bottom parts only	
12	Alma chorus domini	*Gyffard*, i.153, ii.151^v, iii.147^v, iv. 142^v	c	Compline, Whitsun and 3 following days; Compline, Name of Jesus	m?
13	Aurea luce et decore roseo (i)	*H2951*, 66–66^v	a	1st Vespers, Vigil of SS. Peter and Paul. 5s dotted	m
14	Ave maris stella	*H2951*, 68–69	a	Vespers, Annunciation of BVM. 5s dotted	m

No.	Title	Source	Type	Notes	Chant
15	Beata nobis gaudia	H2951, 52ᵛ–53ᵛ	a	2nd Vespers, Whitsun. 5s dotted	m
16	Beata nobis gaudia	C52b21, 189ᵛ	b	Plainsong symbols, mensural cadences. B flat key-signature, with E flats and one E natural	
17	Bina caelestis aulae luminaria (i)	29996, 166	e	Matins, St. John the Apostle. First note not set	m
18	Bina caelestis aulae luminaria (ii)	29996, 167	e	Ibid., Octave Day and Sunday within Octave	t
19	Chorus novae ierusalem	H2951, 43–44	a	1st vespers, Low Sunday. 5s dotted	t8
20	Christe qui lux es et dies	H2951, 34–35	a	Compline, 1st Sunday in Lent. 5s and 3s dotted	m
21	Christe qui lux es et dies	Scot, 95ᵛ	d	B flat at 'lucisque'	m
22	Christe qui lux es et dies	29996, 176	e		t8
23	Christe qui lux es et dies	29996, 10ᵛ and 30513, 35	e		t8
24	Christe redemptor omnium	H2951, 72ᵛ–73ᵛ	e	By Redford	t
25	Christe redemptor omnium	RA56, 31ᵛ	a	Matins, Christmas Day. 5s dotted	m
26	Christe redemptor omnium	29996, 162ᵛ	b	One B flat	m
27	Christe.sanctorum decus	H2951, 70ᵛ–72	e	Lauds, St. Michael Archangel. 5s stroked	t8
28	Conditor alme siderum	H2951, 1–1ᵛ	a	1st and 2nd Vespers, 1st Sunday in Advent. 5s dotted	m
29	Conditor alme siderum	C52b21, ii	a	5s and 3s dotted; 1 square note, some pairs of minims	m
30	Conditor alme siderum	Morley, p. 207	d	Commentary directs downward transposition of faburden by an octave	
31	Conditor alme siderum	29996, 158	e	1st Vespers, 1st Sunday after Octave of Epiphany. 5s dotted	t
32	Deus Creator omnium	H2951, 9ᵛ–10ᵛ	a		t8
33	Deus Creator omnium	C52b21, xivᵛ–xvᵛ	a	Originally only 5s stroked; then plainsong symbols superimposed; some minims	m
34	Deus Creator omnium	C52b21, 200	b	Plainsong symbols with mensural cadences. B-flat key-signature	m
35	Deus Creator omnium	29996, 171	e		t8

No.	Title	Source	Type	Notes	Chant
36	Doctor egregie Paule	H2951, 66[v]–67[v]	a	Conversion of St. Paul. 5s dotted	m
37	Ecce tempus idoneum	29996, 178[v]	e	Vespers, 3rd Sunday in Lent. Incomplete	t8
38	Ex more docti mystico	29996, 174[v]	e	1st Vespers, 1st Sunday in Lent	t8
39	Exsultet caelum laudibus	Pepys, 15[v]–17[v]	c	Lauds, Apostles or Octave of Apostles. By Gylbert Banastre. 3vv.	t8
40	Hostis Herodes impie (i)	H2951, 8–9	a	1st and 2nd Vespers, Epiphany; tune for day, following Sunday and Octave Day. 5s dotted	m
41	Hostis Herodes impie (i)	29996, 169	e	Tune for remaining days of Octave of Epiphany	m
42	Hostis Herodes impie (ii)	29996, 170	e		t
43	Iam Christus astra ascenderat	C52b21, lv[v]–lvi	a	Vigil of Whitsun and 1st Vespers. 5s and 3s dotted; some plainsong symbols and minims	t8
44	Immense caeli conditor	H2951, 19	a	Vespers, feria ii after Epiphany. 5s dotted	m
45	Iste confessor domini	H2951, 89[v]–90[v]	a	1st Vespers and Matins of a Confessor. 3s dotted	m
46	Iste confessor domini	Pepys, 67	c	3vv. Mean slightly closer to chant than discantus	m
47	Jesu nostra redemptio	H2951, 48–49	a	Compline, Vigil of Ascension. 5s dotted	m5?
48	Jesu salvator seculi (i)	H2951, 44–44[v]	a	Compline, 1st Sunday after Octave of Easter. 5s dotted	m
49	Jesu salvator seculi (i)	Pepys, 96	b	Chant fits this monophony slightly better as a Mean	m
50	Jesu salvator seculi (ii)	H2951, 72–72[v]	a	Compline, Octave of Easter week. 5s dotted	m5?
51	Lucis creator optime	29996, 173[v]	e	2nd Vespers, 1st Sunday after Octave of Epiphany; and Trinity to Advent	m
52	O gloriosa femina	H2951, 62[v]–63[v]	a	Lauds, Purification of BVM. 5s dotted	t
53	O lux beata Trinitas	H2951, 55[v]	a	1st Vespers, Sundays from Trinity to Advent. 3s dotted	m
54	O lux beata Trinitas	H2951, 16–16[v]	a	(Marked for 2nd Vespers). 5s dotted	m

No.	Title	Source	Type	Notes	Chant
55	O lux beata Trinitas	Pepys, 61–61^v	b	Ornamental monophonic version of faburden: 3 verses in diminishing proportion. B flats suggest Mean chant	m5?
56	O lux beata Trinitas	Pepys, 11	c	3vv.	t8
57	O lux beata Trinitas	Ritson, 60^v–62	c	2vv.: 3 verses in diminishing proportion. B flats suggest Mean chant	m5?
58	O lux beata Trinitas	Scot, 10	d	4vv.; example of proportions	t8
59	O lux beata Trinitas	Scot, 34^v	d	2vv.; example of melodic inversion	t8
60	O lux beata Trinitas	Scot, 40–40^v	d	3vv.; canon on the faburden	t8
61	O lux beata Trinitas	Scot, 96	d	3vv.; example of faburden	t8
62	O lux beata Trinitas	Scot, 103^v	d	3vv.; example of transposed faburden	t6
63	O lux beata Trinitas	Scot, 103^v–104	d	By Fayrfax. 3vv. example of faburden transposed	t6
64 a-f	O lux beata Trinitas	31391	d	Six canons on first line, five ascribed to 'W. B.' or 'Wm. B.'; probably not Byrd	t6
65	O lux beata Trinitas	Baldwin, 118^v–19	d?	3vv.; imitative fancy by Preston on ornamented faburden	t8
66	O lux beata Trinitas	Baldwin, 122^v–3	d	3vv.; exercise in proportions by John Baldwin. Faburden used twice, but omits line 2 (same melody as line 1)	m
67	O lux beata Trinitas	30513, 31^v	e	By Redford	t8
68	O nimis felix	H2951, 65^v–66	a	Octave of Nativity of St. John the Baptist. 5s dotted	t
69	O pater sancte	C52b21, 189	b	Lauds, Vigil of Holy Trinity. Plainsong symbols and mensural cadences. B flat key-signature, with E flats	m
70	O pater sancte	Pepys, 66	c	3vv.; chant present in Discantus	m
71	O quam glorifica luce	H2951, 65^v–66	a	1st Vespers, Assumption of BVM. 5s dotted	t8
72	O quam glorifica luce	Pepys, 81	b	Unadorned monophony	t8

No.	Title	Source	Type	Notes	Chant
73	O quam glorifica luce	Pepys, 51ᵛ–52	c	3vv.; by Fowler. Rather free: perhaps based on chant in Discantus rather than faburden?	t8
74	O quam glorifica luce	Pepys, 71ᵛ–72	c	3vv.; also rather free at times	t8
75	Primo dierum omnium	29996, 171ᵛ	e	Matins, 1st Sunday after Octave of Epiphany, and Sundays to Lent	t8
76	Quem terra pontus ethera	H2951, 62–62ᵛ	a	Matins, Purification of BVM. 3s dotted	m
77	Salvator mundi, domine	Ryman, 81	a	Compline, Christmas Eve, and many other occasions. 2vv.; black semibreves in score. Textless	
78	Salvator mundi, domine	H2951, 4ᵛ	a	5s and 3s dotted	m
79	Salvator mundi, domine	C52b21, vᵛ–vi	a	Originally 5s and 3s dotted; plainsong symbols and cadential minims superimposed	m
80	Salvator mundi, domine	RA56, 31ᵛ	b	With B flats	m
81	Salvator mundi, domine	Scot, 97	d	Bottom voice has B natural key-signature; as caution against expected B flats of faburden?	m
82	Salvator mundi, domine	29996, 8ᵛ	e	Unusual transposition	t8
83	Salvator mundi, domine	29996, 9	e	E flats	t–2
84	Salvator mundi, domine	29996, 161ᵛ and R1185, p. 285	e	B flats. Late addition to R1185	m
85	Salvator mundi, domine	30513, 42ᵛ	e	By Redford	m
86	Salvator mundi, domine	30513, 66ᵛ	e	By Redford	m
87	Sancte Dei pretiose	H2951, 7–8	a	Lauds, St. Stephen. 5s dotted	m
88	Sancte Dei pretiose	29996, 164ᵛ	e		t
89	Sermone blando angelus	H2951, 44ᵛ–46	a	Lauds, Octave of Easter. 5s dotted	m
90	Summi largitor praemii	29996, 176ᵛ	e	Matins, 1st Sunday in Lent	t8
91	Te lucis ante terminum	29996, 10	e	Compline, Advent etc. when choir is ruled. B flats	m
92	Te lucis ante terminum	30513, 44ᵛ	e	By Redford. Begins with line 2	m
93	Te lucis ante terminum	23623, 165	e	By Bull: presumably the last faburden	m

No.	Title	Source	Type	Notes	Chant
94	Tibi Christe splendor Patris	H2951, 70–70v	a	St. Michael. 5s stroked	m
95	Veni creator spiritus	C52b21, lviiv	a	Matins, Whitsun. 5s and 3s dotted. Stops at 'superna'	m
96	Veni redemptor gentium	RA56, 31v	b	Vespers, Christmas Eve. Wrongly titled 'Deus/ Christe [?] redemptor omnium'. E flats	
97	Veni redemptor gentium	29996, 160	e		m
98	Verbum supernum prodiens	H2951, 1v–2	a	Matins, 1st Sunday in Advent. 5s dotted	t8
99	Verbum supernum prodiens	C52b21, lxv	a	5s and 3s dotted. (Headed 'Lauds, Corpus Christi')	m
100	Verbum supernum prodiens	29996, 158v	e		t8
101	Verbum supernum prodiens	29996, 13v and 30513, 64v	e		t8
102	Vox clara ecce intonat	H2951, 2v–3	e	By Redford	t
103	Vox clara ecce intonat	29996, 159	a	Lauds, 1st Sunday in Advent. 5s dotted	m

II: PROCESSIONAL HYMN 'SALVE FESTA DIES' (various versions and occasions)

Only Nos. 104 and 105 are strict faburdens. Nos. 106–115, though largely in faburden, take occasional liberties (like some of the Magnificat faburdens), and are accordingly placed in parentheses; all are descendants of the 'square' in British library, Harley MS 2942 (f. 121), first identified as the earliest known 'square' by Susan Rankin — it fits the chant, but begins, for example, with a unison instead of a third or fifth, though proceeding thereafter largely in faburden. (The same is true of the bass part of the late fourteenth-century *Magnificat* in Cambridge University Library, MS Kk.1.6 (f. 247), the ancestor of many 'squares' to Tone I that are not quite in strict faburden.)

No.	Source	Type	Notes	Chant
104	B20, 113aᵛ–b	a	'. . . qua sponso'; stops at 'ecclesia'. Faburden copied in dots and plainsong symbols beneath the chant at its sounding pitch in fifths and thirds beneath the chant, so that the scribe found it necessary to add a fifth staff-line. B flats are implied but not written; the first syllable of 'iungitur' has two faburden notes to the single note in the chant. The handwriting looks much earlier than the specimens in 'sight notation' from the early 16th century.	m
105	Scot, 102ᵛ–3	c	3vv.; chant in Discantus	t8
(106)	OL308, end flyleaf	b		t8
(107)	LHS142, back cover	b	Fragmentary paste-down	t8
(108)	L408, 2ᵛ	b		t8
(109)	Pepys, 13ᵛ–14	c	Rather free. 3vv.	t8
(110)	Pepys, 14ᵛ–15	c	Very free. 3vv.	t8
(111)	Pepys, 18ᵛ–19	c	3vv.	t8
(112)	Pepys, 57ᵛ–58	c	4vv.	t8
(113)	Pepys, 81ᵛ–82	c	3vv. Written in plainsong breves	t8
(114)	Ritson, 106ᵛ–107	c	Free in places. 3vv.	t8
(115)	Ritson, 122	c	3vv. Written in 'playne song' notation	t8

III: PROCESSIONAL PSALMS

Faburden was clearly a useful way of singing simple polyphony in the difficult circumstances of a procession (see also categories II and IX). The following two processional psalms were both sung with the refrain antiphon 'Alleluia Alleluia Alleluia' after Vespers on Easter Sunday and daily until the following Friday, 'Laudate Pueri' for the procession to the font, and 'In exitu Israel' during the progress from font to rood-screen.

No.	Title	Source	Type	Notes	Chant
116	Laudate pueri	H2945, 65–66	b	Monophony, copied as palimpsest over erased verses (*alternatim*) in a liturgical MS	m5?
117	Laudate pueri	Pepys, 58ᵛ–61	c	3vv. The incipit 'Laudate pueri Dominum' is given in plainsong in the Mean, transposed to the upper fifth; this is confirmed by the presence of B flats in the faburden voice	
118	Laudate pueri	Gyffard, i. 157, ii. 156, iii. 151, iv. 145	c	By Sheppard. 4vv.; faburden is the bottom voice, with B flat key-signature	m5
119	In exitu Israel	H2945, 67–70	b	As 116, also *alternatim*	m
120	In exitu Israel	Gyffard, i.158ᵛ, ii. 157ᵛ, iii. 152ᵛ, iv. 146	c	By Sheppard, [Thomas] Byrd and Mundy. 4vv.; faburden is the bottom voice	t8

IV: PSALMS

Faburden was no doubt used extensively for antiphonal psalm-singing, but little has survived beyond the Magnificat faburdens and those in III above to show exactly how it was used. Besides No. 121 below, Scottish Anonymous gives five other brief examples to demonstrate the treatment of monosyllables and proper names falling at the end of the half-verse (f.95), of which two may be identified: 'filiorum Edom' is from v.7 of Ps. 136 (Anglican 137), and 'in effrata' is from v.6 of Ps. 131 (Anglican 132).

No.	Title	Source	Type	Notes	Chant
121	Ps. 133, v.3	*Scot*, 95	d	3vv.; Anglican Ps. 134; example of irregular cadence at the half-verse	m

V: TE DEUM

There are eight examples, all from the 16th century. All save that in Scottish Anonymous transpose the following verses up a fifth, relative to their surroundings: 'Salvum fac' (organ settings), 'Aeterna fac', 'Et rege eos' and 'In te Domine' (vocal setting).

No.	Source	Type	Notes	Chant
122	*Scot*, 97ᵛ–98ᵛ	d		m
123	*Gyffard*, i. 2–5ᵛ, ii and iii. 1–4, iv. 2–4	c	4vv.; even-numbered verses only	t–2
124	29996, 22ᵛ	e	By Burton	t–2
125	29996, 20ᵛ and *15233, 8ᵛ*	e	By Redford	m
126	*15233, 2ᵛ* and *30513, 61ᵛ*	e	By Redford	m
127	*30513, 71ᵛ*	e	By Blitheman	t–2
128	*BF156*	e		t–2
129	*BF156*	e		t–2

VI: OFFERTORY

No.	Title	Source	Type	Notes	Chant
130	Veritas mea	29996, 43	e	By Coxsun	t5

69

VII: ANTIPHONS

No.	Title	Source	Type	Notes	Chant
131	Asperges me	L462, 1^V	b	Sung with 2 verses of Ps. 50 'Miserere mei, Deus' and 'Gloria Patri' at sprinkling of water before Mass on Sundays, except from Easter to Trinity	t8
132	Asperges me	Gyffard, i. 5^V, ii-iv. 4	c	4vv.; faburden is bottom voice	m
133	Asperges me	Gyffard, i-iii. 9^V, iv. 10	c	4vv.; faburden is bottom voice	m
134	[Libera nos,] salva nos	ChCh, no. 155 T389, p.181 and Drexel, 74a	c	Sung with Ps. 47 'Magnus Dominus' at Matins, Trinity Sunday. 7vv.; by Sheppard. B Flats; faburden is bottom voice. Starts after beginner's phrase, as does No. 135	t
135	[Libera nos,] salva nos	Baldwin, 110^V and Baldwin, 111	d	4vv.; by John Baldwin. Exercise in proportions	t
			d	4vv.; exercise in proportions	t
136	Miserere mihi, Domine	Ryman, 81	a	Compline Ps.-antiphon, except during week after Christmas. 2vv.; black semibreves in score; textless	m
137	Regina caeli, laetare	H2951, 125^V	a	Processional, Eastertide, BVM. 5s dotted: stops half-way through 'portare'	m

VIII: COMMUNION

No.	Title	Source	Type	Notes	Chant
138	Beata viscera	Pepys, 95^v–96	c	Assumption (also Lady-Mass); Monday in Eastertide; also Annunciation. 3vv.; bottom voice is probably a highly ornamented faburden; chant in Discantus at beginning, less faithfully in Mean, which has incipit transposed up a fifth. B flats	m5

IX: PROCESSIONAL KYRIE LITANIES FOR ROGATIONTIDE

Four of the nine in Sarum use have faburdens surviving, in such numbers as to suggest that the other five may have been sung plain. There are close concordances between certain pairs of sources. The litanies were sung on the three Rogation Days before Ascension Thursday.

No.	Title	Source	Type	Notes	Chant
139	Kyrie . . . qui precioso sanguine	RLe45, 57^v–58 and	b	Copied on same opening as chant. B flat	t8
		Auct, 0. iii	b	Copied on same opening as chant, but a fifth lower than the above. B flat and E flat	m
140	Kyrie . . . qui precioso sanguine	LH5142, cxxx^v and	b	Copied on same opening as chant. B flat	t8
		Kkk55	b	Not seen. Copied 1555–58	t8?
141	Kyrie . . . qui precioso sanguine	Pepys, 12^v–13	c	3vv.; sometimes rather free (cf. 'sanguine')	t8
142	Kyrie . . . qui precioso sanguine	Scot, 96^v	d	3vv. Gives plainsong untransposed. E flat, and implicitly B flat	m

71

No.	Title	Source	Type	Notes	Chant
143	Kyrie . . . . Christe audi nos (i)	L438, 180ᵛ	b	By William Dundy, traceable in 1490s. Called 'ffaburdoun'	t8
144	Kyrie . . . . Christe audi nos (i)	RLe45, 59ᵛ and Auct, 0. iiiᵛ	b	Copied on same opening as chant in each case	t8
145	Kyrie . . . . Christe audi nos (i)	LH5142, cxxxiiᵛ and RB1852	b	Copied on same opening as chant	t8
146	Kyrie . . . . Christe audi nos (i)	Pepys, 17ᵛ–18	c	Not seen. 3vv.	t8?
147	Kyrie . . . . Christe audi nos (ii)	L438, 180ᵛ	b	By Dundy (see No. 144). B natural as unneeded cautionary because of transposition?	t8 (m–4?)t
148	Kyrie . . . . Christe audi nos (ii)	RLe45, 60 and Auct, 0. iiij	b	Copied on same page as chant	t8
149	Kyrie . . . . Christe audi nos (ii)	LH5142, cxxxiiᵛ and RB1852	b	Copied on same opening as chant	t8
150	Kyrie . . . . Christe audi nos (ii)	Pepys, 18	c	Not seen. 3vv.	t8?
151	Kyrie . . . . Domine miserere	L438, 180ᵛ	b	By Dundy (see Nos. 144, 148). B flats and E flats implicit	m
152	Kyrie . . . . Domine miserere	RLe45, 60ᵛ and Auct, 0. iiiᵛ–v	b	Copied on same page as chant. Called 'letania quinta'	t8
153	Kyrie . . . . Domine miserere	Pepys, 55–55ᵛ	c	3vv. B flats, and E flats implied	m

X: UNIDENTIFIED

No.	Title	Source	Type	Notes	Chant
154	[None]	Scot, 54	d	Example of 'faburdoun or faulxburdoun', to show the legitimisation of the fourth; 'Quhan þe barritonant and the descant procedis be ane or ma[n]y saxtis. Than the Voic[e] Jntermediat all wayis obseruand thrid to þe barritonant plesandly sall accord'	
155	[None]	Ryman, 81	b?	All but illegible; could be a faburden, like Nos. 77 and 137, copied on the same leaf	?

73

APPENDIX II

ANALYTICAL TABLE OF SOURCES OF FABURDEN (EXCLUDING MAGNIFICAT)

Type No. Source*	Hymn	Proc. Hymn	Proc. Psalm	Psalm	Te Deum	Offertory	Antiphon	Communion	Litany	Unidentified	Totals
(a): COPIED WITH CHANT											
1 B20		1									1 ⎫
2 Ryman	1						1			1?	3 ⎬ 43
3 H2951	32						1				33 ⎬
4 C52b21†	6										6 ⎭
(b): MONOPHONIES											
5 L462							1				1 ⎫
6 Pepys§	3										3 ⎪
7 Digby	1										1 ⎪
8 OL308		(1)									2 ⎪
9 H2945			2								1 ⎪
10 L408		(1)									3 ⎪
11 L438									3		4 ⎬ 34
12 RLe45	4								4		4 ⎪
4 C52b21†		(1)									3 ⎪
13 RA56	3								3		4 ⎪
14 LH5142		(1)							4		4 ⎪
15 Auct									4		4 ⎪
16 RB1852									2		2 ⎪
17 Kk55									1		1 ⎭

74

											Total
(c): VOCAL POLYPHONY											
6 Pepys§	8	(5)						2		4	⎫ 19
18 Ritson	1	(2)									⎪ 3
19 Gyffard	1							1		2	⎪ 6
20 ChCh										1	⎬ 31
21 T389										1	⎪ 1
22 Drexel										1	⎭ 1
(d): THEORY, CANON											
23 Scot	8		1	1		1	1	1	1		⎫ 13
24 Morley	1										⎪ 1
25 31391	6										⎬ 24
26 Baldwin	2					2					⎭ 4
(e): KEYBOARD WORKS											
27 15233						2					⎫ 2
28 29996	26					2					⎪ 29
29 30513	6					2					⎬ 43
30 BF156						2					⎪ 2
31 R1185	1										⎪ 1
32 23623	1										⎭ 1
Total copies	111	12	5	5	1	10	1	10	1	22	2	175
Close concordances	8	12	5	5	1	3		2		7		20
Total pieces	103	12	5	5	1	7	1	8	1	15	2	155

* For sigla see Appendix III   † Appears under both (a) and (b)   § Appears under both (b) and (c)

APPENDIX III
SOURCES OF FABURDEN (EXCLUDING MAGNIFICAT)

(a) FABURDENS COPIED WITH CHANTS, USUALLY ON SAME STAVE

B20   1. Oxford, Bodleian Library, MS Add. B. 20 (Sarum processional, second half of the 14th century, with additions dating perhaps from the first half of the 15th): contains No. 104.

Ryman   2. Cambridge, University Library, MS Ee. I. 12 (Ryman's MS, 1492: Franciscan poems and carols, with some monophonic and two-part music): Nos. 77, 136, 155.

H2951   3. London, British Library, MS Harl. 2951 (Sarum Hymnal, 15th century, with early 16th-century additions): Nos. 1, 3, 5, 8, 13–15, 19, 20, 24, 27–28, 32, 36, 40, 44–45, 47–48, 50, 52–54, 68, 71, 76, 78, 87, 89, 94, 98, 102, 137.

C52b21   4. London, British Library, printed book C. 52. b. 51 (Sarum Hymnal, Reremund, Antwerp 1528, with MS additions): Nos. 29, 33, 43, 79, 95, 99. See also under (b) below.

(b) FABURDENS COPIED AS MENSURAL MONOPHONIES

L462   5. London, British Library, MS Lansdowne 462 (Sarum gradual, 15th century, with mid-15th-century additions, including 'squares'): No. 131.

Pepys   6. Cambridge, Magdalene College, Pepysian Library, MS 1236 (sacred polyphony, c.1460–70, with some monophonies): Nos. 49, 55, 72. See also under (c) below.

Digby   7. Oxford, Bodleian Library, MS Digby 167 (miscellany of late 15th century with leaf containing stroke notation and a mensural part): No. 9.

OL308   8. Rome, Vatican Library, MS Ottob. lat. 308 (Sarum processional with late 15th-century additions): No. 106.

H2945   9. London, British Library, MS Harl. 2945 (Sarum processional with early 16th-century additions): Nos. 116, 119.

L408   10. Oxford, Bodleian Library, MS Liturg. 408 (Sarum processional of second half of 14th century, with early 16th-century additions): No. 108.

L438   11. London, Lambeth Palace Library, MS 438 (Sarum processional with early 16th-century additions): Nos. 143, 147, 151.

RLe45   12. Oxford, Bodleian Library, MS Rawl. Liturg. e. 45 (Sarum processional with early 16th-century additions): Nos. 139, 144, 148, 152.
             4. See above: Nos. 10, 16, 34, 69.

RA56   13. London, British Library, MS Royal App. 56 (c.1545, mixed polyphony with some monophonies): Nos. 25, 80, 96.

LH5142 14. London, Lambeth Palace Library, Printed Book **H. 5142. P. 1545 (Sarum processional, Reremund, Antwerp, 1545, with MS additions): Nos. 107, 140, 145, 149.

Auct 15. Oxford, Bodleian Library, fragment of printed book with type of Pynson, Auct. T. inf. III 17 4° (undated Sarum processional with MS additions): Nos. 139, 144, 148, 152.

RB1852 16. Paris, Bibliothèque Nationale, printed book rés. B. 1852 (Sarum processional, Reremund, Antwerp, 1545, with MS additions): Nos. 145, 149.

Kkk55 17. Dublin, Trinity College Library, printed book Kk. k. 55 (Sarum processional, Rouen, 1555, with MS additions): No. 140.

(c) FABURDENS EMBEDDED IN VOCAL POLYPHONY (excluding theoretical examples)

6. See above: Nos. 2, 11, 39, 46, 56, 70, 73–74, 109–13, 117, 138, 141, 146, 150, 153.

Ritson 18. London, British Library, Add. MS 5665 (Ritson's MS, late 15th century, mixed polyphony): Nos. 57, 114, 115.

Gyffard 19. London, British Library, Add. MSS 17802–5 (Gyffard Part-books; *c*.1555, sacred polyphony): Nos. 12, 118, 120, 123, 132–3.

ChCh 20. Oxford, Christ Church Library, MSS 979–83 (*c*.1580–1600; sacred polyphony): No. 134.

T389 21. Tenbury, St. Michael's College Library, MS 389 (*c*.1580; sacred polyphony) and companion part-book known as the 'James MS': No. 134.

Drexel 22. New York Public Library, MSS Drexel 4180–85 (*c*.1625; sacred polyphony): No. 134.

(d) FABURDENS (POLYPHONIC) FROM MUSICAL THEORISTS, OR USED AS A C.F. FOR CANONS

Scot 23. London, British Library, Add. MS 4911 (Scottish Anonymous, after 1557; theory): Nos. 21, 58–63, 81, 105, 121, 122, 142, 154.

Morley 24. Thomas Morley, *A Plaine and Easie Introduction to Practical Musicke* (London, 1597; facsimile ed. E. H. Fellowes, London, 1937; reference is to the modern edn. by A. Harman, London, 1952): No. 30.

31391 25. London, British Library, Add MS 31391 (*c*.1600: canons): No. 64 (a–f).

Baldwin 26. London, British Library, MS R.M. 24. d. 2 (Baldwin MS, *c*. 1600; mixed polyphony; all the faburden pieces are didactic): Nos. 65–66, 135.

(e) FABURDENS EMBEDDED IN KEYBOARD POLYPHONY

15233 27. London, British Library, Add. MS 15233 (Redford MS, *c*. 1545): Nos. 125–26.

29996   28. London, British Library, Add. MS 29996 (Tomkins MS, *c*.1545–1650): Nos. 4, 6–7, 17–18, 22–23, 26, 31, 35, 37–38, 41–42, 51, 75, 82–84, 88, 90–91, 97, 100–101, 103, 124–5, 130.

30513   29. London, British Library, Add. MS 30513 (Mulliner Book, *c*.1555–75): Nos. 23, 67, 85–86, 92, 101, 126–7.

BF156   30. Oxford, Brasenose College Library, Fragment 156 (date unknown): Nos. 128–9.

R1185   31. Paris, Bibliothèque Nationale, Fonds du Conservatoire, MS Rés. 1185 (Bull?/Cosyn MS, early 17th century): No. 84.

23623   32. London, British Library, Add. MS 23623 (Messaus MS, 1629): No. 93.

Chapter 4

THE EMERGENCE OF THE IN NOMINE:
SOME NOTES AND QUERIES ON THE WORK OF
TUDOR CHURCH MUSICIANS

Paul Doe

WHEN the modern republication of Renaissance music began in the last century, it was probably inevitable that its editors should opt for complete editions of legendary composers like Palestrina and Lassus. The cult of the individual artist was in some measure a part of the nineteenth-century philosophy of art. As a result, degree candidates in music are annually asked to 'compare the church music of Palestrina and Lassus'. I find myself in strong agreement with Professor Lewis Lockwood who commented, several years ago, that any such comparison is little more than an academic abstraction, only obliquely related to the questions that matter: namely, the very different types of employment and traditions of craftsmanship to which each man belonged. In a sense, any question about a sixteeth-century composer is really about the previous generation and the circle from whom he learnt his trade.

In Britain the habit of selecting named composers was adopted in the 1920s by the editors of *Tudor Church Music*, who searched through dozens of unrelated sources for anything ascribed to Taverner, Tallis or Osbert Parsley, and in so doing more or less compelled their successors to follow the same pattern. Their edition of Taverner (1923) was prefaced by an account of his career which, as one English scholar has recently put it, 'has little value except as dramatic fiction'.[1] Henry VIII's Act of Supremacy of 1534 amounted to a unilateral declaration of independence; and for the rest of his life he successfully held a position of isolation between two opposing forces: the world powers who saw his position as unconstitutional, and the Lutheran Protestants whom he regarded as at least potentially subversive. Taverner's biography makes abundantly clear what E. H. Fellowes failed to recognize, namely that the composer aligned himself with the

Henrician establishment, never showed any serious sympathy for the Lutherans, and probably continued to compose until his last years.

It is very much to the credit of Taverner's editors that his music has been available in print for over half a century. If they had not isolated his music in this way, however, he would probably not have been so misrepresented, for it would have been recognized sooner that there are astonishingly close correspondences between some of the music of Taverner, Tye and Sheppard[2] which seems to date from around 1535–42. (It is tantalizing not to know where they were employed about 1540, although it is known that in 1543 both Tye and Sheppard took up new appointments in institutions[3] which would have demanded a solid record of experience.) My point is that where such a body of music survives mainly in single copies there must be a strong case for publishing intact the sources in which it is found. This was a period when the demands upon a church musician were changing relatively quickly; and it seems reasonable to assume, at least as a hypothesis, that works with close affinities are also close in date of composition. By relating knowledge of changing conditions to the characteristics of the music, and to such little biographical information as has been found, it is possible to arrive at certain provisional conjectures about when it was composed and why it uses particular techniques. Such a 'contextual' approach is vital to any meaningful insight into the art of the past.

For most of the Tudor era the element of personal enterprise was not strong. Any such attitude would have been unbecoming among composers who thought of themselves as craftsmen in the service of the Church, where novelty was resisted as much in music as in any other element of worship. Nevertheless the advent of a Protestant regime in 1547 presented them with an unusual need to adapt; and in this repertory, too, piecemeal publication has obscured at least some of the solutions which they collectively evolved. There are three main sources whose vernacular church music probably belongs wholly to the reign of Edward VI.[4] Each has naturally had the music of Tallis and Tye extracted from it, but only recently have they begun to receive adequate attention as collections.[5] Two are manuscript sets of part-books which have been neglected for several reasons. Each lacks one voice (the Wanley books their Tenor, and the Lumley books their Bass), and in each well over half the contents are anonymous. Both these facts should — but do not — act as a challenge rather than a deterrent to researchers. But perhaps their greatest handicap is the unpretentious nature of their contents, for they have usually been examined by Anglican musicians who approach them with the air of an art-historian making a study of cave-painting, and who have little knowledge of the similarly unpretentious Sarum polyphony from which some of the musical techniques were derived. Brian Trowell[6] has already demonstrated the church musician's craft operating at this very simple functional level; and it was a natural step to use much the same methods for a new liturgy that demanded simple, syllabic and clearly-audible word-setting.

In at least seventeen items of this repertory — twelve canticles and five psalms — a Sarum psalm-tone is used as a tenor.[7] The actual tenor voice survives for only eight, but in the other nine, which are unique to Wanley, the tenor can be restored convincingly by inserting a psalm-tone more or less note by note. Ex. 1 is an anonymous Nunc dimittis from the Wanley books (ff.93, 96, 91) with an editorial tenor identical to the Sarum 1st tone with 5th ending. The technique used is somewhat akin to the type of four-part faburden described by a slightly later theorist,[8] with the top part moving mainly in sixths with the chant. (This example must rank as composed polyphony, but is not very far removed from 'sighted' improvisation.) Another form, distinguished as composition 'upon the faburden', involved the use not of the chant but of the bass-line that resulted from improvisation in two or three parts. Despite the melismatic embellishment sometimes added, the main outline of such a bass is always distinctive. Ex.2 (overleaf) shows that of the 8th tone in another Nunc dimittis in the Wanley books (ff.40, 40, 39[V]), with both a Latin form[9] and also the psalm-tone aligned above it. Imitative polyphony is added above the bass in much the same way as in some Latin pieces of the mid-sixteenth century, such as the anonymous Te Deum which is the first composition in the Gyffard Part-books.[10] In the simpler canticles the faburden-derived voice remained the bass of the texture, but it is quite possible that some further Wanley canticles used a melody of this type as the now missing tenor. It would be splendid if some benefactor would finance the publication of the entire Wanley collection with the tenor stave blank, so that scholars intrigued by such techniques could

Ex. 1

Lord, now let - test thou thy ser - vant de - part in peace: ac - cor - ding to thy___ word.

indulge in detective work. English composers habitually built upon tradition, and the thread of continuity through the Reformation period appears to be stronger than has yet been recognized.

That a more elaborate style of composition existed under Edward VI is clear from the service music of Tallis, Sheppard, Parsons and William Mundy, almost all of which betrays evidence of having been set to the texts of the 1549 prayer-book, and not to the slightly different Elizabethan texts; and again there are such striking similarities of material and method that a close comparative analysis becomes inevitable. It is curious, however, that scarcely any services or anthems can with any confidence be dated in the first half of the reign of Elizabeth I. This apparent neglect was probably due both to the queen's own lack of interest in them and to the increasing puritanism of the English church. Although some of their music may have been lost, composers like Robert Parsons and Robert White seem to have concentrated markedly on vocal music with Latin text, and on similar polyphonic material with no text at all. So far as one can judge, this sort of repertory flowered vigorously between about 1560 and 1575 and then declined sharply, leaving Byrd in a position of relative isolation.

The sources that contain this material, on the other hand, date almost without exception from 1575 or later. They tend to mix —

sometimes in apparently random fashion — both music composed for voices and untexted pieces such as the In nomine. A characteristic example is the 'table' book, British Library Add. MS 31390, which offers a large assortment of In nomines and other cantus firmus pieces, motets, and even some secular vocal music, all copied without text and prefaced by a title page which reads: 'A booke of In nomines & other solfainge songes of v: vj: vij: & viij: parts for voyces or Instrumentes'. From this it seems that the manuscript is an anthology compiled for any *ad hoc* mixture of voices or instruments that happened to be available. Whether 'solfainge songes' implies wordless vocalization must remain a matter for speculation — although Thomas Morley, some twenty years later, referred fairly explicitly to such a practice in discussing the motet:

> But I see not what passions or motions it can stirre up, being sung as most men doe commonlie sing it: that is, leaving out the dittie and singing onely the bare note, as it were a musicke made onelie for instruments . . .[11]

Both these sources, however, merely point to performance habits of the last quarter of the century, when the playing and singing of polyphonic music became a domestic pastime. They give no help in determining what was the primary function of the remarkably large number of In nomines produced in the third quarter of the century, when patterns of music-making could well have been significantly different. It is still widely assumed, for example, that those in consort form were intended for playing on viols; but if so, who played them? To the best of my knowledge no Elizabethan source of In nomines makes any reference to viols, and Add. MS 31390 is the only one that even mentions instruments. Moreover, the prototype of the In nomine is known to have been vocal music, namely an extract from Taverner's 'Gloria tibi Trinitas' Mass[12] in which only three words ('In nomine Domini') are set in highly melismatic fashion to music that lasts for 57 bars in modern transcription. The earliest independent examples are apparently direct imitations of it, and there is no reason in principle why they should not have been vocal like their model: if they were, they could have been sung to the same text, or to no text at all.

Most of these observations have already been made in a paper by Warwick Edwards,[13] whose later dissertation on Elizabethan consort music[14] is the most recent and thorough investigation of the subject, and whose inventory of sources is a model of accuracy and indispensable to anybody working in the field.[15] Despite the various indications of vocal performance, he seems eventually to conclude that the In nomine and its related forms were probably mainly played on viols because of their use of some unvocal idioms and their occasionally very wide compass. Some aspects of the problem, however, may suggest other solutions.

The difficulty of a wide overall compass occurs in only a handful of pieces: the great majority stay within the normal three-octave compass of vocal music. What is perhaps more significant is that a very high proportion are composed in parts whose clefs and individual compasses correspond very closely with those of the Latin motets of the period. The commonest arrangement for five-part vocal music, $G_2/C_2/C_3/C_4/F_4$, is also the one most commonly found in the In nomine, with the proviso that C_2 is usually replaced by C_1 to accommodate the single d'' of the cantus firmus. Moreover the great majority of parts operate within the eleven-note compass of their clef, and do not use ledger-lines to any greater extent than does vocal music. It is difficult to see why so many composers should adopt such apparently vocal limitations if they were not in fact writing for voices; or conversely why, if they were writing for viols, they should select as many as five or six different clefs and use little over half the available compass of each instrument.

Of the In nomine composers up to 1575, every one whose career is at least partly known was also principally a church musician. They include, in alphabetical order, William Byrd, Robert Johnson, William Mundy, Osbert Parsley, Robert Parsons, Thomas Preston, Henry Stonings, Nicholas Strogers, Thomas Tallis, Christopher Tye, Robert White, William Whytbroke and Clement Woodcock. To this tally should be added one foreigner, Alfonso Ferrabosco, who came to England as a young man of nineteen in 1561/2 and finally departed in 1578, leaving behind a son who was to become an eminent musician under James I.

Whatever his other pursuits, Ferrabosco composed a good deal of music in this country, including three In nomines which are certainly by him rather than his son. His reaction to this peculiarly English form is interesting. All three are written in clefs that produce a higher tessitura than the English norm, and whether sung or not they clearly have the brighter sound characteristic of Italian vocal music. Secondly, the opening of one of them (E260, see Ex. 3) is not only very vocal in style but is also reminiscent of Italian settings of the Benedictus, with their curving melodic line for 'Benedictus qui venit' and later repeated-note point for the words 'In nomine Domini'.[16]

Ex. 3

Ex - au - - - - di vo - cem __ me - am

This is one extreme of In nomine style. At the other, there are plentiful examples of writing that would require virtuoso singing, such as the broken-triad triplet patterns sometimes employed to create a final climax. Ex.4 is taken not from an In nomine but from another cantus firmus piece (Parsons, 'Ut re mi fa sol la') whose sole source[17] has marginal comments in two of the part-books: the Altus, for instance, reads: 'If you c[a]nnot singe *the* s[ec]ond p*a*rte let it alonne', which may imply that the owner tried to sing the music, but does not prove that it was written for voices. Similar ambiguities are presented by the In nomines of Tye, most of which have curious enigmatic titles like 'Howld fast' (E295), 'Beleve me' (E289) or 'Crye'

85

Ex. 4

(E291), whose significance has not yet been established.[18] That called 'Crye' has often been cited as a clear instance of an instrumental idiom by virtue of the rapid repeated notes and octave leaps (Ex.5); but even this is not certain, because it is not hard to see this pattern as a mild extension of the bird-mimicry found in Jannequin, or — perhaps more likely — as a 'cry' in the sense of a street cry, of the kind woven into later polyphonic settings. The best-known of these, Orlando Gibbons's 'Cries of London', is not called an In nomine; nevertheless, it does make use of the same cantus firmus.

Ex. 5

More difficult to explain away in vocal terms is another Tye In nomine called 'Rounde' (E301). Assuming that no transposition was intended, its total compass is almost four octaves, from D to c'''. The highest part has an individual range of $e' - c'''$, which seems unlikely for a treble voice. Equally, however, it does not suggest a treble viol, with its highest string normally tuned to d''. Taking the overall style of the piece into account, it seems much more probable that the part was written expressly for a recorder or some other high-pitched wind instrument. The two fragments in Ex. 6 illustrate both the melodic style and the extremes of compass of the music.

Ex. 6

Various features of the style of In nomines have convinced me that a significant number were composed not as 'private music' for viols, but rather as a form of more 'public' music for professional players, who may well have been mainly wind players. The copious references to instruments in Walter L. Woodfill's *Musicians in English Society from Elizabeth to Charles I*[19] make it fairly clear that the gentleman amateur did not normally play the viol before the end of the sixteenth century, when it evidently became a new fashion. Before that, he and his family learnt to play either the virginals or a plucked instrument such as the lute or cittern. Where viols existed, they are more likely to have been played exclusively by professional household musicians, such as the Italians in the royal court[20] and possibly a few others in aristocratic houses. Players of wind instruments, such as the shawm, cornett and sackbut, were likewise restricted to the ranks of the professionals; but they were also very much more numerous and more variously employed. For example, Woodfill[21] is able to list over 30 towns that employed waits by the middle of Elizabeth's reign, and to show that a significant number of private houses also had their own professional groups. Those that did not made a practice of hiring them from elsewhere whenever music was needed for a special occasion. The household accounts give no indication of what music was played, but it can be inferred that such a practice was probably regarded as a normal compliment to a visitor of high rank.

Perhaps understandably, there survive very few musical sources that can be shown to have been used by musicians of this kind. The best candidate is the Lumley books already discussed in a different connection. They were first used for Edwardian church music, but subsequently passed into some private house (probably that of the Earl of Arundel) where their blank pages were filled with instrumental dances and other pieces. Among this material are two In nomines, one by Poynt (E230) and one by Parsons (E327), both apparently early, and 'vocal' in style. The untidy character of these copies makes it very unlikely that they were used by anybody other than the household musicians. Certain other partbooks, such as British Library Add. MS 32377, are similarly 'untidy' and sometimes contain clearer indications of use by wind-players, as for example where a part has been re-written in order (apparently) to eliminate the lowest notes of its compass.[22] Even relatively minor alternative readings can be significant in this context: Ex.7 shows two extracts of an In nomine by Brewster in the form recorded in most sources with, above the stave, the rhythmic variants of a Cantus book which appears to be one of the earliest.[23]

The very style of the music itself, however, can often provide persuasive evidence. All four of Exx. 7–10 are taken from In nomines (E248, 277, 316, 324) which suggest to me that the composer probably had in mind performance by cornetts and sackbuts, or some similar ensemble. The two extracts in Ex.8 are not continuous, the second being from the middle of the piece where the cantus firmus rises to its highest note. Ex.9 is from an anonymous In nomine which frequently comes to a halt on a semibreve chord, making it sound faintly absurd on viols, but very effective played by wind instruments at a brisk march speed and with crisp articulation. The last extract (Ex.10) illustrates another anonymous piece which is in some ways the most skilfully written and impressive of all the In nomines from this early phase, demanding a panache and ringing sonorities that viols simply cannot produce.

Ex. 7
(a)

(b)

Ex. 8

Ex. 9

Ex. 10

I have selected what seem to be fairly convincing examples of a very vocal style on the one hand, and of a more martial or ceremonial manner on the other. Many, naturally, have less well-defined characteristics. It is far from clear, however, whether different styles of writing reflect the succeeding fashions of two or three decades, or different modes of performance, or whether they existed concurrently and were selected to suit the occasion. Is it even possible that two contrasted In nomines such as those of Tallis (E233, 234) were composed and performed as a complementary pair? Certainly there are apparent instances of a different type of 'pairing' in which two pieces, one in duple time and the other triple, use the same voice-disposition and similar thematic material. Such a relationship exists between the two five-part In nomines of William Mundy (E272, 271), and also between two others by Ferrabosco (E258, 259) which can even be performed convincingly in a pavane and galliard rhythm respectively.

Three further observations may be worth adding. One is that many of the dances in the Lumley books were originally composed in four parts but are also supplied with an added fifth part, which is often rather crude and was presumably played only when maximum sonority was wanted. Such a habit may have been more common among household musicians, for there are several In nomines to which the same thing has happened, including the Taverner 'original' and one each by Tallis (E234) and Johnson (E224). Though it does not survive in four-part form, the Brewster piece whose opening is quoted as Ex.7 is probably also in this category: its Tenor II is tolerably well managed for a few bars, but later becomes most ungainly.[24]

Secondly, the use of wind instruments clearly helps to account for the apparently vocal compasses. It is also noticeable, however, that those In nomines which are relatively vocal in style tend to employ a vocal disposition of parts, with different clefs throughout, whereas the instrumental-sounding pieces are more likely to use clefs in pairs. Tye's 'Rounde', for instance, has two high parts both in a G_1 clef, while Parsons even used three pairs of clefs in his six-part piece variously entitled 'Cante cantate', 'Lusti gallant' and 'The songe called trumpetts' (E91). Finally, it is tempting to wonder whether the adoption of In nomines by wind players might be connected with the profusion of major triads so often forced upon a cantus firmus in a minor mode. The first extract of Ex.8 provides a good example, in which the process even results in a diminished fourth between the sixth and seventh notes of the plainsong.

It must be stressed that most of these comments about the In nomine are speculative, because the lack of contemporary evidence forces one to try to draw conclusions almost entirely from the internal evidence of the music. By the time the sources were compiled fashion and taste had already begun to change: the nobility evidently preferred to welcome their guests with the softer sounds of the mixed consort, leaving the music of the previous generation to amateur collectors and performers. Nevertheless the overriding impression of the early Elizabethan period is that men like Parsons and White found themselves serving an Anglican church which did not encourage or even permit elaborate polyphony within its formal worship, although their motets may have been used at the periphery of services in a few choral foundations. As the recognized professional composers, however, they were evidently called upon to satisfy a widespread taste among educated people for 'learned' contrapuntal music; and much of their output, whether texted or not, was probably heard in a variety of fairly formal or even ceremonial situations, and performed by voices or a professional consort. But whatever the relative frequency of different modes of performance, it is difficult to make any case for the regular employment of viols.

NOTES
1. R. Bowers, 'Taverner' in *The New Grove's Dictionary of Music & Musicians* (forth-coming).
2. See N. Davison, 'Structure and Unity in four free-composed Tudor Masses', *The Music Review*, xxxiv (1973), 328.
3. Respectively as *magister choristarum* at Ely Cathedral and *informator choristarum* at Magdalen College, Oxford.

4. The Wanley Part-books (Oxford, Bodleian Library, MSS Mus. Sch. e. 420–22); the Lumley Part-books (London, British Library, MSS R. App. 74–76); and *Certaine Notes* . . . , London (J. Day), 1560, some of the type of which was apparently set up in or before 1552.

5. E.g. J. Blezzard, *The Sacred Music of the Lumley Books* (unpublished dissertation), Leeds University, 1972.

6. See pp. 29 ff. above.

7. Although I had myself identified many of these, the larger count of seventeen results from unpublished research by Dr. John Aplin of Reading University, to whom I also owe the comment about Day's *Certaine Notes* in note 4 above.

8. The anonymous Scottish author of British Library, Add. MS 4911.

9. British Library, MS R. App. 56, f. 23^V (asterisked notes are 'altered').

10. British Library, Add. MSS 17802–5.

11. *A Plaine and Easie Introduction to Practicall Musicke*, London, 1597, p. 179.

12. *Tudor Church Music*, i.148–9.

13. 'The Performance of Ensemble Music in Elizabethan England', *Proceedings of the Royal Musical Association*, xcvii (1970–71), 113.

14. *The Sources of Elizabethan Consort Music*, Cambridge University, 1974.

15. References preceded by an 'E' below indicate the number assigned to a piece in Edwards's thematic catalogue.

16. One source of this piece has the words 'Exaudi vocem meam' underlaid to the beginning of the middle voice, as shown in Ex. 3 (Yale University, Library of the School of Music, Filmer MSS A.11^{a-c}, the words being in MS A.11^C, f. 49^V). In this source the whole piece has also been systematically emended, as though to adapt it to the 'new' text. The same version is in British Library, MS Egerton 3665, f. 67.

17. British Library, Add. MSS 30480–84 (quotation from MS 30481, f. 64).

18. Tye's consort music is published in Christopher Tye, *The Instrumental Music*, ed. R. W. Weidner, New Haven, 1967.

19. Princeton, 1953.

20. A list for 1570 is given in Woodfill, op. cit., p. 183.

21. Ibid., p. 293.

22. Examples are the Treble of Mundy's 'O mater mundi' in Add. MS 32377, f. 23^V, and the two Tenor parts of Brewster's five-part In nomine, which in Dow's part-books (Oxford, Christ Church, MSS Mus. 984–8) have had a good deal of their material interchanged to prevent one of them from going below *f*.

23. Cantus part-book (from the same set as Tenbury, St. Michael's College, MS 389) in the private custody of Mr. Michael James, p. 196.

24. All four pieces have the added fifth part in British Library, Add. MS 31390. That of the Brewster In nomine is found in all four of the complete sources, including Dow's part-books, where it is one of the re-written voices referred to in note 22 above.

Chapter 5

THE MUSICAL THEORIES OF GIUSEPPE TARTINI

D. P. Walker

TARTINI was a remarkably original musical theorist, but he achieved originality at the cost of being archaic — a Renaissance thinker living and writing in the Age of Enlightenment.[1] Moreover he was fully aware of this; he apologizes defensively for using Aristotelian terminology,[2] and there are bitter references to 'this enlightened century' ('questo secolo Illuminato'),[3] which has not even tried to understand his system. In his first published treatise, the *Trattato di musica secondo la vera scienza dell'armonia* (1754),[4] the only modern source he cites is Zarlino, and indeed there is no reason to suppose that he had read any later theorist,[5] though some of Rameau's ideas must have filtered through to him, in particular the concept of a fundamental bass. By the time he published his second work, *De' Principi dell' armonia musicale contenuta nel diatonico genere dissertazione* (1767), he was replying to French critics of the *Trattato*, Jean de Serre and d'Alembert,[6] and was himself criticizing Rameau; but his system was already fixed, and this late reading of modern authors led to only minor adjustments. His reaction to Rameau, when he had read him, was one of unshaken confidence in his own system: 'Where M. Rameau has spoken the truth, he necessarily agrees with the truth of the present system. Where he has spoken falsely, he is necessarily detected by being confronted with the truth of the present system'.[7] Again, although at some period after the publication of the *Trattato* Tartini had at least heard of Kepler's *Harmonice Mundi* (1619),[8] I am sure that the striking likenesses between the musical theories of the astronomer and of the violinist are not due to any direct influence, but to the fact that Tartini's mental world was that of the early seventeenth century.

But Tartini appears much less archaic when compared, not with his

French contemporaries, but with his Italian ones, in particular with two very learned musicians, Francescantonio Vallotti[9] and Giambattista Martini,[10] with whom he was in close and frequent contact. Both these theorists had read Rameau carefully and understood him; but both rejected his system because of its physical basis, namely, the natural series of overtones and the determination of pitch by frequency of vibration rather than by string-length, and, with patriotic conservatism, they kept to the purely arithmetic basis of Zarlino.[11]

The rejection by Tartini of frequency as the determinant of pitch is of importance because it threatens the validity of the mathematical basis of his whole system. Since he thinks of musical ratios in terms of string-lengths instead of frequencies, the concept of musical harmony is for him indissolubly tied to that of harmonic proportion in the mathematical sense, whereas for those of his contemporaries who were thinking in terms of frequencies, harmonic proportions were transformed into arithmetic ones, e.g., the ratios of the natural overtones, which, in string-lengths, give the harmonic series $1, \frac{1}{2}, \frac{1}{3} \ldots$, give, as frequencies, the arithmetic series $1, 2, 3 \ldots$ Since the whole mathematical basis of Tartini's system rests on a descending hierarchy of kinds of proportion: harmonic, arithmetic, geometric, the system loses its main contact with physical realities once it is generally accepted, as it was, at least outside Italy, long before the middle of the eighteenth century, that frequency of vibration in the air is a more fundamental and general cause of musical pitch than length of string.

Tartini argued, as we shall see, that difference-tones, his *terzo suono*, provided the link between his mathematics and the physical cause of musical pitch. But his only defence against the objection that, by contemporary standards, his theory of proportion was upside-down,[12] was an extraordinary argument based on the supposed areas covered by vibrating strings,[13] an argument which shows that he had not even grasped that it is the frequency, not the amplitude, of vibration that determines pitch. Vallotti, who rejected any physical basis for musical theory, including the *terzo suono*, gave a more convincing reason for keeping to string-lengths, namely, that it was not possible to count vibrations, whereas it was possible to measure strings.[14]

This obsolete identification of mathematically harmonic proportion with musically harmonic proportion resulted in Tartini's system linking directly with Zarlino's and, beyond him, with Greek musical theory. And, like any good Renaissance humanist, he claimed for his theories the authority of antiquity, together with the glory of being the first fully to restore this ancient, long lost, true science. Both his wonderful new mathematics, of which his musical theory formed only a small part, and his new theory of the diatonic genus, which was to explain all contemporary harmonic practice, had been known to Plato, and before him to Pythagoras. But, like the Ancient Theologians, they had hidden the core of their knowledge and made public only its outer surface. Tartini has now rediscovered this precious core, developed it, and shown its conformity with modern science and modern musical practice. For he was aware that the ancient theory would require development, since Greek music was not polyphonic; the Greeks used only 'successive harmony' not also 'simultaneous harmony', as we do, though their diatonic scale, like ours, was based on consonances, namely, the harmonic and arithmetic division of the octave into C–F–G–c'.[15]

It seems likely that Tartini's interest in ancient music and the main source of his knowledge of it, apart from Zarlino and Vallotti, came from the Professor of Astronomy at Padua, Gianrinaldo Carli, in whose house, in the 1740s, Tartini attended discussions on music among a circle of scientists and scholars.[16] Carli himself was a wholehearted enthusiast for ancient music, which he believed to have been polyphonic and to have expressed and excited specific emotions; and he was contemptuous of modern music, which, with the exception of a few operas, was totally corrupt, aiming only at pleasure and amusement, and hence subject to fashion, like clothes. He believed that 'music should be sentimental and not a meaningless, purely artificial arabesque'; and, according to him, these views induced Tartini to compose sonatas in a new style, such that like a 'new Timotheus he excited within me, at his pleasure, various feelings, now of joy, now of sadness, now of fury'.[17]

Tartini's views, however, on ancient music and its marvellous effects were those of a moderate musical humanist; which is what one would expect from a reader of Zarlino. The effects must be accepted as historically true on the authority of such great men as Plato and Aristotle; for we have no existing monuments of the music of the ancients, and the details of their modal system are now unknowable. But the possiblity of music producing striking emotional effects is proved by many of Tartini's personal experiences, of which he recounts one. In a *dramma* performed at Ancona in 1714, an unaccompanied bass recitative, of which the text expressed scorn *(sdegno)*, produced such a violent emotional disturbance *(commozione di animo)* that the hearers changed colour and looked at each other in astonishment; and this effect was repeated at all thirteen performances. But such effects differ from ancient ones in two ways: first, they are the result of chance — there are no possible rules in modern music for producing them; second, they are only momentary, unlike the ancient effects, which could profoundly modify the hearers' character.[18] The basic reason why modern music cannot produce specific, lasting effects (the most it can do is to dispose the hearer to a genus of passions, not produce a specific emotion) is that for us music has become an end in itself, dissociated from poetry and philosophy, whereas in antiquity musician, poet and philosopher were the same person: 'music alone, separated from any other consideration whatever, has become our unique end and aim';[19] and in fulfilling this aim of producing pleasing, satisfying music we have succeeded admirably. Nor does Tartini wish to revive the ancient effect-producing music;[20] nor does he think it even feasible — national differences, custom and tradition are such important factors that probably the best ancient music would produce no effect on us.[21]

Our use of polyphony is another cause of our failure to produce the effects. Like Vincenzo Galilei, but independently of him, Tartini considered that plainsong (canto ecclesiastico) has preserved something of the simplicity of ancient music, and might indeed be a descendant of Greek music,[22] though he realized that the Church modes are not the same as the ancient ones.[23] Plainsong is monodic and its rhythm is free, though, unlike ancient music, it does not observe the prosody of the text. The main difference between modern music and plainsong or sixteeth-century polyphony is the frequency and range of modulation; and this is a contributory cause of our failure to produce the effects. His advice on modulation is very conservative: it should be mainly to the dominant and subdominant; one should not modulate abruptly to a remote key; one should keep in the tonic more than in any other key. Tartini is doubtful whether all this modern modulation is natural. Popular song modulates very little, and he has noticed that, when a long pedal-note on the dominant or tonic occurs, usually towards the end of a piece, the audience's attention is aroused — this is because the tonic is thereby established.[24]

Another basic respect in which Tartini is consciously archaic is his use of a threefold scheme of knowledge, of *scienza*, a scheme that becomes explicit in the *Dissertazione* and indeed forms the framework of the whole treatise. The three genera of knowledge are, in Tartini's order:[25]

(1) physical, knowledge of the given facts of nature; what would now be called empirically established scientific knowledge; this is practised by the learned moderns (*i Dotti moderni*).

(2) demonstrative, knowledge obtained by operation of the intellect, that is, mathematical truths, which Tartini assumes to be absolutely certain; this was practised by the ancient Greeks.

(3) musical, knowledge based on sense-experience *(il senso)* and general consent *(consenso commune)*, that is, facts and judgements concerning the practice of music accepted by all experienced musicians; this is practised by the professors of the art of music.

All certainly true propositions about music will be verifiable in all three genera. Any proposition that does not satisfy this condition will be either false or 'of opinion only'. The three genera are a hierarchy, in descending order: demonstrative, physical, musical, in respect of certainty, generality, and, I think, causal priority.

Tartini saw himself as fighting a battle against two classes of opponent, which correspond to the first and third genera of knowledge.[26] First, those scientists who seek to explain musical sound in purely physical, mechanistic terms, based on empirical knowledge of the vibrations in the air and in sounding bodies. Second, those theorists who claim that music is a matter only of feeling and the instinctive judgement of the ear. Both these classes neglect the second genus of knowledge, the demonstrative-mathematical, regarding it as superfluous and irrelevant. Tartini, therefore, though his main aim is to combine all three kinds of knowledge, is throughout his works particularly concerned to defend the validity of the purely mathematical genus and to assert the absolute necessity of including it in any complete musical theory. It might then be thought that his emphasis on the importance of mathematical explanation is due only to this defensive attitude. But this is not, I think, the case, and that he does attribute a real priority to the mathematical genus over the other two becomes clear if one examines his theories in detail, especially those concerning the minor mode and temperament. He regarded the relation of physical-mechanistic explanations to mathematical ones as being the same as the relation of the Aristotelian material cause to the formal cause, and the latter is 'as positive and real' as the former, 'if not more so'.[27]

It is clear that the third kind of knowledge, that based on musical practice, is of a lower epistemological status than the other two in respect of both certainty and generality. It is based on the supposed conformity of human behaviour at all times and in all places — the same kind of argument that was used in natural theology as one of the proofs of God's existence: the *consensus gentium*. This conformity shows that the behaviour in question is natural, in the sense of being a universal psychological datum that can be altered only violently and temporarily. A supremely important example for Tartini of this kind of natural datum *(verità di natura)* is the diatonic genus, which has remained the same from pre-Platonic times until his own day.[28] But Tartini is aware of major historical developments in music, so that the supposed conformity of human behaviour must be limited to allow for such changes. The required limitation is supplied by his demand that the three kinds of knowledge must converge on to a single truth: only those elements of musical practice are natural and remain constant which are based on mathematical and physical truths. Greek music was monodic, part of poetry and philosophy, and effect-producing; ours is polyphonic, an end in itself, and purely pleasurable. The natural element that has remained constant is the diatonic scale, mathematically derived from the harmonic and arithmetic divisions of the octave, and now physically confirmed by the *terzo suono* and overtones.

This third kind of knowledge can also be used in a non-historical way to confirm truths of the other two kinds.[29] For example, Tartini states that he accepts the following propositions from the article on fundamental bass in the *Encyclopédie*:[30] *(i)* untaught people can sing the diatonic scale correctly; *(ii)* untaught people with a good ear sometimes improvise a satisfactory bass to a given tune; *(iii)* that this 'easy, natural' singing of the scale is 'suggested by the fundamental bass'. The first two propositions, claims Tartini, are confirmed by the experience of the whole human species, and the third is a legitimate deduction from them.

Thus Tartini's mathematical and physical explanations of the diatonic scale and the fundamental bass are corroborated by the natural, untaught behaviour of the whole human race. The difference between, on the one hand, what is natural and constant, and, on the other, what is due to art and may evolve historically may be seen in two possible basses to the upper parts shown in Ex. 1a. The fundamental bass is given in Ex. 1b, while musical art also suggests Ex. 1c. The untaught, natural singer will always improvise the former and never the latter.

Ex. 1

I shall deal with the three kinds of knowledge in the order followed by Tartini in both his treatises: first the physical, then the mathematical, and finally musical practice.

Chapter I of the *Trattato*, 'De fenomeni armonici', contains serveral curious errors, some of which he corrected in the *Dissertazione* after they had been pointed out by Jean de Serre. With regard to overtones Tartini believed, at the time of the *Trattato*, that a string produced only the 3rd and 5th partials. If he was experimenting by himself, this would be an easy mistake to make, since the even partials, being octaves of lower notes, are much more difficult to hear.[31] It is, however, odd that he was not led to correct it either by experiments with sympathetic vibration, or by his knowledge of how such instruments as the trumpet or the tromba marina are played. It is odder still that a professional violinist and teacher, writing nearly twenty years after the publication of Mondonville's *Les Sons harmoniques*,[32] should be ignorant of harmonics on the violin.[33] The consequence of this error, though he half-heartedly corrected it in the *Dissertazione*, was that he did not consider overtones a sufficient physical basis for the harmonic series $1, \frac{1}{2}, \frac{1}{3} \ldots \frac{1}{6}$, which he had taken over from Zarlino, and, instead, based the series on difference-tones, his *terzi suoni*.

This phenomenon is quite easy to observe in double-stopping on a violin. If you play a 3rd or a 6th fairly high up and loudly, you will hear a lower note of a bumbling quality but of a definite pitch; the frequency of the lower note will be the difference between the frequencies of the two higher notes. We may then believe Tartini when he claims to have discovered difference-tones by chance early in his life.[34] He communicated his discovery to other musicians and later used it as a guide to intonation when teaching at the violin-school he started at Padua in 1728. As Serre pointed out, in the *Trattato* all the *terzi suoni* are an octave too high, an error which Tartini corrected in the *Dissertazione*.[35] But he also had an incorrect formula for finding their string-lengths. This formula gave correct results only for intervals having superparticular ratios, so that in the natural series of overtones any two successive notes sounded together do in fact give the fundamental, whereas Tartini wrongly believed that any two notes whatever of the series would produce the fundamental. But for Tartini's purposes this mistake was not an important one. Difference-tones do in fact reinforce the overtone series; and it is perhaps legitimate to argue, as Tartini did,[36] that the former provide a surer physical basis for the ratios of consonances than do the latter. For not all musical instruments produce a complete series of overtones, whereas difference-tones, being, as is now thought, caused within the ear, are always the same whatever the source of sound.

There is another group of errors, also pointed out by Serre, caused by Tartini's confusing pendulums with vibrating strings.[37] But these need not detain us, since they had no consequences in the rest of his system. All these mistakes suggest that Tartini's knowledge of musical acoustics was acquired by word of mouth, occasionally supplemented by experiments that were unsystematic and sometimes misleading.

One field in which he did make musical experiments of great originality and interest was the use of the natural 7th, i.e. the 7th partial which gives from a fundamental C a very flat $b'b$. Ptolemy had given scales in which ratios involving 7 are used, and Mersenne had suggested that through long custom such ratios might come to be accepted as consonant.[38] But no one, as far as I know, before Tartini had categorically stated that the natural 7th is consonant,[39] or pointed out the obvious connection between it and the dominant 7th.

Just after his first exposition of the *terzo suono* Tartini asks the question: 'What is the relation of the *terzo suono* to the intervals from which it results?', and he answers it by the following example:

Ex. 2

[terzi suoni]

Of this he states: 'Given these intervals, under which is placed their respective *terzo suono*, this is demonstratively the harmonic bass of the given intervals, and any other bass whatever will be a paralogism'. He then explains that the 3rds at (z) are of the ratios 6:7, and that the $d''\natural$ at (x) is the natural 7th of the bass e. He then continues: 'This interval is extremely easy to play in tune on the violin; it is intended by harmonic nature, because it is made by nature on the tromba marina, the trumpet and the hunting-horn'.[40]

By 'harmonic bass' Tartini means what Rameau and d'Alembert called the fundamental bass, a term he himself later uses. Apart from the above example and a few others to be mentioned shortly, he confines himself to giving the fundamental bass of the major diatonic scale:[41]

Ex. 3

The weak spot in this harmonization, as Tartini points out, is the subdominant–dominant progression at *(x)–(y)*, where he has had inconsistently to put the *g'* below the *b'* in order to avoid consecutive fifths and octaves. According to him, this fault is still worse in the descending scale, where the tritone at *(y)–(x)* is more offensive because the progression is unnaturally moving from the more perfect dominant to the less perfect subdominant. Both these defects could be remedied by inserting the natural 7th, thus:[42]

Ex. 4

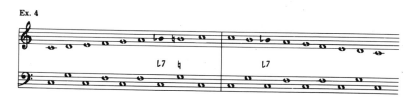

The bass is now a palindrome, and the descending scale is as good as the ascending. If one took the natural 7th as a dominant 7th, the descending scale would be satisfactory and the ascending one very odd. But Tartini does not so take it. He is most emphatic that the natural 7th chord is consonant:[43]

> . . . given [the notes *g'–b'–d''–f''♭*], I say that, combined in any way whatever, they will always have *g* as their *terzo suono*, which is their harmonic fundamental bass. Therefore such a 7th is consonant, not dissonant. Therefore it need not be prepared, nor resolved; it can rise or fall, and, if the intonation is just, it will sound equally well.

He gives two examples of it rising, similar to those in the ascending scale.

Tartini does however connect the natural 7th with the dominant 7th. This connection is of course assumed in the first example above. After assuring us that we should have 'no scruple' in using the above progressions 'when necessary', he continues:[44]

101

The best of it is that more or less the same is done in common practice. On the dominant, which forms the harmonic [perfect] cadence with the tonic, the 7th is used without being prepared. In final cadences it is the almost universal practice to add the 7th to the penultimate note. There is no rule here, rather it is against the rule, since such a 7th is not prepared. But nature is stonger than art.

The difference between *f″* in C major and the natural 7th above *g′* is so slight (63:64) that the ear is little, or not at all disturbed when *f″* is added to the triad *g′–b′–d″*. Hence, for the upper parts of Ex. 5, 'in spite of any rule, there is not and cannot be' any harmonic bass than the one shown.[45]

Ex. 5

One can see here, though Tartini does not mention it, a good reason for insisting on the use of the dominant 7th in such a case: the bass provided by the *terzo suono* (or the overtone series) would be the impossible *c–Bb–c*. Nevertheless Tartini, when giving rules for the use of dissonances, does not give a privileged place to the dominant 7th.[46]

Tartini gives two further musical examples of the use of the natural 7th: the first a harmonization of the Greek enharmonic tetrachord; the second, much longer, a four-part piece in a new scale, in which he uses the chord *f–a–c′♮–d′♯*. This chord, he claims, is consonant, because *f–d′♯* is so near to the natural 7th; he treats it, however, as an augmented 6th, resolving it on to E major. Both these examples were played before professional musicians, who found their effect excellent.[47]

In spite of all this in favour of the natural 7th, Tartini is anxious to preserve Zarlino's harmonic series, which stops short of $\frac{1}{7}$, as we shall see. Also, it is not clear how seriously he was advocating its introduction into general use. In the later treatise, the *Dissertazione*, he is much less favourable to any ratios involving 7; but this may well be only because the *Dissertazione* is a treatise about the diatonic genus.

In the *Trattato* the circle plays a predominant and essential role as the mathematical foundation of the whole of Tartini's system, a system which embraces fields far wider than musical theory. In the *Dissertazione* the circle has almost completely disappeared; but this is not because Tartini has abandoned it, but because he deals with it in another work published simultaneously, a *Risposta* to his critic, Jean de Serre. Of the very long second chapter of the *Trattato*, 'Del Circolo, sua natura, e significazione', Serre wrote: 'Je ne sai s'il s'est trouvé aucun Lecteur qui ait pu soutenir la lecture entière de ce chapitre'.[48] I can claim to be such a reader, but certainly not to have understood it all. The main purpose of the chapter is to demonstrate that the circle is 'intrinsically harmonic', harmonic in the mathematical sense.[49] The circle is chosen because, of all geometric figures, it is the most monadic ('uno in se stesso'). The circle must be inscribed in a square, because straight lines are prior to curved ones; a circle cannot be constructed without a radius.

Tartini considers that the sines of the circle exhibit its specific nature, whereas it has its diameter and radius in common with the exscribed square. The sines are shown to be intrinsically harmonic by the following procedure.

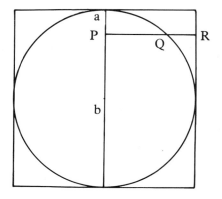

Divide the diameter unequally into a, b, at P. Draw the sine from P to Q, and continue it to meet the side of the square at R, so that PR equals the radius. Then (by Euclid VI, 13) PQ = $\sqrt{ab}$, and PR = $\frac{a+b}{2}$. Tartini then forms what he calls a discrete geometric proportion from a, b, producing four terms: $a(\frac{a+b}{2})$, ab, $(\frac{a+b}{2})^2$, $b(\frac{a+b}{2})$. The harmonic mean, ab, is the sine squared; the arithmetic mean,

103

$(\frac{a+b}{2})^2$ is the radius squared. He has thus succeeded in making the sine into a harmonic mean, but only by squaring it and multiplying the other terms by the radius. What is in fact given in the figure is that the sine is the geometric mean of the two extremes of the divided diameter; one could therefore argue that the circle is instrinsically geometric. Tartini himself raises this objection, and answers it thus.[50]

Since it is true that harmonic mean times arithmetic mean equals geometric mean squared ($\frac{2ab}{a+b} \times \frac{a+b}{2} = ab$), or $H = \frac{G^2}{A}$, and since G = sine and A = radius, which, combined, generate the circle, one can say that the circle is intrinsically harmonic because the sine and radius combined ($\frac{G^2}{A}$) produce the harmonic mean (H). The sine and radius generate the circle in that one can conceive of a quadrant of a circle being built up of an infinite number of sines deriving from an infinite number of divisions of the diameter, the length of the sine being determined by the circumference traced by the revolving radius. Moreover, the sine, being the geometric mean both between the harmonic and arithmetic means of the same extremes ($\sqrt{ab}$ is the geometric mean both of a, b, and of $\frac{2ab}{a+b}$, $\frac{a+b}{2}$), partakes of the nature of both the harmonic and arithmetic means. 'This proposition' says Tartini, 'is in itself, and independently of the musical system, of such and so great importance, that I am sure there is not its equal in all known human sciences'.[51]

So far my audience, though perhaps bewildered and unconvinced, may have some understanding of Tartini's arguments. But in what follows I could not hope even for this modest result. For the rest of the chapter is taken up with extremely complicated attempts to prove the impossible proposition that the radius, diameter and circumference of a circle form some kind of harmonic triad; which 1, 2, 2π evidently do not.[52] I shall therefore pass on to slightly less troubled waters.

The circle is also the basis of Tartini's hierarchy of proportions, an important underlying principle in both his treatises. This descending hierarchy is as follows:[53]

> *harmonic* proportion, rooted in the circle, produces the major triad and the perfect cadence;
> *arithmetic* proportion, rooted in the exscribed square, produces the minor triad and the plagal cadence;
> *geometric* proportion, rooted in the sines, produces the dissonances.

The derivation of dissonance from geometric proportion is based on the fact that any two consonant intervals of the same kind added together produce a dissonance,[54] e.g. two major 3rds produce an augmented 5th, the three notes forming the geometric series 1, $\frac{4}{5}$, $(\frac{4}{5})^2$. There is an unfortunate exception to this statement: the octave; this obliges Tartini to forbid in practice the use of a double octave $(1, \frac{1}{2}, \frac{1}{4})$, though he cannot of course claim that it is in fact dissonant.

In spite of his interest in the natural 7th Tartini was, as I have said, determined to justify Zarlino's *senario*, i.e. to provide some reason for stopping the harmonic series short of $\frac{1}{7}$. This he does by trying to show that its inclusion would involve geometric proportion. But his demonstration, again using the circle, is, apart from other defects, self-contradictory.[55] In the *Dissertazione* he gives interesting hints at other justifications of the 6-system, such as that 6 is a perfect number, being the sum of its factors, 1, 2, 3. The numbers making the basic harmonic ratios, octave 1:2 and 5th 2:3, also add up to 6, whereas the numbers of the basic geometric series, 1, 2, 4, add up to 7. He could have shown how 'the nature of consonance cannot be separated from this basic principle of number'. But since 'this occult science that number contains in itself' is not now understood, he will not venture outside the field of generally accepted matters of fact.[56] One can see here both the very strong attraction that Tartini felt towards numerology, and his sad realization that it would not be accepted by the enlightened century he was living in.

In the *Trattato* Tartini uses the circle also to provide a mathematical basis for the minor mode. But since the series of ratios he requires is so easily and directly derived from the harmonic series, I shall not (you will be relieved to hear) expound his derivation of it from the circle. The series in question is formed by the residues of a string divided harmonically into $\frac{1}{2}$, $\frac{1}{3}$ . . . $\frac{1}{6}$, i.e. $\frac{1}{2}$, $\frac{2}{3}$ . . . $\frac{5}{6}$ (Ex. 6a), as compared with the harmonic series (Ex. 6b).

Ex. 6

(a)

| 1 | $\frac{1}{2}$ | $\frac{2}{3}$ | $\frac{3}{4}$ | $\frac{4}{5}$ | $\frac{5}{6}$ |

(b)

| 1 | $\frac{1}{2}$ | $\frac{1}{3}$ | $\frac{1}{4}$ | $\frac{1}{5}$ | $\frac{1}{6}$ |

The harmonic series belongs to simultaneous harmony, all its intervals having the same *terzo suono*, the low C. The residue series belongs to successive harmony, its intervals giving various and different *terzi suoni*. The former series is the basis of the major mode, which is more natural and perfect than the minor, based solely on the latter series. But the residue-series also contains the major triad, and the subdominant, *F*, which is not present in the harmonic series.[57]

It is from triads on the tonic, dominant and subdominant that Tartini derives the major diatonic scale, as Rameau had done long before him, and also his three cadences.[58] Of these the first two, harmonic and arithmetic, i.e. perfect and plagal, present no problems; but the third, *cadenza mista*, I find entirely baffling.[59] It is from subdominant to dominant, a progression which Tartini himself finds awkward when harmonizing the scale, and which, when it does occur in classical music, is plainly only part of a perfect cadence or one variety of half close.

Tartini's system of cadences points to a basic defect in his general treatment of practical harmony, namely his very archaic conception of the use of dissonances, especially if one compares it with Rameau's remarkable insights into the function of dissonance in determining progressions and cadences and in defining tonality. The rules Tartini gives, in both treatises,[60] for the use of dissonance might come straight out of Zarlino; they codify the practice of a very conservative composer of the mid-sixteenth century.

On the subject of temperament Tartini is equally conservative, admitting its necessity and universal use in the age of the *basso continuo*, but despairing of any rational solution to its problems.[61] He does however come down strongly in favour of the extremely interesting solution to the problem proposed and put into practice by his friend and colleague, Vallotti. This distinguished organist tuned the white notes of his organ in just intonation and let all the errors accumulate in those black notes that are required only in more remote keys, so that, for example F♯ and B♭ were tuned as just major 3rds to D, and G♭ and A♯ were therefore considerably out of tune. This system had the advantage of producing a real effect of key-colour. Vallotti pointed out the pleasure which results

> from the contrast of the greater and less perfection of the chords in the various modulations occurring. If the temperament were equal, or more or less so, there would certainly not be this *chiaro oscuro* which in practice produces an excellent effect.[62]

Tartini then goes on to say that on the violin he is able to play in just intonation, with the help of the *terzo suono*, and that he teaches his students to do so — an important statement, since generations of professional string-players must have passed through his hands.

I have tried in this paper to do two things: first, to show, as others have done in different ways, the originality and interest of Tartini's musical theories, and second, to point out, as few have yet done, the weaknesses in his system. I can perhaps make this second, critical aim clearer by briefly comparing Tartini's system with Kepler's[63] which, though also not without its weak spots, is on the whole much stronger and more convincing.

The main strength of Kepler's musical theory[64] is that it forms part of an all-embracing metaphysical, religious and cosmological system, centred on his God *aei gēometrizōn,* who has created the universe on geometric archetypes and has implanted these in man's soul. If we accept this God, then the order and coherence of the whole system upholds any particular part of it, in this case, Kepler's derivation of musical consonances from the regular polygons inscribed in a circle and the other speculations based on this derivation. Now, in Tartini's published works, this metaphysical-religious framework is entirely lacking; one can only infer, as I have tried to show, the priority of mathematical knowledge over the other kinds, and guess at some Platonic God to account for this priority. But from his letters to Martini, and from the extracts from his *Scienza Platonica* given by Capri, it is evident that Tartini considered his system as a divine revelation, which was destined, by demonstrating the purely mathematical structure and causes of the universe, to defeat the mechanistic and atheistic science of the *philosophes, i Dotti.*[65] But even if Tartini had been able to publish the religious background to his system, this would not, I think, have given it the strength and beauty of Kepler's, for the following reasons.

Though both systems derive ultimately from Plato's *Timaeus* and both are founded on the circle and its properties, they differ fundamentally in that Tartini's is arithmetical, expressed entirely in numbers and explicitly taking number as the highest mathematical reality,[66] whereas Kepler's is geometric and numbers are given a low metaphysical status. Both thinkers refuse to use algebra. For Kepler, since his main demonstrations and analogies are geometric, this matters much less than for Tartini, all of whose arguments would be enormously clearer if expressed algebraically. The dense obscurity resulting from Tartini's numerical presentation of his system is important, not only because it prevented his contemporaries from even trying to understand him, but also because it produced confusion and delusion in his own thinking. At the core of his demonstration that the circle is intrinsically harmonic is the identity: $H \times A = G^2$, which seems to him a discovery of staggering importance. If one thinks of ratios solely in numbers, this identity would not be obvious or easy to discover; it is only if one expresses it algebraically that it becomes self-evident and trivial.

Kepler's God created the universe on the geometric model, co-eternal with Him, of the regular plane and solid figures; Tartini's God created it in number, combining the three proportions, harmonic, arithmetic, geometric. Kepler's system, though extremely complicated in its details, is beautifully simple in its general plan: the plane figures give the ratios exhibited in polyphonic music and in the varying velocities of the planets, and the solid figures, which derive from the plane, give the distances between the planetary orbits. Tartini's system, clogged with arithmetical calculations, painfully produces, at best, true but trivial statements, such as the above identity, and, at worst, arbitrary juggling with numbers, such as the attemps to show that $1, 2, 2\pi$ is some kind of harmonic triad. Where Tartini's system is tidy and logical, as in the derivation from harmonic, arithmetic and geometric proportion of, respectively, major and minor consonances and dissonances, it is musically archaic and unenlightening. Where Kepler's system is illogical and fanciful, as in his sexual analogies drawn from the Golden Section and the Fibonacci numbers and applied to 3rds and 6ths, it is musically illuminating and, in a poetic way, satisfying.

The obscurity of Tartini's writings is certainly not only due to his rejection of algebra. He himself accounts for it in two different ways. First, in his published works, the obscurity is said to arise from the extreme novelty and inherent complexity of his system.[67] Second, in his letters to Martini, in the *Scienza Platonica*, and at one place in the published *Risposta*, he admits to reinforcing the inevitably esoteric character of his new science by deliberate obscurity.[68] He is surrounded by impious materialists who will stop at nothing to suppress, distort or ridicule his system, once they realize that it will utterly refute them. The message, therefore, must be disguised so as to reach only suitable ears. Moreover, some parts of it are so extraordinary that they must be conveyed only by personal interview and be confined to a very few close friends.

Perhaps when all Tartini's unpublished works and letters have been studied we shall know what these important secrets were. At present one can only conjecture that they were of a religious nature. He was deeply convinced of having been favoured with a divine revelation and acutely conscious of the apparent absurdity of a professional violinist claiming to have invented a new mathematical science; but, he writes to Martini:[69]

If God for His greater glory wishes to use the jawbone of an ass (which is what I am) in order to confound the pride of others, are we to suppose that the jawbone of an ass will not produce the effect intended by God?

Near the beginning of his *Risposta* Tartini again emphasizes the apparent absurdity of his claim, and concludes:[70]

Either the Author must consider himself the most solemn fool on earth; or the learned mathematical world is bound to reflect with the greatest possible earnestness on this matter.

I certainly do not think that I have in this paper demonstrated the first of these alternatives, and I have every hope that other scholars, more erudite, more competent in mathematics, and above all with greater knowledge of the manuscript material than I, will make better sense of Tartini's system than I have been able to do. But I strongly suspect that a residue of madness and nonsense will always remain.

NOTES

1. The fullest modern work on Tartini is Antonio Capri, *Giuseppe Tartini*, Milan, 1945. Pierluigi Petrobelli has done valuable work on Tartini's life (*Giuseppe Tartini: le fonti biografiche*, Florence, 1968) and published several articles on him, one of which, 'Tartini, le sue idee e il suo tempo' (*Nuova rivista musicale italiana*, i (1967), 651–75), covers important aspects of his thought omitted in my paper. A. Planchart's article 'A Study of the Theories of Giuseppe Tartini' (*Journal of Music Theory*, iv (1960), 32–61) is quite a full exposition.
   The present paper is based almost solely on Tartini's published writings. There is a large body of manuscript material which I know, if at all, only at second hand. In particular, a late treatise, entitled *Scienza Platonica fondata sul cerchio*, which is certainly of great importance to the aspects of his theory that interest me, was supposed to be in the press in 1976 but has not yet appeared.
2. *Trattato di musica secondo la vera scienza dell'armonia*, Padua, 1754 (facsimile edn. Padua, 1973), p. 31; *De' Principi dell'armonia musicale contenuta nel diatonico genere dissertazione*, Padua, 1767 (facsimile edn. Padua, 1974), p. 113.
3. *Dissertazione*, pp. 37, 71–72.
4. See above, note 2. There is a useful German translation of, and commentary on this: *Traktat über die Musik gemäss der wahren Wissenschaft von der Harmonie*, trans. & ed. Alfred Rubeli, Düsseldorf, 1966.

5. Cf. Tartini's letter of 8 September 1752 to Padre Martini, referring to a mention by Martini of Mersenne: 'Io faccio stato da me solo, e non ho lettura, ne eruditione de sorte alcuna; sicche mi sono affatto incognite tutte le scoperte di tali uomini, e di questi tempi' (*Carteggio inedito del P. Giambattista Martini*, ed. F. Parisini, Bologna, 1888, p. 372).

6. J. A. Serre, *Observations sur les principes de l'harmonie*, Geneva, 1763; J. d'Alembert, *Elémens de musique théorique et pratique*, Lyon, 1762; Tartini, *Riposta alla critica di lui trattato di musica di Mons. Le Serre di Ginevra*, Venice, 1767.

7. *Dissertazione*, p. 82.

8. See Capri, *Tartini*, pp. 490, 493.

9. Cf. Capri, op. cit., pp. 42, 231–4; Rubeli, ed. cit. (above, note 4), pp. 11–12; and below, p. 106.

10. Cf. Rubeli, ed. cit., pp. 18–19, and note 5 above.

11. See E. R. Jacobi, 'Rameau and Padre Martini: New Letters and Documents', *The Musical Quarterly*, 1 (1964), 470–74.

12. Serre, *Observations*, pp. 141–2.

13. Tartini, *Trattato*, pp. 91–92; cf. Rubeli, ed. cit., pp. 140–41.

14. Vallotti, *Della scienza teorica, e pratica della moderna musica Libro primo*, Padua, 1779, pp. 4–5, 58–59.

15. *Dissertazione*, preface (unpaginated); cf. *Risposta*, p. 8.

16. Carli, *Delle opere . . .*, Milan, 1784–7, xiv.332

17. Ibid., p. 333.

18. Tartini, *Trattato*, pp. 134–5.

19. Ibid., pp. 145, 150.

20. *Dissertazione*, p.53.

21. *Trattato*, p. 151.

22. Ibid., pp. 144–5.

23. Ibid., pp. 138–40.

24. Ibid., pp. 146–8.

25. *Dissertazione*, p. 17; cf. *Trattato*, pp. 20–21.

26. *Dissertazione*, pp. 112–13.

27. Ibid., p. 113.

28. Ibid., preface.

29. Ibid., pp. 110–11.

30. *Encyclopédie*, ed. J. d'Alembert & D. Diderot, vii (Paris, 1757), 60 (s.v. 'Fondamental').

31. Rameau (*Nouveau Système de musique théorique*, Paris, 1726, pp. 17–18) admits that even partials are extremely difficult to hear, but considers their existence proved by sympathetic vibration and by the use of organ stops sounding a complete series of overtones.

32. *Sonates à violon seul*, Paris, c.1735.

33. That he did not know them and had not tried to produce them is certain, from the erroneous statement (*Trattato*, p. 10), based on a mistaken theory of vibration, that if on a tromba marina the finger is lightly placed ⅞ of the string away from the nut, no musical sound is produced. Cf. Serre, *Observations*, pp. 113–16.

34. *Dissertazione*, p. 36.

35. Serre, *Observations*, pp. 83–84, 119.

36. *Dissertazione*, p. 112.

37. Trattato, pp. 12–13; Serre, *Observations*, pp. 117–18.

38. Marin Mersenne, *Harmonie universelle*, Paris, 1636 (facsimile edn. Paris, 1965), 'Traité des consonances . . . ', pp. 87, 89.

39. Rameau rejected it; see Matthew Shirlaw, *The Theory of Harmony*, London, n.d., pp. 78, 163.
40. *Trattato*, pp. 17–18.
41. *Dissertazione*, p. 80.
42. *Trattato*, pp. 131–2; *Dissertazione*, pp. 91–92.
43. *Trattato*, pp. 128–9.
44. Ibid., p. 129.
45. Ibid. The other good bass, $c'-d'-a$, is in the minor mode.
46. But cf. *Dissertazione*, pp.88–89.
47. *Trattato*, pp. 127–8, 160–63.
48. *Observations*, p. 121.
49. *Trattato*, pp. 21–22.
50. Ibid., pp. 36–39
51. Ibid., p. 39.
52. Ibid., pp. 27–48, 171–2; *Risposta*, pp. 37–42; cf. Rubeli, ed. cit., pp. 101, 112.
53. *Trattato*, pp. 89–90.
54. Ibid., pp. 73–74. This theory of dissonance is in Zarlino (see Shirlaw, op. cit., pp. 33–34). Vallotti (op. cit., pp. 92 f.) also derives dissonances from geometric proportion.
55. *Trattato*, pp. 56–59.
56. *Dissertazione*, pp. 47–49.
57. *Trattato*, pp. 66–68; *Dissertazione*, pp. 60–64.
58. *Trattato*, p. 98; *Dissertazione*, pp. 66–67, 71–71, 75.
59. *Trattato*, pp. 102–3.
60. Ibid., pp. 78–82; *Dissertazione*, p. 104.
61. *Trattato*, pp. 99–100; *Dissertazione*, pp. 109–10.
62. *Trattato*, p. 100.
63. Benjamin Stillingfleet, in his *Principles and Power of Harmony* (London, 1771, pp. iv–v, 17), notes the likenesses between Kepler and Tartini, both of them deriving from the same Pythagorean–Platonic tradition. Vallotti (op. cit., pp. 59, 60–61) dismisses both Kepler's theory of consonance and Tartini's circle-theories in the same words: 'una pura e mera analogia'.
64. See D. P. Walker, 'Kepler's Celestial Music', *Journal of the Warburg and Courtauld Institutes*, xxx (1967), 228–50.
65. See Capri, op. cit., p. 498.
66. *Dissertazione*, pp. 29–31.
67. *Trattato*, p. 171; *Risposta*, pp. 7, 12.
68. See Capri, op. cit., pp. 419, 449, 496; *Risposta*, p. 7.
69. Martini, *Carteggio*, pp. 334–7.
70. *Risposta*, pp. 7–9.

Chapter 6

TRECENTO ANGELS
AND THE INSTRUMENTS THEY PLAY

Howard Mayer Brown

IN the early fourteenth century, angels in Italian art began to take a more active part in adoring Christ and the Virgin Mary than they had ever done before.[1] Thirteenth-century angels were content merely to hold up drapery or to stand silently by. But shortly after 1300 heavenly messengers can be seen to weep for the crucified Christ, to offer flowers to the Virgin and Child, or to play musical instruments. Indeed, for the next 200 years and more angels form the most numerous, and therefore the most important, class of musicians in Italian art. For that, if for no other reason, we need to understand their role. Why were they depicted playing instruments, and how did artists choose the particular groups of instruments angels were given to play?

Reinhold Hammerstein, in his magisterial study on angelic music,[2] furnishes a satisfactory answer to our first question. Biblical, as well as didactic and literary texts of the Middle Ages all describe the angelic choirs praising Mary or the Trinity in the court of Heaven. Jacobus de Voragine, for example, in his *Golden Legend*, the thirteenth-century book of saints' lives which had such an extraordinary success in the late medieval world and which served so many artists as a source for their images, describes how, as the Virgin was about to ascend into Heaven, 'Jesus came with the ranks of angels, the troop of the patriarchs, the host of the martyrs, the army of the confessors, and the choir of the virgins: and all took their places before the throne of the Virgin, and their voices mounted in sweet and solemn song'.[3] Dante described the Archangel Gabriel appearing in the Heaven of the Fixed Stars as a glowing torch; he circled Mary, singing a melody incomparably more beautiful than anything heard here on earth; and he was answered by all the angelic choirs: 'Thus the circling melody impressed itself, and all the other lights made sound the name of Mary'.[4]

And some of the laude in the mid-fourteenth-century laudario now in the Biblioteca Nazionale in Florence describe how the angels and saints sing and dance in praise of Christ:[5]

> Versi ed afinati canti
> fanno li angeli co' sancti;
> utti sono isplendienti,
> chiari sança tenebrore,

or the Virgin Mary:[6]

> No' vi facciam preghiera
> e all'alto re del cielo, che nne chonduca
> a questa luce chiera,
> là've sonno li vangelista e Marco e Luca
> et sonnvi tutt'i sancti
> che fanno i dolçi canti:
> davanti alla regina fanno dança.

Painters of the *trecento* attempted, then, to translate into visual terms the ineffable melodies of the angelic choirs, especially when they celebrate the Virgin Mary, whose cult enjoyed great vigour, not least among the confraternities of lauda singers that sprang up everywhere in Italy during the thirteenth and fourteenth centuries. One of the Florentine confraternities met regularly in the chapel of Orsanmichele, where the frescoes adorning the walls and ceiling were planned, at the end of the fourteenth century, by the novelist Franco Sacchetti. His Poem 'Capitolo dei Bianchi' — one of the few surviving documents of the time explaining the iconographical programme of so large a work — explicitly confirms the function of musical angels in surrounding and praising the Virgin. Addressing Mary directly, Sacchetti brags of the 'piu notabili' saints, 'degni e venerabili', depicted among her followers, and he describes how

> . . . ne la volta di sopra stellifera,
> Atorniato con stormenti e citera,
> Son pinti i tuo'angeli, che suonano,
> E ne pilastri ancora, che t'adorano.

The nature and the placement of the images, he tells Her, were designed, among other reasons, to make manifest Her glory and to display Her miracles ('per dimostrar la gloria, / Li miracoli tuoi disporre').[7]

In fact, musical angels are most apt to appear in one of three Marian scenes: the Virgin enthroned holding the Christ Child, Her Assumption, or Her Coronation in the court of Heaven. Almost all the literary sources (except, of course, Sacchetti) describe the angelic choirs as merely singing, whereas artists show them playing instruments. The explanation for this anomaly seems obvious and simple: the change comes about in transforming words into visual images. Musical instruments are much more vivid and immediate symbols of heavenly praise than open-mouthed angels, who may or may not be singing. The central panel of the Baroncelli polyptych in Santa Croce, Florence, attributed to Giotto and his assistants, and showing the Coronation of the Virgin, is presumably meant to depict singing angels.[8] But the same point is made more strikingly and unambiguously by the side panels of the same polyptych and the much more pedestrian Assumption (Plate I) by Niccolò di Ser Sozzo Tegliacci which forms the title page of a collection of Sienese civic documents dated 1332 to 1336 — to name but two of the many *trecento* paintings that depict angels playing instruments.[9]

Hammerstein has pointed out that Tegliacci shows the entire hierarchy of nine angelic orders.[10] Only the lowest of them actively make music. The angels and archangels play instruments, while the princedoms and powers sing, surely some indication of the relative place of the two kinds of musical activity in *trecento* life. The higher orders of angels, the virtues, dominations, and so on, are shown as progressively more thoughtful, passive and inward looking, until finally at the top the seraphim, closest to the Godhead, are hardly more than disembodied ideas of angels. Tegliacci's explicit treatment of the angelic hierarchy helps us, then, to understand better his other Assumption, now at San Gimignano.[11] The second is but an abbreviation of the first. Instead of four ranks of angels on either side of the Virgin, the San Gimignano Assumption shows only three; and instead of four players and four singers, the San Gimignano Assumption shows only two of each, in a single row. But both paintings 'mean' the same thing. The hierarchies of angels adore the Virgin, the lower orders by actively singing Her praises.

Tegliacci, like many other *trecento* artists, showed angels playing musical instruments in groups of four. In attempting to explain the choice of four musicians, Hammerstein recalls the tradtional image of Christ in majesty within a mandorla, surrounded by the symbols of the four evangelists.[12] In the more familiar and human world of the early fourteenth century, Christ and the evangelists were transformed into the Virgin Mary, adored by four musical angels. Hammerstein's

PLATE I

Niccolò di Ser Sozzo Tegliacci, 'Caleffo dell'Assunta', detail
Siena, Archivio di Stato

PLATE II

Niccolò di Cecco del Mercia, assisted by Sano and Francesco Fetti, Assumption

Prato, Cathedral

point is best supported, though, not by Tegliacci's Assumption, but by those works of art more closely resembling older pictures in the disposition of their images, that is, with a central figure in a mandorla flanked by smaller figures at each corner, for example, the relief in the Chapel of the Cathedral of Prato that preserves a reliquary containing the Girdle of Our Lady, which she sent down from Heaven to Doubting Thomas on earth (Plate II).[13] It depicts the Queen of Heaven handing her belt to St. Thomas, while musical angels in each corner play gittern (that is, mandora), psaltery, fiddle and lute.

The theory that there is a meaningful relationship between these two iconographical motifs, Christ with his evangelists and Mary with her musical angels, is all the more convincing since one of the earliest *trecento* pictures with musical angels — a leaf from a lauda manuscript written in the first third of the fourteenth century and now in the Pierpont Morgan Library in New York (Plate III) — shows not Mary, but Christ in Majesty.[14] He is flanked by four angels, two at the bottom playing psaltery and fiddle, and two disembodied seraphim at the top. Given the uncertainty of dating early *trecento* works of art, it is not possible to argue that the illumination represents an interim stage between the earlier Christ with evangelists and the later Mary with musical angels. But the illumination does at least make plausible the notion that the artists themselves were conscious of the relationship between the motifs.

Recognizing the similarity of Christ with his evangelists and Mary with Her musical angels, however, does not really offer a convincing explanation of why the transformation should have taken place. Hammerstein has left out a crucial step in chronicling the history of these images, by failing to take into account the most important context in which groups of four musicians appear in earlier medieval art. King David, son of Jesse and author of the psalms, was often portrayed in the Middle Ages, especially in frontispieces to psalters and illustrations of Psalm 1, with his four musicians: Asaph, Ethan, Heman and Idithun. Although all four of David's assistants are mentioned in the Scriptures, they are never described there together as the unified group they appear to be in so many manuscript illuminations. Hugo Steger has identified the source of this iconographical theme as one of the most widely distributed psalm commentaries in the Middle Ages, *De Psalmorum libro Exegesis*, at one time ascribed to the venerable Bede.[15] Pseudo-Bede explicitly linked the psalmist to four assistants, and he even specified which instruments they play: David the psaltery and his four assistans 'cymbala,' 'cyrnira' (apparently a Latin corruption of 'kinnor', the Hebrew word for lyre),

PLATE III

Anon., Christ in Majesty, detail
New York, Pierpont Morgan Library, MS M.742

118

'cithara' and 'tuba'. Some of the manuscript illuminations even quote or paraphrase pseudo-Bede, but few if any of the medieval artists followed the commentator in assigning the instruments he names to the figures they depict; more often the illuminators included in their pictures instruments they knew from real life, or instruments they had copied from earlier illustrations of the same scene.

Steger argues that David was associated with four musicians in order to strengthen his image as a precursor of Christ, following the medieval tradition that attempted to find antecedents for New Testament figures in the Old Testament. Since Christ had his four evangelists, his precursor, David, was given four musicians. It is easy to see, then, why *trecento* painters turned to an iconographical motif borrowed from the Book of Psalms, 'the principal source of Christian devotional material' in the Middle Ages and an obvious place to find images for praising God (or Christ or the Virgin Mary).[16] And it is easy to see why *trecento* artists transformed one of the most widespread musical images of the Middle Ages — that of David and his four musicians, originally devised as a way to connect visually the psalmist with his successor, Christ — into the best means of showing Mary, also of the tribe of Jesse, being adored by the angelic choirs. What better source of praise than the psalms, and what better way to show angels singing — that is, playing instruments — than to borrow the most obvious and common image of the praise for heavenly things, namely, David with his four assistants?

Angels playing musical instruments began to appear in Florentine paintings and manuscript illuminations during the second quarter of the fourteenth century, in works by the followers of Giotto and by Pacino di Bonaguida and his workshop. For example, Bernardo Daddi, the Florentine who transformed Giotto's massive forms into refined and lyric paintings, and his assistants and followers in the 1330s and 1340s regularly included groups of four musical angels in their depictions of the Virgin and Child and the Coronation of the Virgin.[17] In Daddi's hands, the motif often involved a standardized group of instruments. He and his circle painted angels playing two portative organs and two fiddles, as in the San Pancrazio polyptych now in the Uffizi, or else they adopted some slight variant of this scheme, such as two portatives, fiddle and psaltery, or two portatives, fiddle and tambourine, as in the fragment now at Christ Church, Oxford (see Frontispiece).[18] While the Sienese, Ambrogio Lorenzetti, also opted for a symmetrical arrangement of musical angels in his imposing Maestà at Massa Marittima, he did not adopt Daddi's grouping of instruments, choosing instead two fiddles, psaltery and lute.[19] So far as I can see, the only other artist to include groups of four angels in paintings made before 1350 was Allegretto Nuzi, the first painter from the Marche to assimilate Tuscan style, whose work was especially influenced by Bernardo Daddi. But Nuzi's angel quartets follow Lorenzetti's disposition of instruments more closely than Daddi's, although Nuzi seems not to have had a fixed conception of which instruments angels should play. In his London Virgin and Child he chose two fiddles, a double recorder and a tambourine; in the Southampton Coronation two fiddles, a double recorder and a portative organ; and in the Coronation that forms a part of the fresco in the Church of San Domenico in Fabriano, near Lucca, he showed angels playing fiddle, double recorder, lute and tambourine.[20]

In fact, apart from Daddi's conventional grouping of two portative organs and two fiddles, fourteenth-century artists seem to have had no rigidly fixed idea of which instruments quartets of angels should play while adoring the Virgin, although most were inclined to arrange the instruments they chose symmetrically. And painters throughout the rest of the century continued to exercise complete freedom of choice by depicting the most varied instrumental quartets.[21] At least, I can find no principles guiding their decisions. They did not translate pseudo-Bede's enumeration of the instruments played by David's assistants into *trecento* terms. So far as I know, there are no medieval psalm commentaries which assign angels particular instruments; the patristic fathers supposed that the angels sang. And the scorings shown in fourteenth-century paintings do not correspond with any systematic classification of instrumental types known to *trecento* musicians,[22] or to any I can devise myself.

Thus Daddi's scoring involving only two instruments, organs and fiddles, disposed symmetrically on either side of a central figure, is the only conventional scheme — that is, the only scoring that recurs a number of times — in *trecento* works of art. In fact, groups of two angels, playing an organ and a fiddle, can also be seen in a number of *trecento* paintings, especially those showing the Virgin and Child. Indeed, two angels more often form the requisite chorus of praise than four in the *trecento,* and whereas the quartets of musical angels remained a predominantly Tuscan motif throughout the century, duetting angels, who also first appear in Tuscany, soon spread to every part of Italy, even before 1350. Many angelic duets fall into one of two simple categories. In the first, a psaltery is joined by a fiddle, as in Niccolò di Pietro Gerini's Coronation now in Montreal (Plate IV).[23] The second and much larger category takes in all those paintings which show one angel playing a portative organ and the other a

PLATE IV

Niccolò di Pietro Gerini, Coronation of the Virgin, detail
Montreal, Museum of Fine Arts

stringed instrument, either a fiddle, as in Daddi's quartets and Giovanni di Bartolomeo Cristiani's St. John enthroned (Plate V); or else a lute, a psaltery or a gittern.[24] Both these groupings — psaltery with fiddle and portative organ with a stringed instrument — inevitably recall the words of the psalms.

Of the fifteen psalms that mention musical instruments, three exhort the reader to praise God with 'cithara' and 'psalterio' exclusively, and three others mention only one or the other of those two instruments. Psalm 150, the last in the Book of Psalms and musically the most comprehensive, enjoins 'everything that breathes' to praise the Lord, first with 'tubae', then with three pairs of instruments — 'psalterio et cithara', 'tympano et choro' and 'chordis et organo' — and finally with 'cymbalis benesonantibus' and 'cymbalis jubilationis'. One of the three pairs of instruments — 'tympano et choro' — does not lend itself well to the sort of illustration of angelic

121

PLATE V

Giovanni di Bartolomeo Cristiani, St. John Evangelist enthroned
Pistoia, S. Giovanni Fuorcivitas

praise I have been describing, especially since 'chorus' was often translated as dance from the Middle Ages on.[25] But the other two pairs match the principal categories of angelic duets in *trecento* paintings remarkably well. Both 'psalterio et cithara' and 'chordis et organo' exactly describe the instruments in the pictures. The first category, represented by a relatively small group of paintings, might even be redefined to include psaltery and lute, and psaltery and gittern, or almost any combination of two stringed instruments, such as two lutes, two fiddles, fiddle and lute, gittern and fiddle or lute, and so on. Any such combination might reasonably translate 'psalterio et cithara' into *trecento* terms, for both words seem to have been applied to a variety of stringed instruments throughout the Middle Ages.

Groups of two or four instruments played by angels are much more common in *trecento* paintings than any other combinations. Both duets and quartets appear at the very beginning of the tradition of actively musical angels, that is, in the 1320s and 1330s, and they are to be seen in some of the most important and influential paintings by predominantly Tuscan painters of the generations following Giotto, painters such as the Florentines Bernardo Daddi, Giovanni del Biondo, Jacopo Casentino, Orcagna and the Master of the Fabriano Altarpiece (Puccio di Simone). Both groupings of two and four angels seem to reflect, if not always to translate literally, psalms or commentaries on them, sources highly approprate for depicting the ways we should praise God 'in his sanctuary . . . in his mighty firmament, . . . for his mighty deeds . . . [and] according to his exceeding greatness', to quote Psalm 150.

The motif of musical angels could, however, be varied considerably. Sometimes, for example, instead of depicting only four angels, artists doubled the number, and showed four angels on either side of the Virgin Mary. In his mystical marriage of St. Catherine (Plate VI), dated 1359, for example, Lorenzo Veneziano arranged the angels exactly symmetrically, with corresponding figures to the right and left of the Virgin, each playing shawm, lute, psaltery and gittern, with a ninth angel in the foreground holding portative organ. Similarly, the Coronation of the Virgin in Budapest, sometimes attributed to Giotto but more probably by one of his followers, includes angels disposed symmetrically in front of the throne, although those on each side do not play precisely the same instruments. Working outwards from the central combination of lute and portative organ, the two fiddles match one another, but a shawm on the left is balanced by a double recorder on the right, while the two angels at the ends both play tambourines.[26]

In order to add pomp and circumstances to their vision of the

PLATE VI

Lorenzo Veneziano, Mystical Marriage of St. Catherine
Venice, Accademia

Virgin's coronation, *trecento* painters also added to the standard group of four angels two or four trumpet players, as in the Coronation of the Virgin in Berlin by a follower of Bernardo Daddi and Giovanni del Biondo's version of the same scene.[27] The trumpeters often stand at the outside edges of the group of musical angels, symmetrically arranged, sometimes with the bells of their instruments crossed. They look, in fact, very much like courtly trumpeters playing for royal coronations on earth, or like civic musicians performing for some important municipal occasion,[28] and so it is clear that artists added these loud sounds to the predominantly soft music of the normal angelic quartets in order to emphasize that the Virgin's coronation, like those on earth, took place in an atmosphere of courtly ceremonial. They simply translated celestial events into mundane terms. The court of Heaven, the artists seem to be saying, is incomparably grander than anything we know, and yet it is not completely different from the imperial, royal or even municipal splendour that fourteenth-century Italians could occasionally see in real life.

There are as well a few *trecento* paintings, though surprisingly few, in which three, five or seven angels adore the Virgin, or where groups of six or eight cannot be analyzed easily as variants of the more conventional combinations of two or four.[29] I suspect that these exceptional paintings 'mean' the same thing as the others, and that their 'meaning' is not at all incompatible with my interpretation of the duets and quartets. I take it, at any rate, that in selecting but eight instruments to praise God, the author of Psalm 150 made use of the rhetorical device of synecdoche; he used examples to represent a greater whole. All instruments, the psalmist implies, should be used to praise God. In singling out two of them, or four, *trecento* painters evidently intended us to recall the words of the psalms, or David's four assistants. And the relatively large group of paintings that depict crowds of angels — six, seven, eight, nine or even more — adoring the Virgin by playing musical instruments, convey the idea even more directly that 'all breathing things' should offer praise.

Nine or more angels appear in fourteenth-century paintings as early as the groupings of two or four angels. All three variants of the same theme seem to have grown up in Tuscany during the second quarter of the century. For example, the manuscript page from an antiphonary showing Christ in Majesty (Plate VII), now in the Cleveland Museum of Art, dates from the first third of the fourteenth century.[30] It shows a row of angels at the top of the page celebrating the mystery seen below. The Cleveland page is unique, so far as I know, in presenting this particular arrangement of figures. Northern European and

PLATE VII

Florentine illuminator, *c.*1330, Christ in Majesty, detail
Cleveland, Museum of Art, MS 39.677

English manuscripts of the thirteenth and fourteenth centuries often include crowds of angels or spectators watching the main action going on below them, but that composition is uncommon in Italian illuminations. Each of the nine angels may represent a single order in the angelic hierarchy. Be that as it may, nine angels constitute a crowd. Crowds of musical angels appear, too, in a composition of the Virgin's Assumption painted about 1340 (Plate VIII), which Millard Meiss attributes to a Sienese master influenced by Simone Martini, in which the angels fly in a circle, seen in perspective from above, an arrangement imitated a number of times in later paintings.[31] From mid century on, in fact, some painters chose to assemble large flocks of angels — normally ten or twelve but occasionally as many as 21 — to offer praise, especially at the Coronation of the Virgin. A follower of Giotto, perhaps Taddeo Gaddi, for example, depicted fourteen angels in more or less symmetrical arrangement — pairs of trumpets,

126

PLATE VIII

Sienese painter, *c*.1340, Assumption of the Virgin, detail
Munich, Alte Pinakothek

shawms and fiddles and single psalteries and portative organs on each side, with a bagpipe thrown in for good measure — in the Baroncelli polyptych, dating from the 1330s and now in Santa Croce, Florence.[32] Nardo di Cione's Paradise in the church of Santa Maria Novella in Florence is similarly peopled with flocks of musical angels, although their instruments should be identified with caution, since the central figure plays what can best be described as a violin, doubtless the result not of Nardo's prescience but of an overzealous modern restorer.[33] In Venice, Paolo Veneziano painted several Coronations (among them, that shown in Plate IX) adorned with large numbers of angels, generally disposed in fours, playing a relatively exotic collection of instruments, including wing-shaped psaltery, harp-psaltery, and bladder pipe.[34] In Siena, Lippo Vanni crowded nineteen angels playing instruments and three singing into his chapel of San Leonardo al Lago.[35] And in northern Italy the Paduan Master of the Padiglione found space for at least 21 in his fresco showing the Coronation of the Virgin in the Cathedral of Venzone.[36]

It seems plausible to suppose that the artists themselves had a quasi-encyclopedic intent in depicting these large groups of angels — they wished to portray all instruments praising God — even though their primary goal was doubtless simply to dazzle and astound the viewers; in any case they certainly did not intend their works to be didactic or encyclopedic in any narrowly technical sense. But musicians today can use their paintings — indeed, must use them in the absence of any other sort of evidence — to form some more or less precise notion of the instrumentarium available to fourteenth-century Italians. We may be slightly naive in wishing to take literally the intentions of *trecento* artists, but their works furnish the best information that has come down to us about the kinds of instruments musicians played. And no other sources supply us with so many details about the instruments themselves — their shapes, the number of fingerholes and strings they had, where the stringholders went, and so on — and about the way they were played — hand and body positions, presence or absence of bows and plectrums, and so on. For us, these paintings are the visual equivalents of those written encyclopedias of the sixteenth and seventeenth centuries. Students of fourteenth-century music must rely on the admittedly somewhat ambiguous testimony of Taddeo Gaddi, Lippo Vanni, Lorenzo Veneziano and other *trecento* painters, rather than on the more technically secure information supplied later by Virdung, Agricola, Trichet, Praetorius, Mersenne and the other organologists of the Renaissance and early Baroque periods.

PLATE IX

Paolo da Venezia, Coronation of the Virgin, detail
New York, Frick Collection

My method presupposes, of course, that *trecento* painters depicted the instruments they knew from real life, a basic assumption difficult to prove or disprove.[37] At the very least, though, that hypothesis is consistent with the known facts. Painters during the first half of the fourteenth century made sacred legends more familiar and more real than ever before. They turned biblical stories into homely, intimate events that constantly recur in human lives. They showed laymen, saints and other characters in their narratives wearing contemporary clothing. Whereas they recalled biblical texts and medieval commentaries on them in selecting the number and kinds of musical instruments they included in their works, the artists did not illustrate the texts literally, nor do the particular instruments they depicted show the influence of the ancient world or of earlier representations. In short, the nature of *trecento* painting suggests that artists did indeed depict the instruments they knew, though not necessarily playing in ensembles fourteenth-century audiences could have heard, save perhaps in some few exceptional instances.

If flocks of angels give us a fair consensus of what *trecento* painters thought were the principal instruments of their times, then we can draw both positive and negative conclusions from their testimony.[38] On the positive side, we can know that portative organs were the principal keyboard instruments used in the performance of *trecento* music, fiddles the principal bowed string, and lutes, gitterns (that is, mandoras),[39] psalteries and harps the principal plucked strings. We

129

have seen that trumpets appear not infrequently in paintings of the Coronation of the Virgin, with or without nakers. Angels also play shawms and bagpipes, sometimes grouped together in suggestively realistic ensembles. If the painters are to be believed, double recorders — two independent instruments separated from one another by a 30 to 45 degree angle — must have been the principal soft wind instrument of the *trecento,* for no others can regularly be seen in the mouths of angels. And tambourines and cymbals, along with nakers, added the percussive element in the angelic orchestras.

Many pictures offer relatively imprecise impressions of the instruments. Painters obviously did not intend to present technically accurate working drawings and, taken as a group, they supply us with quite a lot of conflicting evidence. Nevertheless, artists working in various parts of Italy at different times during the century are consistent enough in the details of instrumental structure they supply that we can with some confidence go even further to describe the most important features of the principal instruments. Thus portative organs often had two rows of open flue pipes, with twelve to fifteen pipes in each row. If the range were completely chromatic, the normal disposition gives a compass of about two octaves or slightly more, almost certainly at four-foot pitch. Some of the larger portatives had three or more stop knobs at one end, and hence a part of the instrument could be blocked off. On some, the stop knobs may have activated the one or more drones that tower over the other pipes on the larger instruments.

Normally fretted, fiddles appear in a variety of sizes but most often in the same oval, slightly waisted, shape. They are shown with three to six strings, but most of them either have four strings or four over the fingerboard and a fifth running beside the fingerboard, presumably to serve as a drone. They are variously pictured with curved bridges, apparently flat bridges and with string holders that seem to have feet in place of bridges. Angels tell us that *trecento* lutes, most of them unfretted and played with a plectrum, were usually supplied with four double courses, or three double courses and a single top string. Gitterns were similarly fitted with four double courses, but they are normally shown with frets. Incurved trapezoidal psalteries — instruments in the familiar shape of a pig's snout — predominate in pictures, although some angels play trapezoidal psalteries without incurved sides, or semi-trapezoidal or rectangular instruments. Fourteenth-century psalteries were usually played against the chest, long end up, sometimes with one and sometimes with both hands. Most angels use at least one plectrum, but quite a few use two, and a few angels apparently pluck their psalteries with their fingers. Most psalteries were strung with from seven to about 22 triple courses. Many have between eleven and fifteen, giving the diatonically tuned instrument a compass of an octave and a half or slightly less. Some harps evidently had a similar range, while others, with twenty to thirty strings, must have been able to play diatonic notes within a range of three octaves. Angelic harpists invariably use both their hands; they could, then, have played more than one melodic line at a time.

Similar sorts of observations — none readily apparent from other kinds of evidence — could be made about each of the principal instruments on my list. If I am correct in supposing that *trecento* painters intended to show us all instruments in common use at the time, then we can also make negative conclusions. Presumably the instruments they did not include did not exist in the fourteenth century or else they were not common or not important enough to be included in schematic enumerations. The complete absence of such instruments as the cornetto and the transverse flute, and the scarcity of other instruments, such as the rebec, the hurdy gurdy and the recorder, inevitably lead to the conclusion that those instruments were either rare or unknown in Italy during the fourteenth century.[40] At the very least, we might assume as much until conflicting evidence comes to light to modify our conception of the *trecento* instrumentarium.

One or two pictures of a particular instrument tell us little save that the instrument was uncommon. The hurdy gurdy in Puccio Capanna's Glorification of St. Francis can scarcely have been made up out of the artist's imagination,[41] and yet some reason needs to be put forward to explain why similar instruments do not recur in other paintings. The guitar-like instrument in Nardo di Cione's Paradise in the Strozzi Chapel in Santa Maria Novella, Florence,[42] may be the product of some modern restorer's fancy, like the 'violin' played by the angel in the centre of the same fresco. The cittern with its characteristic winged tips in Gentile da Fabriano's Coronation of the Virgin in Milan may be some sort of missing link between earlier and later Italian citterns.[43] And the *ala bohemica*, the wing-shaped psaltery found almost exclusively in Germanic art of the period, but played by one of Paolo da Venezia's angels, doubtless reflects the northern influence on that painter's work, or, perhaps even more likely, the cosmopolitan character of his native Venice.[44] Paolo included as well in several of his paintings triangular psalteries or harp-psalteries (instruments played like a harp but with a sound board beneath the strings), found nowhere else, that may indicate some otherwise unknown local usage, or the painter's fertile imagination, or a reference to some as yet unidentified text. Whatever the explanation of these anomalies, the isolated appearances of unusual instruments in *trecento* paintings — the hurdy gurdy, the guitar, the cittern, the *ala bohemica*, the triangular psaltery and the harp-psaltery — argues strongly against their being considered a regular part of Italian musical life in the fourteenth century.

Similarly, various wind instruments appear only once or twice or not at all in *trecento* paintings, and they can therefore be excluded, at least provisionally, from the mainstream of Italian music. One or two curved horns — probably animal horns — suggest the pastures or the hunting field more than any sort of more formal music making, although they are the closest things to cornetti to be found in paintings of the time. Paolo da Venezia painted one angel playing a bladder pipe, and its rustic connections are suggested by the only other Italian bladder pipe known to me from the fourteenth century, in the hands of a shepherd adoring the Christ Child.[45] Transverse flutes, on the other hand, seem to have been completely unknown in Italy. Played in Etruscan times and in the Byzantine colonies in Sicily, they seem to have been carried along with other Byzantine artifacts to Germany as early as the eleventh century (hence, probably, the term 'German flute'), and then they came down the Rhine into the rest of northern Europe during the fourteenth century.[46] No trace of them survived in Italy. If the transverse flute was played there at that time, it cannot have been considered important enough to have been included among all the instruments praising God.

Nor does the recorder seem to have played an important part in the musical life of the *trecento*. It is, of course, more difficult to distinguish recorders from shawms and cornetti in paintings — they all tend to look rather alike — than to identify the various stringed instruments. Shawms, on the other hand, have a very characteristic profile, with their flared bells, conical tubes and pirouettes, and artists usually show angels playing them with puffed cheeks, an indication that a relatively high degree of wind pressure is necessary to make them sound; in any case, angels playing double recorders and tabor pipes never puff their cheeks, so presumably recorder players did not need to do so either. The shape of the instrument and its playing technique, then, usually indicate that *trecento* painters intended to depict shawms, and not recorders, although a few paintings leave ambiguous the exact nature of the wind instrument, and a few paintings include a wind instrument that cannot be a shawm, a trumpet, a tabor pipe or a double recorder, and may therefore be a single recorder. The earliest unambiguous picture of an Italian recorder — in which the fipple mouthpiece is clearly depicted — known to me is a Virgin and Child in the Museo Nazionale in Palermo, painted by the Pisan Turino Vanni, born probably around 1349 and documented from 1390 to 1427.[47] Two angels make music; one plays a cylindrical recorder, and the other a double recorder, in which the fipple mouthpieces can also be seen. But before the middle of the fourteenth century, a series of related paintings also include an instrument that might be a recorder. The Sienese Assumption of about 1340, now in Munich, in which the angels dance and play instruments in a circle around the Madonna, includes an instrument that can be directly compared with both a shawm and a set of double recorders (see Plate VIII above).[48] At the right front of the circle an angel plays an instrument with a long narrow, apparently cylindrical, tube that resembles much more closely one of the two double recorders immediately to the angel's left than the squat, markedly conical shawm seen being played in the upper right corner. When the Master of the Ovile Madonna painted his version of the same composition, he depicted the same kind of instrument in the same position.[49] But when Andrea di Bartolo reworked the composition, he omitted the ceremonial trumpets and shawm in the background and depicted an angel at the front of the circle playing an instrument markedly more conical than the set of double recorders next to it, but apparently without a pirouette.[50] When Francesco di Vanuccio attempted the same scheme,[51] though, he clearly intended to depict a shawm, it seems to me, since the instrument has such a pronounced flaring bell, completely unlike its neighbouring double recorders, even though a pirouette cannot be seen, at least not in the reproduction available to me. It is almost as though the anonymous Sienese master of about 1340 and the Master of the Ovile Madonna were depicting an instrument familiar to them, but when Sienese artists copied their composition they inserted an instrument they knew, the shawm, for the mysterious original instrument of a sort they had never seen. Ultimately, some more positive explanation of the presence of a recorder — if that is what it is — in two Sienese paintings of the mid fourteenth century must be found; but since they are the only two painters before the very end of the century who considered the recorder important enough to be included in their conception of 'all instruments', we are safe in assuming in the meantime that the recorder played no important role in the performance of *trecento* music. That conclusion is surprising, not only because we are inclined to suppose that the recorder played in all music written before 1750 for the irrelevant and illogical reason that the instrument has enjoyed such a renascence in the twentieth century, but also because the principle of the whistle flute was clearly known and understood in the *trecento*. A very short pipe (presumably of the whistle flute variety) played with tabor makes its appearance among the angelic instruments in a few fourteenth-century paintings;[52] although it may be significant that, like the recorder, the combination of pipe and tabor seems to have been known mainly by Sienese painters. And surely some fourteenth-century Italian performer of the double recorder tried playing one of his set of pipes alone; but if the practice became widespread, no evidence has survived to document it.

Determining the principal instrumental types of the *trecento* is, of course, merely the beginning of the search to know precisely how the music of the period sounded. In the first place, detailed studies of each instrument need to be made, to refine our knowledge of their structure and their musical capabilities. More important, we need to discover how each of them was used. Which of the instruments, for example, normally performed the polyphonic music that has survived? Did courtly society in the Veneto and Lombardy use instruments different from those common in republican Florence? Did the ordinary citizens of Tuscan and Umbrian towns play instruments different from those cultivated by rich merchants and their families, by disenfranchised clothworkers, or by small farmers and peasants who lived in the countryside near larger towns? Some of these and related questions will be relatively easy to answer. Trumpets and drums, for example, playing fanfares that have left no traces in extant musical manuscripts, had an important role in adorning some of the ceremonial occasions of *trecento* life, in church, at court, in councils of state and in the banqueting hall. Among other things, tambourines accompanied dance songs, as we can see, for instance, in Ambrogio Lorenzetti's magnificent fresco depicting good government, showing the happy citizens literally dancing in the streets.[53] Professional minstrels, the *giullari*, accompanied themselves on the fiddle, and doubtless other instruments as well, and mastery of the fiddle, as well as the lute, would have been considered a desirable social accomplishment by members of the upper classes, if Boccaccio's *Decameron* is to be believed.[54] In short, having established the kinds and qualities of instruments in fourteenth-century Italy, we need to discover how those instruments helped to enhance the presentation of music at all levels of society.

NOTES

1. A point made, for example, in George Rowley, *Ambrogio Lorenzetti*, Princeton, 1958, i.60.

2. *Die Musik der Engel: Untersuchungen zur Musikanschauung des Mittelalters*, Berne & Munich, 1962. See also Emanuel Winternitz, 'On Angel Consorts in the 15th Century', in his *Musical Instruments and their Symbolism in Western Art*, New York, 1967, pp. 137–49; and Victor Ravizza, *Das instrumentale Ensemble von 1400—1550 in Italien*, Berne & Stuttgart, 1970. Ravizza's work is marred, however, by his naive assumption that scenes with musical angels depict reality.

I have omitted from consideration one important class of musical angels: those playing long, straight trumpets (or, occasionally, curved horns) on the Day of Judgement. They begin to appear in Italian art in the thirteenth century, but they do not seem to have influenced angels shown in Marian scenes. On non-musical angels in art before the fifteenth century, see Gunnar Berefelt, *A Study on the Winged Angel: the Origin of a Motif*, Stockholm, 1968, which includes an extensive bibliography of earlier studies of the subject.

3. *The Golden Legend of Jacobus de Voragine*, trans. Granger Ryan & Helmut Ripperger, London, 1941, ii.451. The original Latin appears in Jacobus de Voragine, *Legenda aurea*, ed. T. Graesse, 3rd edn., 1890, p. 506.

4. *Paradiso*, Canto 23. The translation is from *The Divine Comedy*, trans. John Carlyle & Philip Wicksteed, New York, 1950, p. 547. On music in Dante, see Kathi Meyer-Baer, 'Music in Dante's Divina Commedia', *Aspects of Medieval and Renaissance Music: a Birthday Offering to Gustave Reese*, ed. Jan LaRue, New York, 1966, pp. 614-27, and Guido Salvetti, 'La Musica in Dante', *Rivista italiana di musicologia*, vi (1971), 160–204.

5. *La Lauda e i primordi della melodia italiana*, ed. Fernando Liuzzi, Rome, 1935, ii.26–28.

6. Ibid., ii.142–6.

7. See Werner Cohn, 'Franco Sacchetti und das ikonographische Programm der Gewölbemalereien von Orsanmichele', *Mitteilungen des Kunsthistorischen Instituts in Florenz*, viii (1957/59), 65–76. In the sixteenth century Giorgio Vasari described how the fourteenth-century Sienese painter Pietro Laurati 'depicted a truly angelic and divine joy in a choir of angels flying in the air about a Madonna. As they gracefully dance they appear to be singing, and whilst they are playing various instruments they keep their eyes fixed and intent on another choir of angels, sustained by a cloud of almond shape bearing the Madonna to heaven, arranged in beautiful attitudes and surrounded by rainbows' (*Le vite de' più eccellenti architetti, pittori e scultori italiani*, ed. Gaetano Milanese, Florence, 1878 ff., i.474; trans. William Gaunt as *The Lives of the Painters, Sculptors and Architects*, London, 1963, i.100).

8. The central panel is reproduced in Bernard Berenson, *Italian Pictures of the Renaissance. Florentine School*, London, 1963, i, Pl. 63; and Richard Fremantle, *Florentine Gothic Painters*, London, 1975, Pl. 24. The entire polyptych is reproduced, among other places, in *The Complete Paintings of Giotto*, ed. Andrew Martindale & Edi Baccheschi, New York, 1966, pp. 118–19, which includes a brief note about its history and the various attributions scholars have made.

9. Millard Meiss (*Painting in Florence and Siena after the Black Death: the Arts, Religion and Society in the Mid-Fourteenth Century*, Princeton, 1951, pp. 169 f.) dates the

Assumption ten years later than other scholars, on stylistic grounds. Some of the earliest representations of angels playing instruments illustrate the 24 Elders of the Apocalypse worshipping the Lamb of God (Revelations v.8) or the harpers harping and singing a new song before God (Revelations xiv.2–3). But Hammerstein (*Musik der Engel*, p. 196) points out that in Italy instruments were not shown in such scenes. I have been unable to find any evidence of an Italian concern for Apocalyptic angels playing instruments (except, of course, for those sounding trumpets at the Last Judgement). One of the few references to the music in Revelations in an Italian source is a passing reference to the harpers harping a new song in *Meditations on the Life of Christ: an Illustrated Manuscript of the Fourteenth Century*, ed. Isa Ragusa & Rosalie B. Green, Princeton, 1961, pp. 380–81, where they are mentioned along with the music sung after the crossing of the Red Sea and the songs and dances of David leading the ark of the covenant, all of them cited as examples of thanksgiving to God.

10. Op. cit., pp. 224–5. On the codification of the hierarchy of angels by pseudo-Dionysius the Areopagite in the fifth century see, among other sources, James Hall, *Dictionary of Subjects and Symbols in Art*, New York, 1974, p. 17. Jacobus de Voragine (*Legenda aurea*, p. 512) once makes use of the term 'citharisando' to describe the way in which the powers praise Mary.

11. Reproduced in Bernard Berenson, *Italian Pictures of the Renaissance. Central Italian and North Italian Schools*, London, 1968, ii, Pl. 357. The San Gimignano Assumption may, however, have been trimmed.

12. Op. cit., p. 224.

13. Attributed to Giovanni Pisano in Hammerstein, op. cit., Pl. 87, and to Niccolò de Cecco del Mercia with assistance from Sano and Francesco Fetti in Giuseppe Marchini, *Il duomo di Prato*, Milan, 1957, Pl. 19.

14. The page, from MS M. 742 of the Morgan Library, contains the beginning of the lauda 'Alta trinita beata', found complete in the Florentine laudario and published in Liuzzi, *Lauda*, ii.18–20.

15. Hugo Steger, *David Rex et Propheta*, Nuremberg, 1961, pp. 74–75, 113–17.

16. James W. McKinnon, 'Musical Instruments in Medieval Psalm Commentaries and Psalters', *Journal of the American Musicological Society*, xxi (1968), 4. For an interpretation of patristic commentaries on music, see also McKinnon, *The Church Fathers and Musical Instruments* (unpublished dissertation), Columbia University, 1965, and 'The Meaning of the Patristic Polemic against Musical Instruments', *Current Musicology*, i (1965), 69–82.

17. Meiss, *Painting in Florence and Siena*, p. 6.

18. Attributed to a painter of the Florentine school, *c*.1340–50, in J. Byam Shaw, *Paintings by Old Masters at Christ Church, Oxford*, London, 1967, No. 5. The central panel of the San Pancrazio polyptych is reproduced in Berenson, *Florentine School*, i, Pl. 177, and Richard Offner, *A Critical and Historical Corpus of Florentine Painting*, III/iii (New York, 1930), Pl. 14, and III/viii, Pl. 5. A Coronation with angels playing two portatives, fiddle and psaltery is reproduced in Offner, *Corpus*, III/v, Pl. 22. Other paintings by Daddi and his circle showing four angel musicians include two reproduced ibid., III/iv, Pll. 36 & 42.

19. Reproduced in Rowley, *Lorenzetti*, i, Pl. 5, and ii, Pll. 23, 61 & 63–66.

20. The first two paintings are reproduced in Berenson, *Central Italian and North Italian Schools*, ii, Pll. 206 & 214. The Fabriano fresco is reproduced in Raimond van Marle, *The Development of the Italian Schools of Painting*, v (The Hague, 1925), Fig. 78.

21.　For a selection of angel quartets, see, for example, Fremantle, *Gothic Painters*, Pll. 176–8, 242, 353, 512, 514–15, 633, 665, 739 &c.

22.　That is, *trecento* painters did not, as far as I can see, paint representative examples of the three classes of instruments (wind, percussion and instruments of tension) cited by Boethius and Cassiodorus. On these classifications, see Oliver Strunk, *Source Readings in Music History*, New York, 1950, pp. 85 & 89, and the illustrations in Joseph Smits van Waesberghe, *Musikerziehung: Lehre und Theorie der Musik im Mittelalter* ('Musikgeschichte in Bildern', iii/3), Leipzig, n.d., Pll. 89–90, 95–96. Nor did *trecento* painters illustrate the classification system explained by Marchettus of Padua in his *Lucidarium*, in which music is divided into three classes, harmonic (that is, produced by voices), organic (produced by human breath or air, as in wind instruments) and rhythmic (produced without breath, as in stringed instruments). On this classification, see Jan. W. Herlinger, *The Lucidarium of Marchetto of Padua: a Critical Edition, Translation and Commentary* (unpublished dissertation), University of Chicago, 1977, First Treatise, Chaps. 7, 8, 12 & 14.

23.　For some other paintings showing angels playing psaltery and fiddle, see Berenson, *Florentine School*, i, Pl. 319; Enzo Carli, *Pittura Pisano del Trecento: la seconda metà del secolo*, Milan, n.d., Pll. 144–5; van Marle, *Italian Schools*, iii, Fig. 286, iv, Fig. 77, v, Fig. 164; and Charles Seymour, Jr., *Early Italian Paintings in the Yale University Art Gallery*, New Haven & London, 1970, No. 31.

24.　For some other paintings showing angels playing a portative organ and a stringed instrument, see Berenson, *Florentine School*, i, Pll. 224 & 314; Fremantle, *Gothic Painters*, Pll. 239, 242, 354, 355 & 454; and Offner, *Corpus*, III/ii/2, Pll. 50–51, III/vii, Pl. 40, & IV/ii, Pll. 3/16 & 12.

25.　See Hammerstein, *Musik der Engel*, pp. 28–29. On 'chorus' as a bagpipe, bladder pipe or plucked stringed instrument, see Andreas Holschneider, 'Instrumental Titles to the Sequentiae of the Winchester Tropers', *Essays on Opera and English Music in Honour of Sir Jack Westrup*, ed. F. W. Sternfeld, Nigel Fortune & Edward Olleson, Oxford, 1975, pp. 12–14.

26.　Reproduced in Berenson, *Florentine School*, i.135; Miklós Boskovits, *Early Italian Painting: Budapest Museum of Fine Arts*, Budapest, 1966, No. 5; and Hammerstein, op. cit., Pl. 95.

27.　The Berlin painting is reproduced in Offner, *Corpus*, III/iv, Pl. 35, and van Marle, *Italian Schools*, iii, Pl. 221. The Giovanni del Biondo painting is reproduced in Offner, *Corpus*, IV/iv, Pl. 29, and Fremantle, *Gothic Painters*, No. 490.

28.　See, for example, the illumination in Milan, Biblioteca Ambrosiana, MS 6, showing the coronation of Gian Galeazzo Visconti in 1395, reproduced in Emma Pirani, *Gothic Illuminated Manuscripts*, London, 1970, Pl. 41; and the painting on the cover of a collection of Sienese civic documents, dated 1385, showing Government restored to power holding in check the citizens of Siena, while four municipal trumpeters play, reproduced in Enzo Carli, *Le tavolette di Biccherna e di altri uffici dello Stato di Siena*, Florence, 1950, Pl. 18.

29.　For some paintings showing three or five musical angels, see Berenson, *Central Italian and North Italian Schools*, ii, Pll. 512–13 & 515; Berenson, *Florentine School*, i, Pl. 368; Berenson, *Venetian School*, Pll. 21 & 29; van Marle, *Italian Schools*, iii, Fig. 336, and iv, Figs. 31, 37, 88 & 89; and Rodolfo Pallucchini, *La pittura veneziana del trecento*, Venice & Rome, 1964, Pll. 369, 604, 609 & 706.

30.　Shelf-mark MS 39.677.

31.   On this painting (in the Alte Pinakothek in Munich) and the tradition of depicting the Assumption in this manner, see Hermann Beenken, 'Das Urbild der sienesische Assuntadarstellungen im XIV. und XV. Jahrhundert', *Zeitschrift für bildende Kunst*, lxii (1928/29), 73–85; Ernest T. Dewald, 'The Master of the Ovile Madonna', *Art Studies*, i (1923), 45–54; Hammerstein, op. cit., Pl. 86; and Meiss, *Painting in Florence and Siena*, Pl. 22.

32.   Reproduced in *The Complete Paintings of Giotto*, pp. 118–19.

33.   Reproduced in Berenson, *Florentine School*, i, Pl. 194; Fremantle, *Gothic Painters*, No. 297; van Marle, *Italian Schools*, iii, Fig. 258; and Offner, *Corpus*, IV/ii, Pl. 10.

34.   Below the detail shown here, flanking the figures of Christ and the Virgin, are two more angels with portative organs. The complete painting (now in the Frick Collection in New York) is reproduced, among other places, in Berenson, *Venetian School*, Pl. 10; van Marle, *Italian Schools*, iv, Fig. 6; and Michelangelo Muraro, *Paolo da Venezia*, University Park, Pennsylvania & London, 1970, Pll. 120 & 122. Two other paintings by Paolo showing crowds of angels are reproduced in Muraro, *Paolo*, Pll. 77–78, 133–5.

35.   Reproduced in Enzo Carli, *Lippo Vanni a San Leonardo al Lago*, Florence, n.d., and Frederico Ghisi, 'An Angel Concert in a Trecento Sienese Fresco', *Aspects of Medieval and Renaissance Music*, pp. 308–13 and Pll. 18a–d.

36.   Reproduced in Luigi Coletti, *I Primitivi*, iii: *I Padani*, Novara, 1947, Pl. 69b.

37.   In the sixteenth century, Vasari seems to have believed the same thing, to judge from his remark that Simone Martini painted an Assumption in the Camposanto at Pisa, which shows the Virgin 'borne to heaven by a choir of angels, who sing and play so naturally that they exhibit all the various expressions which musicians are accustomed to show when playing or singing, such as bending the ear to the sound, opening the mouth in various ways, raising the eyes to heaven, puffing the cheeks, swelling the throat, and in short all the movements which are made in music' (*Vite*, i.552; *Lives*, i.131 — see note 7 above).

38.   The list of principal instruments and the brief comments about the structural features of some of them are derived from an examination of about 500 *trecento* paintings, a corpus of iconographical material that ought to be published. Many of the pictures are reproduced by Berenson, Fremantle, van Marle and Offner. I intend to publish more detailed studies of individual instrumental types or groups of instruments based on this material as well as on evidence gathered from literary sources, some of which contradicts or supplements in an important way the iconographical evidence (see note 40 below).

39.   Laurence Wright has argued convincingly that the instrument usually called 'mandora' in the musicological literature (a small, plucked lute-like instrument with a round back and sickle-shaped pegbox) ought to be called 'gittern' (in Italian, 'chitarra'), the name by which it was known in the Middle Ages ('The Medieval Gittern and Citole: a Case of Mistaken Identity', *Galpin Society Journal*, xxx (1977), 8–42).

40.   The working hypothesis that the rebec is not one of the principal stringed instruments of the *trecento* may have to be modified, since it does appear in *trecento* literature. It is included, for example, among the instruments listed in the poem *L'Intelligenza*, sometimes attributed to Dino Compagni, as appropriate for a court; see A.-F. Ozanam, *Documents inédits pour servir à l'histoire littéraire de l'Italie*, Leipzig & Paris, 1897, p. 406. The comic Florentine worker Calandrino plays a rebec in Boccaccio's *Decameron;* see Howard Mayer Brown, 'Fantasia on a Theme by Boccaccio', *Early Music*, v (1977), 335. And Filippo Villani in his eulogy of Francesco Landini

(*Liber de civitatis Florentiae famosis civibus*, Florence, 1847, p. 34) lists the 'ribeba' as one of the instruments the composer had mastered. Moreover, the poet Francesco di Vannozzo's implicit claim that he introduced the harp into Italy from France in the second half of the century needs to be investigated more thoroughly. The claim is made in the series of sonnets exchanged between his lute, his harp and himself, published in *Le rime di Francesco di Vannozzo*, ed. Antonio Medin, Bologna, 1928, pp. 51–58. See also Ezio Levi, *Francesco di Vannozzo e la lirica nelle corti lonbarde durante la second metà del secolo XIV*, Florence, 1908, pp. 343–8.

41. The fresco, in the church of S. Francesco al Prato in Pistoia, is reproduced in Hammerstein, *Musik der Engel*, Pl. 68. The hurdy-gurdy shown there differs considerably from the more elegant instrument sculpted about 1360 by Orcagna, now in the National Gallery in Washington, reproduced in Georg Kinsky, *A History of Music in Pictures*, London, 1930, Pl. 42/4.

42. For reproductions of the Nardo di Cione fresco, see note 33 above. For an unusually good comparison of a *trecento* musical instrument before and after modern restoration, see Leonetto Tintori & Eve Borsook, *Giotto: the Peruzzi Chapel*, New York, 1965, Pll. 50–53.

43. The Gentile da Fabriano painting is reproduced in Berenson, *Central Italian and North Italian Schools*, ii, Pl. 529. On the winged tips of citterns, see Emanuel Winternitz, 'The Survival of the Kithara and the Evolutions of the English Cittern: a Study in Morphology', *Musical Instruments and their Symbolism*, pp. 57–65. A number of medallions in the lower church in Assisi, S. Francesco, show prophets holding cittern-like instruments painted by followers of Giotto.

44. See Muraro, *Paolo da Venezia*, Pll. 77, 113–14, 120.

45. Ibid., Pl. 120. The other painting, a scene from the story of the birth of the Virgin, is in the National Gallery, London (reproduced in *National Gallery Catalogues: Earlier Italian Schools*, London, 1953, ii.433–6).

46. See Howard Mayer Brown, 'Flute', *The New Grove's Dictionary* (forthcoming).

47. Reproduced in Stefano Bottari, *La pittura del Quattrocento in Sicilia*, Messina & Florence, 1953, Pl. 6.

48. On the Munich Assumption and its related paintings, see note 31 above.

49. Reproduced in Beenken, 'Urbild', p. 76; Dewald. 'Ovile Madonna', Fig. 30; and van Marle, *Italian Schools*, ii, Fig. 216.

50. Reproduced in Beenken, 'Urbild', p. 76; Dewald, 'Ovile Madonna', Fig. 31; and Berenson, *Central Italian and Northern Italian Schools*, ii, Pl. 423.

51. Reproduced in *A Loan Exhibition: the Art of Painting in Florence and Siena from 1250 to 1500. In Aid of the National Trust and the National Art-Collection Fund*, London (Wildenstein), 1965, Pl. 78.

52. For example, Plate VII; the paintings mentioned in notes 35, 48 & 49 above; and the painting by Meo da Siena and his assistants, in Subiaco, Sacro Speco, reproduced in van Marle, *Italian Schools*, v, Fig. 28. The fresco in the lower church of San Francesco in Assisi, depicting St. Francis in glory, and attributed to followers of Giotto, shows an angel in the upper left corner playing a short instrument, like a tabor pipe, but with no tabor. It is reproduced in Giovanni Previtali, *Giotto e la sua bottega*, Milan, 1967, Fig. 316.

53. Reproduced in Rowley, *Lorenzetti*, i, Pl. 7. and ii, Pl. 157.

54. See Brown, 'Fantasia on a Theme by Boccaccio', pp. 324–41. See also Giuseppe Vecchi, 'Educazione musicale, scuola e società nell'opera didascalica di Francesco da Barberino', *Quadrivium*, vii (1966), 5–29, which quotes the remarks of Francesco da Barberino (1264–1348) that singing, playing musical instruments and dancing modestly were desirable social accomplishments for the middle and upper classes in early fourteenth-century Italy. Francesco states that well-born ladies may play in polite society the psaltery ('mezzo cannone'), the fiddle ('viuola'), the harp ('arpa') or 'd'altro stromento onesto e bello e non pur da giollare'. By implication, then, many of the other principal instruments of the *trecento* ought not to be played by upper-class amateurs; they were appropriate only for professional *giullari*. That trumpets, nakers, shawms and bagpipes are not fit for the drawing room should surprise no one. On the other hand, Francesco's remark is especially useful in that it allows us to infer that the gittern and double recorders were the instruments of professionals, a conclusion supported by pictorial evidence, for example, the two *giullari* playing those instruments in the fresco in Assisi painted by Simone Martini, depicting St. Martin's investiture as a knight, reproduced, among other places, in Berenson, *Central Italian and North Italian Schools*, ii, Pl. 123, and van Marle, *Italian Schools*, ii, Figs. 137–8. Francesco may have left the lute off his list inadvertently, for we know from the *Decameron* that it was played by elegant amateurs.

Chapter 7

FANTASY AND ORDER IN BEETHOVEN'S PHANTASIE OP.77

Hugh Macdonald

BEETHOVEN'S PHANTASIE Op.77 for piano presents a number of problems which admit no easy explanation; or rather, it presents a single considerable problem which can only be solved if we jettison a number of cherished views about criticism, analysis and musical response. It is a short piece which might be thought innocuous enough to be left in the general obscurity in which it lies, but it has the potential to explode the whole network of modern criticism. Of course it would be typical of Beethoven to undermine many of our long-established notions with a piece such as this, and that is what I believe it does.

The Phantasie was composed in 1809. On 22 December 1808 Beethoven gave the famous concert that included the first performances of the Fifth and Sixth Symphonies, the Fourth Piano Concerto, various vocal pieces and the Choral Fantasy, Op.80. He also played a 'Phantasie' for piano alone, which may or may not bear any relation to the Phantasie under discussion. Most probably it was improvised, as we know that he improvised the opening cadenza of the Choral Fantasy. This cadenza was written down in 1809, and the Phantasie was probably composed at the same time, along with the Fifth Piano Concerto and the two piano sonatas Op.78 and Op.79. It was published in 1810. By any standards it is a most extraordinary composition. Since C.P.E.Bach the title fantasia or fantasy had embraced all kinds of freely composed pieces which belonged to no recognised category of composition; Mozart's and Schubert's fantasies can be, structurally, very loose. But the Phantasie Op.77 is, even within this tradition, the most violently disconcerting of any. It begins in G minor and ends in B major; in between it passes through D minor, A flat major and numerous other unrelated keys. It has no thematic skele-

141

ton, the tempo fluctuates wildly. Pauses, cadenzas, flourishes and violent changes of dynamic and direction abound. Only two clear formal elements can be isolated: one is the descending (and sometimes ascending) scale, like a harp glissando, which is heard at the beginning, the end and elsewhere in between (Ex.1). The other is the set of variations in B major which begins at bar 157 and which makes the composition inconsistently inconsistent by introducing the semblance of musical order into what has begun as a totally disorderly piece.

The Phantasie has turned out to be one of Beethoven's least known compositions, but by no stretch of the imagination can it be called dull or commonplace. It has been neglected by critics, scholars and pianists probably for the very reason that it is so baffling, for there are doubtless as many responses to this piece as there are listeners. The questions it poses are, among others, the following: Why does it begin, after the scale, with a cadence rather than a theme? Why is that cadence immediately repeated a tone lower? Why does the D flat section occur where it does (bar 6)? Why should Beethoven introduce a banal little folkish melody at bar 15 and abandon it with such violence at the switch to D minor (bar 37)? Why does the same D minor section move abruptly into an A flat Adagio, of all things, which in turn fails to establish any but the most transitory existence? Why does the B minor 'più presto' section (bar 102) introduce a quasi fugal texture? And why, ultimately, should all this scrambling and switching conclude with a serene but not particularly profound (by Beethoven's standards) set of variations in, of all keys, B major?

What can we say? We can turn away baffled and even repelled, as perhaps many have. Or we can follow Czerny, as most critics do, in describing it as an example of Beethoven's art of improvisation. Czerny is good authority, of course, but one should pause for a moment to ask why Beethoven should improvise in a style so much more disorderly than usual. He was certainly capable of improvising without abrupt shifts of tempo and material, and could surely improvise whole movements in the same key and tempo if he wished. The implication of Czerny's comment is that Beethoven was a highly undisciplined improviser, which is hard to believe.

Alternatively one may see the piece as the enactment of a drama. Wilhelm de Lenz, who lived a good deal closer to Beethoven's age than we do, described the Phantasie as some kind of medieval legend which Beethoven was relating, incident by incident, although he was no more specific than that.[1] Even Tovey, in a 1923 programme note, attaches descriptive significance to the opening phrases:[2] the scales, he says, are a 'note of interrogation' and the adagio cadence that follows is 'an expression of resigned hopelessness'. To the piece's extraordinary structure he shows no reaction save to say that the B minor 'più presto' section leads somewhere, that is to say into the B major variations, unlike all the preceding passages, 'all these questions and efforts', as he calls them.

Paul Bekker, who is generally sound on Beethoven's improvisatory pieces, has another poetic interpretation (written in 1912):[3] 'Has the Soul found its balance and rest?', he asks. No, is the answer. But Bekker also strikes a more modern note with an attempt to demonstrate the unity of the Phantasie:

> The B major melody, the kernel of the whole, is developed organically from the apparently insignificant one-tone motive. The way that the characteristic opening scale frequently reappears in fresh guise, framing the whole from first to last and adapted to each change of mood, makes it absurd to speak of the whole as a haphazard, luxuriant mosaic of ideas. Despite its multiplicity of theme-materials, the Phantasie possesses an inner unity and displays a readily recognizable and highly poetic sequence of thought throughout.

This seems to be the first attempt to make structural sense of the piece, although no deeper analysis is attempted.

A more recent writer, Jürgen Uhde,[4] attempting similarly to interpret the form, concluded that not the one-tone motive, the major and minor second, was the important interval, but the third. Uhde sees the chaotic tonality as a reflection of improvising and treats the opening scale not as an occasional recurrent event but as a thematic motive with transformations as an arpeggio (Ex.2) and as a scale

Ex. 2

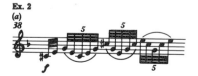

(Ex.3). In other words it breeds anything in the piece which descends or ascends, whether it is a scale or not. The only element not related to it is the occurrence of repeated notes in both the A flat Adagio and in the B major variation theme, a reference that has hitherto gone unnoticed (Ex.4). Uhde then explores the motivic use of the third in, for example, the B flat section at bar 15 and in the variation theme. Once again this is not very searching analysis, but it does lead him to the fantastic conclusion that it proves that in Beethoven the function of a passage is more important than its beauty or any other intrinsic qualities. In fact this is not a conclusion at all; it is a tendentious attitude which is given only the slightest support by the presence of major and minor thirds and ascending and descending scales in the Phantasie — as though any work of Beethoven could be declared innocent of major thirds, minor thirds and scales.

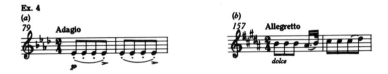

A further approach to the Phantasie is provided by a short paper published in the 1970 Bonn *Kongressbericht* by Jürgen von Oppen,[5] which places it against the context of the Fifth Piano Concerto, whose slow movement has many points of resemblance with the B major variations, and which was composed at about the same time. More boldy he relates the B major tonality to the F sharp sonata Op.78 and the high $e'''b$ on which the Phantasie begins to the E flat tonality of the concerto. This putative kinship with adjoining compositions is also evident from the sketchbooks, two of which contain material for Op.77. They reveal work on Op.73 (the concerto), the Phantasie Op.77, the sonata Op.79 and the Choral Fantasy, Op.80, in progress simultaneously, or at least interlocking. Beyond placing the work in its chronological background and pointing to elements which Beethoven notated in isolation (for example, the harmonic shift in bar 37), the sketches provide little help and certainly no illumination about the piece's structure or purpose.[6]

How then is the Phantasie to be understood and studied if the search for structural logic is unavailing? My own answer may seem unduly negative, but it can be argued as a positive solution. The only workable interpretation, it seems to me, is to regard the piece's disunity, diversity, illogicality, inconsistencies and contradictions as themselves the principal idea of the piece. The unspoken assumption has been that because it lacks the formal balance and clarity usually found in Classical music it is a bad piece, however we circumlocute that judgement. Now Beethoven, as we all know, was quite capable of composing poor music, though the works that fall into that category are generally dull and obvious. The Phantasie is not dull and it is anything but obvious. Furthermore there can be no question of Homer nodding while he let pass an unworthy product; it is put together in Beethoven's full maturity and in full consciousness of what he was doing. His genius consists precisely in his capacity to surprise and astonish, and all his finest works do exactly that in a fine balance with giving us what we do expect. In the Phantasie his urge towards the unpredictable, which is pronounced in all his music from Op.1 onwards, becomes the *raison d'être* of the piece. Its purpose is to revel in strangeness, to mislead our dull brains and to leave us baffled and breathless. It is defiantly dotty and illogical. Here Beethoven is taking a particular principle — the principle of disunity — to an extreme, and would surely smile at our well-meaning attempts to find the structural point of the work and our absurd talk of 'progressive tonality',[7] 'inner unity' and the even more absurd search for structural seconds and structural thirds. The point of the work is that it has no structural point.

There seems to be no way of judging the Phantasie except as a deliberate attempt to stress the disruptive elements of music. It is so narrowly aimed at this uncomfortable target that it cannot possibly be counted among Beethoven's greater works, but it does illustrate his command of musical resource, in that when he wished to contradict the usual patterns of classical order he was able to do so in characteristically extreme fashion.

The lesson to be learnt from this is that the more we recognise Beethoven's supreme mastery of musical material and his consciousness of his own power, the more we must acknowledge that our habitual criteria of excellence (and its opposite) are false. If structural coherence is to be applauded, incoherence must be condemned. We have no grounds for condemning the Phastasie for being structurally incoherent since that is, if I am right, the main purpose of the composition. It follows that structural coherence and logical patterns of form are not the invariable touchstones of quality they are generally supposed to be. We have long taken coherence for granted as a musical virtue because it is so rewardingly to be observed in the great works of the German classical tradition. But how much coherence do we really want? How much can we stand? When does too much coherence become obviousness? The banalities of second-rate music are frequently the banalities of over-coherence, of knowing all too certainly what will happen next. The bones extrude all too plainly from the flesh.

The notion that unity, as a special manifestation of coherence, is the essential hallmark of a great work of art must surely be abandoned. For so long now this quest for the unity of every great work has been as stubborn as the alchemist's pursuit of gold, and equally fruitless. There have been endless self-satisfied discoveries of hidden unities in one masterpiece after another. We have been shown relationships between themes that would make any listening musician's hair stand on end. Everyone will have his own favourite examples; perhaps it is a sufficient example to cite Rudolf Reti's claim that the 'Joy' theme of the Choral Symphony with its predominantly stepwise movement is related thematically to the striding arpeggios which open the first movement.

We need above all to recognise the true balance between like and unlike, between resemblance and difference, between unity and contrast. Music, like any art, requires the artistic mixing of these opposites. It is strange that the principle of contrast embodied most obviously in such phenomena as the concerto principle and in sonata form has been so little understood by those who have wished to show that two elements which the composer clearly places in opposition to each other are in fact united and related. Why may they not be allowed to remain contrasted? To concentrate on unity without looking for the real contrast of disparate elements is to misunderstand this balance.

If we abandon the search for hidden and inner unity the advantages are striking and numerous. For one thing we will no longer have to say, like Bekker, that the Phantasie Op.77 has inner unity, when it obviously has not. It will be possible to discuss a work's heterogeneous elements without feeling obliged to restore it to grace by asserting its unity. An anonymous programme note for *Die Zauberflöte*, [8] which intelligently and lucidly pointed out that in this opera there is to be

146

found an extraordinary mixture of musical elements and styles: fugue, chorale, *Volkslied*, aria, hymns, coloratura, *Singspiel*, pantomime, religious and Masonic symbolism and so forth, nonetheless felt obliged to conclude that 'the opera has an unmistakable unity' — and so, the writer might have gone on to say, it is safe to listen to, it has passed its trial. In truth *Die Zauberflöte* is a work of many very great qualities, but unity is not one of them.

The following is an extract from a recent programme note for Monteverdi's Vespers:[9]

> What is so remarkable about the Vespers is not merely the diversity of character of the movements or the jostling of styles within them, but also the fact that they are for the most part built up throughout of extremely brief musical paragraphs; one phrase tends to follow on another with astounding rapidity and often with startling contrast too. The conscious unifying forces are there, as I have attempted show, but they lie mostly beneath the audible surface.

One senses how uncomfortable that writer was to have drawn attention to contrast and diversity, and so felt obliged to add that the Vespers are redeemed by inaudible unifying forces.

Another advantage of releasing the concept of unity from the unhappy burden it has to bear would be to rid musical literature of the lengthy analyses of great works which claim to prove that they are great works. Schenkerian analysis is too often applied to the 'Hammerklavier' Sonata, to the *Tristan* prelude and to *Verklärte Nacht*, but never, as far as I am aware, to the works of Rutini or Raff or Rheinberger or Respighi, presumably because the analyst is afraid that the music of these worthy composers might reveal hidden cross-relationships between themes and movements and so betray their unity.

We will no longer be asked to believe that intervals of seconds, thirds, fourths, tritones, fifths, sixths or sevenths are structurally important when they are, as we all know, the very bricks from which the building is constructed — not just one building but every building. We will no longer have to worry about those passages in great works where something extraneous and inexplicable happens. A good example may be found in the Choral Symphony's last movement when quite suddenly the melodic shape of Ex.5a is followed at once by a very curious sequence (Ex.5b). Then the phrase is never heard again in the rest of the movement. This is one of innumerable passages in Beethoven where structuralist explanations will only create confusion

and heresy, whereas to accept such events purely as events, without a logical or sequential framework is to widen our experience of music.

We will no longer need to prove, for example, that the *Ring* has a fixed and logical key-scheme when it is plain that it has not. Tonality in the *Ring* is of course fundamentally important, especially for purposes of colour, characterisation and drama, but it is not logical. It is based on both unity and contrast and above all on intuition. The fact that Wagner was prepared to admit transposing certain passages of *Tristan und Isolde* says more for his practical sense of the theatre than for his obedience to modern critical designs.

The inexplicable in music is not something to be afraid of, as it is in science or politics, but an essential part of its nature. It is everywhere we look and is the source of much of what we love and admire most. Debussy spoke of the mysterious element of composition and of his fear of fracturing that mystique. Burney, on the other hand, asserted that music could be decompounded, as in chemistry, and measured for its various ingredient elements. Modern criticism has strayed too far from Debussy and too far beyond Burney in the sophistication of techniques for decompounding music, hopeful perhaps that it will yield the same spectacular results as in modern biological analysis. Schoenberg said that a piece of music was like a biological specimen in being made up of innumerable cells, each of which carries a unifying genetic imprint. The analogy is striking but not proven, since it is clearly nonsense to suggest that all the minutest details of a piece of music possess a unifying and identifying imprint. There is, on the contrary, abundant evidence of foreign cells among the parent cells, that is, works which contain within them disruptive and heterogeneous elements which are there because the composer put them there, and for no other reason. Musicology will tell us, often with mind-bending amplitude, what exactly the composer wrote. It will often tell us when he wrote it, where he wrote it, with and for whom he wrote it, for what functional, pecuniary, symbolic, personal or other purpose he wrote it and what he was attempting thereby to achieve. But the belief that it can tell us why he did what he did is the most pernicious heresy of our century. We shall never know why the 'Eroica' begins on two firm E flat chords or why the close of Brahms's Third Symphony is soft, not loud, or why the Rhine sounds on a low E flat in *Das Rheingold*, not a low D flat, or why Mozart begins and ends his operas in the same key while Beethoven and Verdi do not.

There is a further objection to the elevation of unity to a place of honour in modern criticism. In the eighteenth and nineteenth centuries the concept of unity is of course occasionally found in critical writing, but as a conscious objective in the minds of artists and composers it is essentially twentieth-century property, part of the legacy of a desire to impose a structured unity most clearly exemplified in Schoenberg's methods. In this area the critic is bound to measure the music's achievement in terms of perceptible unity as a legitimate criterion of excellence. But to what extent may a post-Schoenbergian, post-Freudian or even post-Hanslickian conception of musical structure be applied to earlier music, to Bach, Beethoven and Berlioz? Historical music is wedded indissolubly to its own time. We are familiar with authentic texts and authentic instruments and authentic performance practice; much of our efforts are directed towards promulgating these very things. But we have as yet no conception of authentic criticism. We use mid-twentieth-century psychology to unravel mid-eighteenth-century music and the result is inevitably absurd.

To arrive at a technique of authentic criticism we need to do the same kind of patient work of reconstruction as that needed for the study of performance practice. We have to go beyond studying the critics of the appropriate period, we have to reconstruct the attitudes and assumptions against which the composer was writing. We do not reproduce them but we base our own responses on the most enlightened type of critical response that the composer himself could have hoped for. We should not cheat on a composer by expecting his music to perform the tricks expected of music of our own time. We must hear the music through the composer's own ears, so far as that is possible.

This concept of authentic criticism and authentic response has wide implications that cannot possibly be pursued here. But it is worth asking how one might devise an authentic criticism of, for example, the Phantasie Op.77 with which this paper began. The first thing, as I have suggested, is to stop looking for post-Beethovenian and un-Beethovenian criteria and to clear our minds of critical debris accumulated in the last 170 years. We then have to recognise Beethoven's capacity to encompass the rational and the irrational side by side in music, some of which admits explanation, some of which does not. Very little of the Phantasie can be explained, in any useful sense. Every time Beethoven misleads his audience, the solution lies not in themes or motives or cells or key-structures but in the simple fact that he is deliberately deceiving us. The more nonsense we offer by way of interpretation the more his cruelly effective sense of humour has triumphed.

NOTES

1. *Beethoven et ses trois styles*, Paris, 1855, p. 195.
2. Reid Orchestral Series, 10 February 1923, reprinted in T. K. Scherman & L. Biancolli, *The Beethoven Companion*, New York, 1972.
3. *Beethoven*, Berlin, 1912; English translation, London, 1925, p. 90.
4. *Beethovens Klaviermusik*, i: *Klavierstücke und Variationen*, Stuttgart, 1968.
5. 'Beethovens Klavierfantasie Op.77 in neuer Sicht', *Bericht über den internationalen musikwissenschaftlichen Kongress Bonn 1970*, ed. Carl Dahlhaus & others, Kassel &c., n.d., pp. 528–31.
6. The sketches for Op.77 are described in Gustav Nottebohm, *Zweite Beethoveniana*, Leipzig, 1887, p. 274, and in J. S. Shedlock, 'Beethoven Sketches Hitherto Unpublished', *The Musical Times*, 1 (1909), 712.
7. Philip Barford, 'The Piano Music – II', *The Beethoven Companion*, ed. Denis Arnold & Nigel Fortune, London, 1971, p. 192.
8. Chelsea Opera Group, Oxford Town Hall, 1973.
9. Programme note by Philip Brett, University of California, Berkeley, 22 August 1977.

Chapter 8

ANALYTICAL THINKING IN THE FIRST HALF OF THE NINETEENTH CENTURY

Ian Bent

THE STUDY of musical theory is one of the oldest and most scholarly branches of musicology. We are now in what might be called the third generation of editing activity (if we can regard the work of Gerbert, Coussemaker and LaFage as the first, and that of the earlier editors of this century such as Cserba, Rohloff, Steglich and Vivell as the second). The volumes of *Corpus scriptorum musicae* already stretch away behind us. Possibly some of the editing and re-editing is happening too soon; perhaps we should take stock more critically of what survives before we rush into editorial print.

There are signs that a new understanding of theoretical material has been emerging in the last ten years, an understanding of theory as a continuous process rather than as individual treatises at discrete points in time. The concept of transmission has emerged — not transmission at a gross level, but the transmission of small clusters of words, of single expressions or of ideas. This work is happening mostly in the medieval world, especially in the recent work of Hans Heinrich Eggebrecht, Fritz Reckow and Frieder Zaminer, and in the *Handwörterbuch der musikalischen Terminologie*. When we come to the theory of the nineteenth century, there may be very little case for editions as such. But there is important work to be done in tracing the history of terms and of ideas in the modern field. What we need is a systematic distributional analysis of the contents of theoretical writings, at least from 1750 and stretching up into the twentieth century.

As a way of pointing towards the work to be done, I propose to sample here the analytical thinking in a small group of theoretical publications between approximately 1750 and 1850. First I should like to consider one central and very familiar aspect of musical theory in this period, namely the attitude of writers to the concept of form, as reflected in treatises by August Kollman,[1] Carl Czerny[2] and Adolf Bernhard Marx.[3] Later I shall examine more briefly two specific cases, both of them comparatively obscure, one from the beginning of the period and one from the end: the technique of permutations and the use of harmonic reduction.

August Kollmann's *Essay on Practical Musical Composition* of 1799 comprises twelve chapters, of which the first is entitled 'Of the Plan for a Piece to be composed'. The other chapters then discuss sonatas, symphonies, concertos, fugues and so forth, concluding with a chapter on style. Kollmann opens his first chapter by stating that in order to compose a piece one must first consider its 'intended *nature*'; this done, one must determine the '*means* by which it can be made to answer its purpose' — 'and this', he declares, 'is what I call forming a *Plan* of it'. This preliminary consideration of the piece to be composed covers its 'Length and Disposition; its Modulation; its Character; the instruments or Voices for which it is to be composed; and all such other Circumstances'. In other words, before the invention of musical material begins, the scope and nature of the piece ought to be apparent from the purpose which it is to serve, even down to details of its structure; for Kollmann says that in specifying the 'Length and Disposition of a Piece' the composer will decide how long it is to be, how many movements it will have, and how many sections each movement will contain; and then 'what Subjects, Periods, and Passages . . . will be best'.

Kollmann then proceeds to the tonal structure, or what he calls the 'Modulation of a Piece'. He first draws out a three-part scheme: 'every movement is considered as a piece in itself; and has three particular objects in its modulation, viz. first, the *setting-out*; secondly, the *elaboration*; and thirdly, the *return* of the modulation'. He exemplifies how this scheme works with short movements made up of a single section or two sections, and for longer movements in two sections. However, he then goes on to speak of 'three sorts of elaboration', and immediately declares that: 'Each section may be divided into two *subsections*, which in the whole makes *four* subsections'. The first subsection he calls the '*proposition*'; its purpose is to establish the 'key, mode, and character of the piece', and it remains in 'the principal key', ending with a 'half cadence'. He goes on:

> The *second* subsection begins . . . to enlarge upon the first proposition, in the *nearest* points of view; which is what I call the first sort of elaboration . . . it admits of touches in any other key . . . . The *third* subsection, or first part of the second section, enlarges on the first

proposition in all those more or less *distant* points of view . . . . It is therefore the place where real digressions to other related and foreign keys are most at home; and comprehends what I call the second sort of elaboration . . . . The *fourth* subsection once more resumes the first propostion, and still enlarges upon it in such *nearest* points of view, as are opposite to those of the second subsection; which is what I call the third sort of elaboration.

How are we to reconcile Kollmann's five terms — 'setting-out', three 'sorts of elaboration' and 'return' — with his four 'subsections'? The answer appears to be that he is dealing with two quite separate schemes. One is a tonal scheme and is made up of three 'objects in . . . modulation'; the other might loosely be called a thematic scheme, despite Kollmann's tonal commentary to it, and is made up of four 'subsections'. If we try to superimpose these schemes we arrive at something like the diagram in Fig. 1.

Fig. 1

Thematic:	*Proposition*	1st sort	*Elaboration* 2nd sort	3rd sort	('subsections')
Tonal:	*Setting-out*	*Elaboration*		*Return*	('objects in . . . modulation')

Kollmann's three-part scheme superficially recalls J. G. Sulzer's plan under 'Anlage', in the *Allgemeine Theorie der schönen Künste* (Leipzig, 1771–4): the trinity of *Anlage, Ausführung* and *Ausarbeitung* — in fact inappropriately, but we shall return to Sulzer in a moment. His four-part scheme recalls, much more suitably, the rhetorical schemes of the Baroque theorists and particularly the six-part scheme set out by Mattheson in *Der vollkommene Capellmeister* of 1739. The third section of Mattheson's scheme was in fact called the *Propositio*. Indeed, Kollmann's four subsections are quite close to Matthesons's scheme shorn of its two introductory sections (p. 236): *Propositio–Confirmatio* ('the artistic strengthening of the proposition')–*Confutatio* ('the resolution of objections')–*Peroratio* ('the end or conclusion of our musical oration', which customarily re-used the material of the first section — though this was of course in Mattheson's case not the *Propositio* but the *Exordium*).

Kollmann's overall procedure is in fact very close to Sulzer's trinity. In particular, Sulzer's *Anlage* is very near to Kollmann's 'Plan'.

As Sulzer says:

> In the *Anlage* the plan of the work is determined, with its principal sections; the *Ausführung* gives each principal section its shape; and the *Ausarbeitung* works out the lesser relationships, assembles the smallest units each into their rightful place and best form.

What Kollmann is doing becomes clear from his preface, where he says:

> I have endeavoured not to waste room with the descriptions of mere *Forms*, which have been hitherto in the different sorts of musical pieces; but to teach *Principles*, on which every branch of composition depends, and according to which the known forms of a piece may be varied, as well as new forms invented.

Kollmann's view of form, then, is an admixture. It has a Baroque concept still at heart, and still with vestiges of rhetorical language in its description; but this is projected on to a Classical three-part tonal structure, with the underlying concept of tonal movement implicit in the words 'setting-out' and 'return'. And the whole is exemplified by reference to works not only by Bach and Handel, but also by Haydn and Mozart, and by the generation of Beethoven, Clementi, Dussek and others. It is highly determinate. It pronounces laws. Like Sulzer, Kollmann is concerned with universal procedures, not with forms themselves. As Sulzer says, the artist 'should not only apply the greatest exertions of his spirit to the *Anlage*, which is the most important part, but also not let himself proceed to the other parts of the task until he is content with the first'. (How similar this is to Ebenezer Prout's statement, a hundred years later: 'We cannot conceive of a painter going to his easel and beginning to work on his canvas without having decided what was to be the subject of his picture. Nobody but a lunatic would set to work before he made up his mind whether he was going to paint a bit of "still life", a portrait, a landscape, or a piece of architecture. A composer goes to work on the same principle . . . '![4])

In sharp contrast to Kollmann's attitude is that of A. B. Marx. Marx was of course a polemicist for the new, the romantic view of form, and his views are well known today. Form, he said, is a 'self-determining', a 'being oneself and being different from others'. Form is not the opposite of content but the specification of it. Musical substance, in origin shapeless, is only fired with spirit and becomes music through the medium of form. Hence form is not external, not arbitrary. 'The number of forms is unlimited'; there are ultimately no laws governing what form a particular compositon should take.[5]

Marx's discussion of sonata form is rightly celebrated. But it is significant that in his first brief description, tucked away at the back of the second volume (1838) of his *Lehre von der musikalischen Komposition* in its first edition, he offers one page of formal instruction on the form in the major key and follows it by twice as much on possible ways of deviation from the ground-form, stressing always that the spirit may lead the composer in some other direction. Marx acknowledged that there were similarities in form between pieces, but denied strongly that forms were as a result 'routines' through which composers worked. Content was not really separable from form. Even so, the very appearance of similarities suggests that 'there must be some rationale underlying these moulds, some concept which is of broader significance, greater strength and longer duration'.[6] Thus Marx denied form as convention and proposed for it an epistemological basis. Forms are patterns abstracted from past practice, rather than conscious guidelines; they represent deep-seated principles of organization which analysis uncovers.

Czerny was clearly acquainted with this new approach to form. 'These forms', he says, 'are by no means of arbitrary creation: they were invented, improved, and extended by degrees, and in the course of time, by distinguished geniuses'. But then he relapses into an eighteenth-century concept, justifying forms by their naturalness, and drawing a parallel with other arts: forms 'depend as much on natural laws, as those rules by which the painter must dispose his groups and figures, the architect his pillars and columns, and the poet the incidents of his narration or his drama'.[7] Czerny seems at one moment to accept freedom and originality, but at the next moment limits this freedom to the invention of material only. Quite unlike Marx, with his view of the fusion of substance and form in one spiritual act, Czerny declares that the development of musical material 'must assume a determinate *form*, and the composition must therefore belong to a *species* already in existence: consequently, in *this* respect, no originality is, in general, necessary'.[8] Indeed, with a nod towards the nineteenth-century image of genius he issues a warning against the dangers of innovation in the area of form: 'even in this case it is always a hazardous undertaking for the composer, as the present age, in the first instance, and afterwards futurity, decides whether these innovations are actually to be considered of real advantage to the art'. The worst criticism that can be made of a work is to be told: 'Your work . . . contains much that is new and beautiful: but alas! the new therein is not beautiful, neither is the beautiful, new'.[9]

In one respect, at least, Czerny was markedly different from Kollmann. He certainly did not spurn 'mere *Forms*'. Indeed, his treatise is a veritable compendium of forms, including exotic dances such as the bolero, fandango and tarantella, and a section on Russian national dances. But each is *pre*scribed, not *de*scribed. The display is not one of an infinite variety of infinitely variable forms, but rather of a dazzling array of highly fixed forms. And he harks back to Kollmann's universalism in saying: 'There are . . . a tolerable number of different forms in music. These, however, are reducible to a far lesser number of each principal forms, as are totally different in their structure from one another' — not a single underlying procedure, as with Kollmann, but several fundamentally different procedures, an idea which Marx had accepted when he spoke of a number of *Kunstformen*. But Czerny shows his impatience, not satisfaction, with the situation, quite out of the blue, when discussing the form of the Etude. Commenting that the Etude threatens to supplant other forms in popularity, he says: 'For as we are unfortunately not very rich in varieties of musical forms, and as the names *Sonata, Variation,* Rondo &c already begin to grow old; we find the title *Study (Etude)* very acceptable . . . '[10] His observation on the small number of forms that are really different is, then, not a declaration of orderliness, nor is it a statement of epistemological universals; it sounds more like a cry of frustration.

On the subject of key-scheme in sonata form Marx is again of interest. He shows how the main thematic material is announced in the principal tonal areas of the home key, and that the form explores all the related key areas in some order or another, all in due proportion. He then spells out this proportion:[11]

> But the tonic key occupies the most prominent position. For it predominates in the first half of the first section and in the whole of the third, the dominant in the second half of the first section. Thus the tonic key rules at the beginning and end, as is appropriate. The dominant can be extended from the close of the first section into the second section, and is touched upon in the third section. None of the other keys ever becomes more than a point of modulation, though in the transitions they can be dwelt upon for longer. In this way no key is forgotten, and none is used in ill-timed repetition.

This is an extraordinarily eighteenth-century deterministic view for Marx to adopt. His tonal hierarchy is not essentially different from the one delightfully illustrated by Joseph Riepel almost a century earlier.[12] Riepel's 'Master' (*Praeceptor*) — for the treatise is in the old-fashioned dialogue form — offers to his 'Pupil' *(Discantista)* a symphonic Allegro with the key-scheme C–G–C, and makes an analogy by referring to the tonic as the 'farmer' and to the dominant as the 'servant'. But the ever-eager Pupil is not satisfied with this, and counters:

> But our farmer, who is put in charge of the farm by the Baron, has a steward and a housekeeper, and a milkmaid, and a day-labourer, and an errand-girl; and he sometimes gets help from his neighbour, *die schwarze Gredel*. The farmer is the first to get to work and the last to leave, and the most industrious of all.

'Yes', replies the Master, 'and this is the best picture of tonal order we could possibly have':

> The key of C is the farmer, G is the steward, A minor the housekeeper, E minor the milkmaid, F the day-labourer, D minor the errand-girl; and C minor is the housekeeper of E flat, because she can sometimes help the farmer, so we call her *die schwarze Gredel*.

The master then gives musical examples illustrating the role of each of these, and concludes: 'You see that the farmer, the key of C, often appears in the middle, each time that he wants to give new orders or pass on new information. In other words, he must not be out of sight or out of earshot. Everything turns on him'.

Apart from its amusement value, Riepel's parable puts tonal order into a rational order of society in which everything has its precisely defined role to play; and it illustrates the idea of animating, personifying, tonal movement, glimpsed in Kollmann and the idea of 'setting-out' and 'return'. Riepel's work also gives rise to the first of my special cases, namely that of permutation technique. For in his table of contents to Chapter 2 of the *Anfangsgründe* there appear rather improbable entries (it is impossible to translate them literally):[13]

> *Mathematical Reckoning* is of no help to composition. It is a preposterous myth, sheer fanciful nonsense, to say that this or that distinguished person learnt to compose by means of it . . .
> *The Unique Technique of Permutation,* by means of which one can invent more than 99 themes in a single day, is at least 99 times more beneficial to composition than the much-vaunted mathematical reckoning.

Riepel's Master begins with his Pupil's name:

> You are called *Jacob*, and your surname is *Rab*. Now *Rab* comprises three letters, *R*, *a* and *b*. These letters can be re-arranged six times . . . : *rab, rba, arb, abr, bra, bar.*

He then sets out a huge table giving the number of permutations of elements from 1 to 50, and the Pupil experiments with the permutations of his surname with an added final 'e' — Rabe — and with his first name, Jacob. Then the Master comes to the point:

> Just as with letters, so too with musical notes: two notes can be re-arranged twice, three notes six times, four notes 24 times, and 50 notes as many times as that unpronounceable number at the bottom of the permutation table.

The Pupil tries it first with the two notes C and D, and obtains C–D and D–C. He then tries it with C, D and E, and produces six permutations. And then he tries the rather more interesting exercise of taking four notes and two different note values. C and E he makes crotchets and D and F quavers, and he produces 24 permutations, all under the time signature 6/8, eight of which form syncopations across the middle of the bar (Ex. 1).

Ex. 1

But, the Pupil complains, several of these permutations are too 'strange' to be used. 'No trouble', replies the Master:

> You simply pick out the best . . . . All I have to do is to look at the four notes in your 24 permutations, take a bar here and there from them, add one or two quite different bars to them, and in a moment I have 24 beginnings for a theme. I will make this clear to you by marking the new bars with a cross, and your bars with the numbers that you have already assigned them.

And with this he produces two phrases (Ex. 2), in both of which the first and third bars come from the table of permutations, and are numbered accordingly, while the second and fourth are newly supplied, and are marked with crosses.

Ex. 2

He then goes on to use up eight more permutations, making four new phrases out of them (Ex. 3). At this point he explains that he has exhausted all of the six permutations which begin on C. From now on he will have to begin with newly composed bars and incorporate the remaining permutations into the middle of each phrase. This he then does. When the Pupil exclaims 'Amazing!', he responds quite curtly, 'It's not amazing, it's entirely natural'.

Ex. 3

159

The lesson then continues until the Master takes things a stage further:

> PRAECEPTOR: Now just as with notes, so too I can re-arrange whole bars in permutations — so far as tonal progression and melody will allow.
> DISCANTISTA: I can imagine that, too. Five names — Jacob, Philip, Hansmichel, Gerhard, Adam — could be re-arranged 120 times, just as if they were single letters.
> PRAECEPTOR: And if I wanted to re-arrange the letters of these names as well as the names themselves, a huge number [of permutations] would result.

This prompts a veritable dissertation from the Pupil in which the full vista of permutational possibilities opens up before his eyes. It dawns upon him that it offers not a mechanical way of generating compositions by rote, but an inexhaustible means of varying a theme once it has been written, and making it into an extended composition; not only that, but also a means of singing an aria with inexhaustibly changing variations.

How does this strange phenomenon fit into the history of musical theory? There is no trace of it in Sulzer. Nor is there in Heinrich Christoph Koch's *Musikalisches Lexikon* of 1802. (In both of these the word *Verwechslung* refers to harmonic writing and denotes transfer of a dissonance to another part; Sulzer also uses it for chordal inversion. Koch, in his *Versuch*, employs it also for enharmonic change and for change from major to minor key.)[14] Two things come to mind. The first, more obviously, is a possible connection with Baroque improvisation. (Permutations, after all, are an important element of the classical Indian musician's daily practice, and often come through in his performance of the opening improvisatory *alap* of a raga.) Another possiblility is a connection with the spate of dice compostion which occurred in the mid-eighteenth century. Kirnberger's *Der allezeit fertige Polonoisen- und Menuettencomponist* of 1757 is perhaps the most celebrated example: it lays down a fixed chord scheme for the dances, and supplies motifs for each bar from which the user selects by throwing a dice.[15]

But I prefer first to look a little further at Riepel, then to look in a quite different direction. First to later in Riepel's second chapter, where he presents a quite remarkable account of cadential structure in music, including the use of repetition to extend a phrase beyond its notional four-bar norm.[16] Moreover, Riepel's fourth chapter, published in Augsburg in 1765, is interesting especially for its exposition of melodic 'figures' — *Figuren* — not as rhetorical Baroque devices but as units of formal construction. Taking an aria melody, he shows how a single figure can be used to create an extended melodic line by means of sequential movement, and then combines two figures in the same way.[17] Though the melodies remain Baroque in character, the exposition of method is astonishingly modern.

Secondly, I would turn to the aesthetic concept of unity as it was developing in writings of the period. Sulzer's wonderfully lucid definition of 'Einheit' states that to the philosopher 'perfection and . . . beauty consist of diversity bound together in unity'. Only when the constituent parts of a thing exist together in interrelationship, so that we perceive the whole rather than the parts, does that thing possess unity. Koch in his *Musikalisches Lexikon* clarifies the musical application of this by stating, also under 'Einheit', that a piece must have unity of material and also unity in the presentation of that material. Koch criticizes composers who 'string ideas and thoughts one after another, ideas which when considered on their own are beautiful'. And in his *Versuch*, Koch in 1787 exemplifies the principle by showing how a Minuet by Haydn has only one main idea, an idea which is modified in various ways, including inversion; and how as a result the piece has 'the most perfect unity'.

> One can see that even a single phrase is sufficient to form a small composition of this sort if the composer knows how to bring it back in such different transformations and interrelationships that the whole in its unity nevertheless acquires the necessary diversity.[18]

So Riepel's permutations can be seen as a very early theoretical move towards unity of material, one which perhaps takes a practice from the past and turns it to a new purpose — and one which incidentally delightfully anticipates the teachings of Schoenberg, the ideas of 'thematic process' and other modern practices.

My second special case takes us forward in time again to Czerny's *School of Practical Composition*, and again to his discussion of the Etude.

> A well written Study is generally based on some determinate melody, and then the figures are only a variation of the same. This melody may be either a two-part theme . . . or it may take the form of an Andante, an Allegretto, a Rondo &c. . . .

This 'determinate melody', on which a Study is generally based, is further defined as the 'groundwork' of the Study. Czerny seems to have two kinds of groundwork in mind: either a 'ground-melody' or a 'ground-harmony'. In other words, underlying a Study there is usually either a skeletal melody with harmonies, or piece of counterpoint, or otherwise a succession of chords. This skeleton is fleshed-out with what he calls the 'moving figure' (shades of Riepel again!).

Part of Czerny's purpose is to get the student to prepare a skeleton of this type for himself and then clothe it with figuration as a Study. But as an intermediate stage toward this, he encourages the student to take a known Study, reduce it to its skeleton, and then write his own Study on it, 'which, however, in respect to the ideas, melodies, and passages, must be entirely different from the chosen original'.[20] But Czerny sees a larger value in this procedure than merely as a compositional device. He observes to the pupil 'how extremely useful and requisite it is, for him to write out similar ones of very many distinguished compositions'. He continues: 'By this procedure the pupil will with delight become acquainted with the internal structure of the most admirable compositions, and frequently remark with surprise, on what a simple, though firm and symmetrical basis, the finest and most intellectual works of the great masters rest'. Czerny does not only have small-scale compositions in mind. When he speaks of 'distinguished compositions', he continues 'such as Mozart's and Beethoven's Sonatas, Quartetts and Symphonies'.

Czerny himself offers five examples of such reduction, one to a short composition of his own, one to a Clementi sonata slow introduction, one to a Cramer Study, one to a Chopin Study and one to the first Prelude of Book I of Bach's '48'. With one exception, each proceeds bar-by-bar. The Chopin reduction consists of block chords, mostly in semibreves and minims. The Bach Prelude has its note-values reduced to half, so that two bars of the original combine to form one bar of the reduction. In both these cases Czerny gives the entire skeleton, followed by the first couple of bars of the original to show the figuration. He advises:

> For this purpose, knowledge, care and a great deal of penetration into the spirit of the music is required, in the case of complicated pieces, in order thus to divest the melodies and figures of all ornaments, and to reduce them to their *most simple* harmonies. In so doing, particular care must be taken to write out each chord in the position which perfectly answers to the melodic idea of the composer.

This can be seen in Ex. 4, which shows bars 40–42 of Chopin's Study Op. 10 No. 1 (Ex. 4a) and Czerny's reduction of them (Ex. 4b). Czerny has raised the bass line to a higher octave, compressed the

Ex. 4

right-hand passage-work into the middle register, discarded inessential notes — the B's, for example, in bar 40 — and re-ordered the texture into continuous slow-moving lines. The reduction of the Clementi slow introduction in a sense goes slightly further, in that it is free from the strict measure of bar lines. The thirteen bars of the original are reduced to seven block chords. (Ex. 5 shows the first five bars of the piece superimposed on Czerny's entire reduction.) Again inessential notes — or perhaps one should say progressions that are structurally of only local significance — have been discarded.

Ex. 5 (a)

INTRODUZIONE   CLEMENTI

Clearly, what Czerny is doing is related to fundamental bass practice as it derives from Rameau and comes through into our period with Kirnberger and with Kollmann's earlier harmony treatise. And yet what he does with the Bach Prelude, for example, is worlds away from Kirnberger's analysis of the B minor fugue from Book I in 'Die wahren Grundsätze zum Gebrauch der Harmonie', published as an addendum to *Die Kunst des reinen Satzes* in about 1775. The latter is an immensely cumbersome apparatus of six staves on which a bass presenting the roots of the implied chords is set out twice with different degrees of figuring, and then a dense harmonic matrix is created with further heavy figuring. Czerny's reductions are not at all restricted to root-position chords, and they greatly simplify the original rather than complicating it. He describes his process as . . .

> the *anatomy* of the pieces, by which the pupil becomes acquainted with the plan, the construction, the melody, the harmony, the course of the ideas, and, generally, with the particular thoughts of the composer, in essential points, and distinguishes them from all exterior embellishments calculated only for effect.

Czerny's final judgement is arresting and prophetic of the view of Schenker. 'A piece whose skeleton is unrhythmical or without meaning', he says, 'must ever be ranked as a failure.'[21]

All three aspects of musical theory discussed in this paper reveal a process of change, of genuine development, in musical thinking during the period in question. Kollmann, Marx and Czerny, the writers considered under the first, general heading of attitude towards form, were all concerned with the training of musicians to write music. But whereas Kollmann, in the first half of the period, laid down determinate procedures for the production of pieces of music, Marx, at the end of the period, offered a limitless field, with infinite possibilities. So in Marx the examination of existing pieces of music takes on a different function and is much more disinterested. And my two specific cases, of permutation and reduction, are two discrete points along a line — a technical line — that runs parallel to the aesthetic line from Kollmann, through Czerny to Marx. Permutations are generative, reduction is reflective.

In conclusion, reference must briefly be made to one further aspect of theory that is another symptom of the general trend, namely the use of musical examples. In Riepel's *Anfangsgründe* all the examples are the author's own. Koch's analysis of a Haydn Minuet has already been mentioned, and this is only one of a score of examples, all of them sections or complete forms, which Koch cites in his third volume of the *Versuch* — examples taken from C. P. E. Bach, Benda, Graun, Rosetti, Scheinpflug and Stamitz. Nonetheless, the vast majority of Koch's musical examples are unidentified and were apparently devised by him to suit his own purpose. Out of 900 examples in the treatise as a whole, less than 30 are ascribed to composers. The proportion is increased tenfold in a very significant treatise not so far mentioned, Antoine Reicha's *Traité de mélodie*.[22] This treatise stands on a line of essentially melodic and structural treatises from Riepel and Koch through to Lussy and ultimately Riemann. It comprises a volume of text and a separate volume of beautifully engraved musical 'plates'. The latter is almost an historical anthology of music from the previous 60 or 70 years, presenting melodies by some fifteen composers, including Handel, Gluck, Haydn, Mozart, Piccini and Cimarosa, and submitting them to graphic segmental analysis into structural units — *dessins, rythmes, périodes* and *parties*, punctuated by *cadences* of various strengths. And finally when we arrive (yet again) at Czerny, virtually all the musical examples are drawn from extant works — the older forms exemplified by Bach, Handel and Albrechtsberger, the newer forms by Haydn, Mozart, Beethoven, Rossini, Bellini, Weber, Meyerbeer and others.

So we have a spectrum from none in Riepel to 3 per cent in Koch to 30 per cent in Reicha and to 98 per cent in Czerny. Not all of this is evidence of a growing faith in the past as a model for the present. Reicha and Czerny were writing for students who already had the basic elements, who knew simple harmony and counterpoint. Reicha was in any case only dealing with melody, and was seeking to create for melody a critique as searching as those in existence for poetry and rhetoric. So he was doing something already more lofty. And Czerny makes it plain at the outset that he is dealing with higher matters than mere rudiments. This naturally leads them into more extended musical examples where, even in Koch, quotation of an existing piece is more likely. But for all that, even Koch in his third volume, in which he too is dealing with higher matters, uses only 15 per cent of ascribed musical examples. Reicha and Czerny must have believed there was virtue in citing extant music. Reicha actually draws attention to this feature in two ways: at the end of his preface, by listing the composers quoted, and on the title page, by speaking of the whole of the treatise as being 'appuyé sur les meilleurs modèles mélodiques'. They must have had some feeling that studying the music of at least the recent past was a valuable activity. And this is not surprising when we think of the rise during this period of musical-historical studies — itself only part of a much bigger rise in consciousness of the concept of history.

NOTES

1. *An Essay on Practical Musical Composition*, London, 1799.
2. *School of Practical Composition*, London, 1849.
3. *Die Lehre von der musikalischen Komposition, praktisch-theoretisch*, Leipzig, 1837–47.
4. *Musical Form*, London, 1893, p. 1.
5. 'Die Form in der Musik', *Die Wissenschaft im neunzehnten Jahrhundert, ihr Standpunkt und die Resultate ihrer Forschungen*, ed. J. A. Romberg, ii (Leipzig, 1856), 21–48; see pp. 25, 27.
6. *Lehre von der musikalischen Komposition*, ii (1838), 7.
7. *School of Practical Composition*, i.1 f.
8. Ibid.
9. Ibid., i.218.
10. Ibid., i.90.
11. *Lehre*, ii.499.
12. *Anfangsgründe zur musikalischen Setzkunst*, Regensburg &c., 1752–68, Chapter 2: *Grundregeln zur Tonordnung insgemein*, Frankfurt, Leipzig &c., 1755, pp. 65 ff.
13. Riepel's *Verwechslung* I translate as 'permutation' (hence *Verwechslungskunst*, 'permutation technique'), the verb, *verwechseln*, as 're-arrange'. For the discussion of permutation technique, see pp. 25–32.
14. H. C. Koch, *Versuch einer Anleitung zur Composition*, Leipzig & Rudolstadt, 1782–93, ii.261, 196.
15. See Stephen A. Hedges, 'Dice Music in the Eighteenth Century', *Music & Letters*, lix (1978), 180–81. In discussion Claude Palisca drew attention to the relationship between permutations and the *combinatoria* discussed by Athanasius Kircher in *Musurgia universalis* (1650) and by Mersenne in *Harmonie universelle* (1636); and also the *inventio* discussed by Heinichen in *Der Generalbass in der Komposition* (1728) and by Mattheson in *Kern melodischer Wissenschaft* and also in *Der vollkommene Capellmeister* (1739). See also ' "Ars combinatoria": Chance and Choice in Eighteenth-century Music', *Studies in Eighteenth-century Music: a Tribute to Karl Geiringer on his Seventieth Birthday*, ed. H. C. Robbins Landon & Roger Chapman, London, 1970, pp. 343–63.
16. pp. 36–65, *passim*.
17. pp. 81 ff.
18. *Versuch*, iii (1787), 58 ff.
19. Op. cit., i.90.
20. This process of reduction and re-composition is perhaps reminiscent of Kirnberger's *Methode Sonaten aus'm Ermel zu Schüddeln* (1783), though the technique involved is different. See William S. Newman, 'Kirnberger's *Method for Tossing off Sonatas*', *The Musical Quarterly*, xlvii (1961), 517–25.
21. *School of Practical Composition*, i.97 f.
22. Paris, 1814.

Chapter 9

SELF-ANALYSIS
BY TWENTIETH-CENTURY COMPOSERS

László Somfai

THERE IS a tacit understanding among professionals in musicology that the composition itself, the score, is the only authentic form of a composer's creative communication, whereas his explanatory and analytical remarks about his work, so unprofessional in most cases, have to be placed among supplementary, secondary sources of historical value but of fading attraction. 'Self-analyses' — to use the term for all sorts of written and spoken, public and private statements of the composer about his work — are dutifully quoted in biographies, programme notes and popular music literature. Nevertheless, musicologists, specifically those who are involved in stylistic, aesthetic and theoretical studies, usually prefer the conceptual, the more detailed, more technical (or philosophical) 'professional' studies to the self-analyses of the composer.

Before a survey, classification and evaluation is attempted, a general question should be raised: what is the intention and the greatest possible achievement of any expert analysis of a musical composition written by an outsider? An analysis, naturally, is just one feasible *interpretation* of a complex work of art; a subjective exploration, an argumentative arrangement of only those phenomena which are considered by the analyst as essential, structural, or individual. An interpretation which, however, is often believed by its writer as if it has solved a musical problem with full authenticity and with creative power — in a way similar to the composer's own solving of musical problems in his work. No professional analytical writer thinks that his best work can soon lose its relevance and become a period piece, because a next generation will inevitably discover newer and, even if less exhaustive, better analytical methods. Yet the fate of an outsider's interpretation is exactly that. In addition, while its analytical method and terminology quickly grow obsolete, neither does it retain the 'historical authenticity' possessed by the composer's self-analysis.

If an outsider points out that the form of Webern's Variations for Orchestra, Op.30, is reminiscent of certain classical formal models or procedures, this is just a subjective statement, not very informative, and will lose its relevance as soon as a subsequent analysis describes the structure in a more specific way. But if Webern himself declares that 'Fundamentally my "Overture" [meaning his Op. 30] is an "Adagio"-form, but the recapitulation of the principal theme appears in the form of a development, so this element is also present; Beethoven's "Prometheus" and Brahms's "Tragic" are also overtures in Adagio-form and not in "sonata-form"!!!',[1] this statement by the composer will not be outdated by time and by better and better analyses. For it is a fact, objective and not unimportant, that Webern — using certain traditional terms, identifying those with classical examples — thought his Variations aptly characterized by such a comparison. Very probably he was aware of the analogy even during the process of composition. At any rate, the composer left a somewhat enigmatic message of primary importance, which has to be examined and will be re-interpreted as long as there is an analytical interest in the structure of his Op.30. What is the use of the message though, if one is not familiar with the traditional Viennese terminology, including 'Adagio-form' and 'Andante-form', and with the specific internal terminology and workshop discussions of the Schoenberg circle?

The Webern example highlights the root of the problem of dealing with authentic but really 'historical' self-analysis. Before making use of isolated data one has to investigate carefully the theoretical background of the composer; next the terminology — what he learned and what he possibly introduced himself — in the original language and wording, because it may be crucial; and finally circumstances in which he made the self-analytical statement. If the process is to be so complex and time-consuming, will we nevertheless persist in turning to the composer's self-analysis for enlightenment?

One more preliminary example may serve as a warning: the case of Bartók's short introduction to the structure of his *Music for Strings, Percussion and Celesta* entitled 'Aufbau der "Musik für Saiteninstrumente" ', written in German in 1937 and printed in the Philharmonia miniature score edition in the same year, with a miserable English translation and a somewhat better French one provided by the publisher. It appeared unsigned alongside Philharmonia's standard biographical introduction, and only recently has it been recognised as being by Bartók himself—long after Ernő Lendvai's exhaustive analysis, including detailed examination of the monothematic relationship between the four movements, and long after the 'discovery' of a so-called 'bridge-form' in Bartók's music. In certain details this single column of self-analysis, which escaped the notice of the professionals, is more substantial and informative than Lendvai's half-a-book-long analysis nearly twenty years later[2] and its subsequent revisions (to mention only the most significant critical literature). For example, Bartók disclosed that in the development of the second movement there is not only a reference to the theme of the first, which is obvious, but also an 'allusion to the principal theme of the fourth movement'. More important, however, is the fact that in this analytical note the terminology is carefully selected and every statement weighed, rejecting contemporary misinterpretations and criticism, and that Bartók here identified some important, consciously used structural procedures in his work. It is revealing, for instance, that he defines the tonality of each movement, and that sonata-form terminology is used for the second movement, as against the more schematic descriptions of the others, including the invention of the term 'Brückenform' ('bridge-form') for the A–B–C–B–A pattern of the third movement. Important analytical statements, apart from those on the monothematic correspondences, are the comment that in the second movement 'the recapitulation transforms the 2/4 rhythm of the exposition into a 3/8 rhythm' and the remark that the final section of the last movement 'introduces the principal theme of the first movement, but now in an extended diatonic form instead of the original chromatic one' — two procedures characteristic of many of Bartók's works but as yet inadequately covered in recent analytical literature. In short, this one-column description by Bartók is a masterpiece in its genre and an inexhaustible authentic source for further, more detailed analyses.

It goes without saying that, in spite of illuminating details of occasional novelties, the quoted examples, like the majority of self-analyses dating from the first half of the present century, are commentaries rather than genuine analyses of the structure or of the compositional method applied. At this stage it is essential to distinguish in general between the self-analysis of the Schoenberg–Bartók–Stravinsky generation and that of the Messiaen–Boulez–Stockhausen–Xenakis period.[3] From the point of view of the historical musicologist there are at least three areas of basic differences which cannot be neglected: the composer's personal attitude to the task of analyzing his own work; the intended purpose and subject-matter of his analysis; and the standard, the degree of professionalism and originality, compared to the best analyses of contemporaneous musicology.

In terms of attitude, the first generation mainly believed in the specialization of roles inherited from the late nineteenth century — that the composer was best advised to leave the performance and the analytical-aesthetic introduction of his work to professionals, because it did no good to his image for him to talk publicly about his craft and technique. Consequently, if he agreed to make a self-analytical statement at all, he usually delivered simply what he was asked for, be it programme note, preface, essay or lecture; in any event he used traditional methods and did not search seriously for new approaches that might have been more adequate. The composer of the second generation, however, the *avant garde*, since the music of the Schoenberg generation had failed to win assimilation into the standard Classical/Romantic repertory, turned his attention to those — both musicians and listeners — who were really interested in modern art. He could consequently pursue his analysis unfettered by old inhibitions; after all, he was the only competent spokesman for the concept, the structure and the intended manner of performance of his piece.

In terms of purpose and subject-matter, composers of the first generation were usually concerned with discussing only certain traditional aspects of the music, such as the work's motivation and history of composition, its thematic characteristics and form — and they carefully employed the formal terminology familiar from writings about classical forms. The composer wanted his work to be regarded as an ordinary piece of music, which could be understood on the same terms as any Classical or Romantic composition. He was also convinced that total appreciation of a complex new musical work should come about through careful listening, by following the musical events in the tempo of the performance — if necessary, of course, by repeated concentrated hearings. Less idealist was the next generation, and probably more sensitive to the spirit of the times: people may not wish to hear a piece more than once but may be interested in reading an introduction, if it explains the curious title of the work, if it discloses structural principles, formulated in a scientific way, if it explains extra-musical (e.g. linguistic, mathematical etc.) pre-compositional considerations; then the reader may visualize his personal image of the composition beforehand which will be checked and reconsidered during performance — an exciting two-stage process of cognition. Consequently the self-analytical statement will not refer to classsical analogies, to outdated musical terms that are no longer of any more than symbolic relevance, but should be precisely factual, pointing out the work's important individual features and original concepts. Typically, many major works of the *avant garde* and experimental music written since the 1950s bear extra-musical or enigmatic titles which, from the listener's point of view, require explanation. It is also a fact that these works usually have some central structural, technical or performing pattern, a real 'invention', and the composer is anxious to announce it to his fellow-composers — for he knows from experience that new concepts and patterns often spread faster than the music itself.

In the third area of basic differences, the degree of professionalism and the relationship to contemporaneous musicological analysis, the stratification is even more obvious, though of course many composers of the second generation have retained the post-Romantic attitude. Certainly, Schoenberg sent his pupils to Guido Adler to study musicology; he himself wrote important essays and textbooks on music theory; every member of his school was an excellent teacher of composition. Hindemith, again, was an influential theorist. Bartók represented real professionalism in ethnomusicology. Nevertheless, in the stylistic analysis of modern music the composers of the first generation can hardly be regarded as professionals. They were not innovators; their terminology was an extension of traditional theoretical vocabulary as taught in conservatories rather than an extension of up-to-date musicological methods. When Schoenberg and his generation began to write self-analytical programme notes, they set out from the pattern and motivic presentation of Kretzschmar's *Konzertführer* and from the vocabulary of Riemann (not being familiar with the most advanced nineteenth-century analytical methods incorporated into large biographical studies). The genuine evolution of their self-analyses as time went on was due to inner improvement. It is significant that they were not at all impressed by musicological approaches that concentrated on internal aspects of structure, such as the analyses of Heinrich Schenker — though these were discovered by the next generation of *avant-garde* composers and theorists.

In contrast, the theoretical training and expertise of the generation of Boulez, Stockhausen and Xenakis are highly professional. After World War II it was natural that the *avant-garde* composer should study musicology — or higher mathematics, information theory or computer techniques. In addition he became expert in acoustics and sound engineering.He extended his professionalism to embrace the performance of well demonstrated lectures, the analysis of serial music and the elucidation of his own composing technique for other composers. Compared to contemporaneous historical musicology, it is not just that his terminology and vocabulary sound more 'scientific'; in fact he has succeeded in defining neglected parameters of the world of sound, and his considerations of new facts, relationships and patterns have been highly instructive, if at times provocative. And he has dealt not only with his own works but with the music of Webern, Stravinsky and their contemporaries as well. The musicologist who concerns himself professionally with modern music obviously cannot neglect the self-analysis of second-generation composers; but there is also much to be learned by the music historian who is directly involved only in the structural analysis of music of the past.

To sum up, the historical stratification of twentieth-century self-analysis is not simply a difference of generations; the attitude, the aim and the degree of technical demands and expertise have changed completely. First to require closer examination, before any attempt can be made at classification, is the generation of Schoenberg, Bartók and Stravinsky.

In general the self-analytical material of the first generation falls into four classes. The order of their treatment here corresponds more or less to the progression from the purely descriptive to more conceptual and structural analysis.

1. Traditional descriptive notes written for the general public, published in periodicals and programme booklets or accompanying gramophone records.

2. Formal summaries ('Formübersicht', 'Aufbau') in miniature scores, intended for trained musicians and students.

3. Introductions to the work or to the composer's personal style in the form of a lecture, broadcast talk, interview, article, open letter etc.

4. Structural or conceptual explanations for professionals, in the form of notes or a letter (sometimes published) to the interpreter, to a friend of the composer, etc.

Before the four classes can be considered, it needs to be said that the situation in regard to their sources is a very confused one. There is no reliable specialist bibliography; most of the material has to be assembled from biographies, programme booklets and periodicals; the texts are often available only in corrupt versions or in translation. Editions of composers' writings such as the volume devoted to Nono[4] would be well worth while. For practical reasons the examples considered in the present paper quote mainly from the self-analyses of Schoenberg, Berg, Webern, Stravinsky and Bartók. But even in these cases there is hardly a so-called critical edition that can be regarded as a good enough source. Neither edition of Schoenberg's writings,[5] for example, contains the original English versions of some of his programme notes.[6] Similarly inadequate is the published Bartók material. The two standard collections[7] are unilingual, so that neither contains the original versions of texts written in French and German, and both are incomplete (for example, the programme notes on the First and Second Orchestral Suites, unsigned in the printed sources, are missing), not to mention problems of authenticity.[8] In the case of Stravinsky the question of authenticity scarcely needs to be raised here, with so many languages and versions and co-authors involved.

Traditional descriptive notes form probably the most extensive class of self-analysis of the first generation. This group could be subdivided further, according to the amount of technical matter (including music examples) employed and the degree of independence from the conventions of the programme note. Around 1905–10 the typical programme note followed the conventional pattern but with a tendency to focus on more specifically musical features, consisting of a list of main themes together with a few words about the form, motivic relationships or programmatic interpretation. This was the pattern used by Schoenberg writing about his First String Quartet in 1906,[9] by Bartók in 1904 for his symphonic poem *Kossuth*, in 1905 and 1909 for the First and Second Orchestral Suites and in 1910 for the Rhapsody for Piano and Orchestra.[10] Apart from the note in French on the Second Piano Concerto, which the numbering of the music examples reveals to be a rough draft for a carefully planned self-analysis,[11] programme notes from Bartók's later years are short and reticent, and without music examples (Sonata for Two Pianos and Percussion, 1938; Concerto for Orchestra, 1944). Schoenberg's later, retrospective analytical notes (*Pelleas* and the Chamber Symphony, 1949; *Verklärte Nacht*, 1950) are disappointing, representing the conventions of the turn of the century. The *Notes on the Four String Quartets*[12] form the most confusing Schoenberg material, on the one hand manifesting basic concepts and characterizing the nature of his musical thinking, and on the other hand intermingling personal reminiscences and outdated thematic descriptive methods with important self-analytical comments. Stravinsky was too astute and strong-minded to be drawn into writing standard narrative descriptions. But the notes written for the late Columbia recordings (e.g. for *Petrushka* in 1960) and for the first performances of his late works, especially from the exemplary note on the Cantata (1952)[13] onwards, are all individual and of vital importance, as are the retrospective analytical notes of his later years.[14]

As an appendix to the first class, the phenomenon of indirect self-analysis should also be considered. Willi Reich's Berg monograph of 1963[15] contains two important analytical texts that must be accorded a high degree of authenticity, even though neither is at first hand: the analysis of the the concert aria 'Der Wein', written by Reich under the supervision of the composer himself, and Reich's edited transcription of Anton Webern's oral analysis of the Violin Concerto. There are further second-hand sources in the Bartók literature. In the case of the Fifth String Quartet Bartók's sketchy description of the form was subsequently used for an expanded version written and signed by an acquaintance, the music critic (and composer) Alexander Jemnitz.[16] A programme note on the Dance Suite for a Berlin Philharmonic Orchestra performance on 5 October 1925 similarly contains some of the composer's own material; presumably Bartók declined to write detailed notes himself, but he sent some information and the incipits of the main themes, and these were incorporated in facsimile into the rather mediocre note by Rudolf Kastner. Both of these are unreliable sources, but for the historian they are useful data in the chain of the complete documentation.

Our second class, consisting of formal summaries in miniature score, is a much smaller group, inspired by Philharmonia pocket scores, a subsidiary of Universal Edition, the principal publishers of Schoenberg's circle. The reason why composers were generally unwilling to write and sign introductory notes under the title 'Formübersicht' or 'Aufbau' was that the notes could easily have been identified as an organic part of the composition itself. The three Viennese masters were typical in their reluctance to provide such summaries; they placed the matter in the trusted hands of pupils and friends like Erwin Stein, Felix Greissle and Paul Pisk, whose introductions can in most cases be considered as authenticated texts. The unsigned *Formübersicht* of Schoenberg's [First] Chamber Symphony (Philharmonia No. 225) must have been approved by the composer; and in the case of the Wind Quintet (Philharmonia No. 230) it was again Schoenberg speaking, through his son-in-law Greissle. The best pocket-score introductions to the music of the Viennese school, and the most precise in terminology, are those of Erwin Stein.[17] Other house composers of Universal Edition, like Zoltán Kodály in his introductions to the *Dances of Marrosszek*, *Dances of Galánta* and *A Summer Evening*,[18] tended to use the pocket-score preface for artistic confessions rather than formal summaries. Kodály's friend Bartók was originally opposed to explaining himself in the score, and in 1929 rejected the proposal that he should write the introduction to the first edition of his Fourth String Quartet. But on becoming acquainted with the insubstantial Philharmonia prefaces to the Dance Suite (Arthur Willner) and the Third Quartet (Dr. A. P. = Paul A. Pisk) he changed his mind. In January 1930 he sent the text of a note on the *Aufbau* of the Fourth Quartet, and subsequently he wrote the analytical note to the *Music for Strings, Percussion and Celesta* already mentioned.

In the case of Bartók — a composer so uncommunicative about his work — it is worth mentioning that there are further peripheral but interesting circumstantial clues as to how the composer 'analyzed' the form of his music, or at least how he arranged a movement in intelligible sections. Given careful historical treatment, such hitherto unexplored evidence can amount to a complementary source of information. One problematical example is the placing of rehearsal cues in a score, whether in the form of letters or figures or selective bar numbers — providing the arrangement is the composer's own, and providing the bar numbering is selective, not purely mechanical. In Bartók's case there are four types of arrangement, different in the amount of information they offer and unpredictable in their chronological sequence. Even the first type, customary around 1900, with large rehearsal figures at points where a passage can easily be started again, can be instructive in controversial questions such as how Bartók interpreted the continuous form of his Third Quartet, played without a break (since the work consists of four sections of equal rank, he begins a new sequence of rehearsal figures for each). The method found in the late Universal Edition scores, consisting of routine bar numbering combined with rehearsal letters and indications of duration between landmarks, expresses clearly the main formal articulation. And the scheme adopted in the later Boosey & Hawkes scores in fact represents a detailed guide to the form in the small and medium term: selective bar numbers (e.g. in the first movement of the Divertimento bars 8, 14, 19, 25, 29, 33 and 42) act as suitable rehearsal marks and also indicate small-scale articulation; indications of duration at the end of sections (for example 1′ 32″ up to the second subject, 1′ 14″ from there to the end of the exposition, etc.) show the articulation on a larger scale. Needless to say, this sort of self-analytical information can only be used in conjunction with a comparative study of all relevant sources.

Introductions to a work or to a composer's personal style in the form of lectures, interviews and so forth, representing our third group, again come in a rich variety of types. The leading figures of the first generation reacted differently and unpredictably, depending on their personal circumstances and attitudes. In 1928, for example, Bartók in his American lecture-recital[19] spoke primarily about his experiences in folk music, mentioning only casually similar phenomena in his own harmony and melody. Later, however, in his Harvard Lectures of 1943,[20] detecting prejudice and losing his patience, he went into details of his concept of tonality and modality, his 'polymodal chromaticism', and his rhythmic resources. Alban Berg set an example to his friends when he agreed to deliver on a lecture tour a paper on his new opera *Wozzeck*.[21] Following his example, Schoenberg accepted an invitation from Hans Rosbaud to give broadcast talks in Frankfurt in association with concert performances (in 1931 on the Variations for Orchestra, in 1932 on the Orchestral Songs, Op. 22).[22] The analysis of motivic development in the first song is one of Schoenberg's most significant statements, illuminating important aspects of his concept of composition. The Variations also gave rise to an interview with Erwin Stein[23] which demonstrates how good and informative an interview for the general public can be if the interviewer is an expert and the dialogue so to speak pre-composed. Apart from several further types in Schoenberg, represented in *Style and Idea*, which would need detailed individual consideration, the largest and most colourful group of this class is the Stravinsky material, bedevilled as it is by the problems of joint authorship and so forth — a tangle that will need rigorous textual criticism. In any event, the volumes of dialogues between Stravinsky and Robert Craft represent an abundant source of authentic information which in many respects shocked the world of professional stylistic analysis (one need only think of the supposed debt of his music to folksong). Stravinsky was also the author of the most fascinating variety of provocative writing and manifesto, such as 'Some Ideas about my Octuor' (1924), his 'Warning' about classicism (1927) and his concept of prosody in 'Perséphone' (1934).[24]

While it is relatively easy to select, classify and evaluate the self-analytical material of this third group that derives from Schoenberg's circle and from Bartók and Stravinsky, the writings, interviews, memories and diaries of other composers present much greater variety — and pose many more problems of value and relevance. To take but one example, in the case of Charles Ives one is faced with the contrast between the painstakingly polished public voice of the *Essays before a Sonata* (1920) and the private savagery of the posthumously published *Memos*.[25]

Our fourth group of first-generation self-analyses, comprising structural and conceptual explanations for professionals, fortunately needs no introduction here; this is the familiar material, since such writing attracts the attention of the musicologist. It was Alban Berg, probably the most imaginative composer of his generation in devising analytical models, who took the decisive step. His 'open letter' to Schoenberg[26] was historic in being the first piece of self-analysis in which real issues of a particular concept of composition were aired publicly in an adequately professional manner. (That in no way alters the fact that Berg's confession was motivated by a kind of exhibitionism.) Subsequently the key figure was the violinist Rudolf Kolisch, Schoenberg's brother-in-law, who as a pupil, friend and member of the family persuaded the Viennese trio to reveal their secrets. It was for him that Berg wrote the often quoted 'nine-page' analysis of the *Lyric Suite*.[27] Again it was Kolisch who was the recipient of Webern's famous letter of 19 April 1938 containing the description of the String Quartet, Op. 28, at that time still with the first and second movements in the reverse order.[28] Kolisch's attempt to persuade Schoenberg to talk about the note-row and structure of his Third Quartet did not succeed — unless it can be counted an even greater success to have provoked Schoenberg's famous dictum: ' . . . my works are twelve-tone *compositions*, not *twelve-tone* compositions'.

Some of Stravinsky's late notes contain valuable conceptual comments, but in general it is difficult to find instances of conceptual or structural self-analysis outside the Schoenberg circle to equal those already quoted. Elsewhere the material is either fragmentary and in need of interpretation, as with Bartók's remarks on pieces of his *Mikrokosmos*,[29] or alternatively consists not of retrospective self-analysis but of pre-compositional planning and sketching — an even more interesting phenomenon but a different one. Looking back, one can see that throughout the first generation's period of activity — in spite of islolated master-analyses such as Hindemith's explanation of his revised (1948) version of *Das Marienleben*[30] — there was only a single new technical procedure that attracted widespread interest, namely twelve-note serialism. But Schoenberg, the commanding personality of the school, repeatedly refused to discuss technical matters in public as a supposed approach towards a better understanding of modern composition. And this attitude, being generally accepted by the rest of his generation, naturally discouraged self-analysis.

In conclusion, a few recommendations for consideration. Schoenberg, Bartók and Stravinsky are by now the classics of the present century, and for the self-analytical writings of this generation there are three requirements. A bibliographical record is needed of all the surviving material, including that of minor composers and marginal cases. There should be critical editions of the self-analytical material of individual composers, including variants, biographical information and commentaries as necessary. And composers' statements about their own music now require historical and analytical assessment, and to be considered alongside contemporary and more recent analytical writing on the same subjects.

In the case of the second generation it is easy to be swayed by personal taste — and to be paralyzed by the forbidding appearance of much recent self-analytical writing. But the music historian must acknowledge that recent compositions are by no means necessarily self-explanatory creations in sound, which can be appreciated and judged simply by uninformed listening; frequently some previous knowledge of the music's conceptual make-up is indispensable. It is true that composers' self-analyses are not always wholly reliable; they may, for instance, misuse Schenkerian methods, misinterpret Webern's serial technique, or be obviously biased in some respect. But the historian's task is to study the theoretical attitudes of the composer, not to judge them, and there should be little danger of his being misled. Unfortunately, perhaps, one class of self-analysis that must be included as an indispensable source is the really complex scientific presentation familiar from the studies of Xenakis, which can be more instructive than commentaries written in the trade jargon of musicology. In any event, we cannot neglect to study the self-analysis of the composer before defining our own analytical procedures.

1. Anton Webern, *Der Weg zur neuen Musik*, ed. W. Reich, Vienna, 1960, p. 67.
2. *Bartók stílusa*, Budapest, 1955.
3. There is of course a third 'generation' of critical texts and writings, those of composers who (to borrow the subtitle of Michael Nyman's book) may be referred to as 'Cage and beyond' — the radical experimental trend that led to all kinds of indeterminacy, mixed media, minimal art and so forth. But that is beyond the scope of the present paper.
4. Luigi Nono, *Texte: Studien zu seiner Musik*, ed. J. Stenzl, Zurich, 1975.
5. *Style and Idea: Selected Writings of Arnold Schoenberg*, ed. L. Stein, 2nd edn., London, 1975; *Gesammelte Schriften*, i: *Stil und Gedanke; Aufsätze zur Musik*, ed. I Vojtěch, n.p., 1976.

6. The notes to *Verklärte Nacht, Pelleas und Melisande* and the Chamber Symphony have been reprinted in connection with the Columbia recordings, *The Music of Arnold Schoenberg*, vols. ii & iii (M2S 694 & M2S 709).

7. *Bartók Béla Összegyűltött Irásai*, ed. A. Szőllősy, Budapest, 1967; *Béla Bartók Essays*, selected & ed. B. Suchoff, London, 1976.

8. See my review in *The Musical Times*, May 1977.

9. See U. Rauchhaupt, *Schoenberg, Berg, Webern: die Streichquartette. Eine Dokumentation*, Hamburg, 1971, p. 11.

10. *Kossuth* and the Rhapsody in *Bartók Összegyűltött Irásai*, pp. 767, 774; the Orchestral Suites in manuscript in the Bartók Archives, Budapest. The explanation of the thematic relationships between the five movements of the First Suite is especially revealing.

11. See L. Somfai, 'A rondó-jellegű szonáta-expozíció Bartók 2. zongoraversenyében', *Muzsika*, August 1977, pp. 16–20.

12. For the 1936 version see Rauchhaupt, op. cit.; the 1948 version in German translation in *Gesammelte Schriften*, i.409.

13. See E. W. White, *Stravinsky: the Composer and his Works*, London, 1966, p. 429.

14. See the notes on *Pribaoutki, Symphonies of Wind Instruments, Jeu de Cartes, Orpheus, The Rake's Progress* etc. in I. Stravinsky & R. Craft, *Themes and Episodes*, New York, 1966.

15. *Alban Berg: Leben und Werk*, Zurich, 1963.

16. Bartók's original (1935) in *Bartók Essays*, p. 414; Jemnitz, 'Béla Bartók, V. Streichquartett', *Musica Viva*, April 1936.

17. For examples of the *Formübersicht* type see Schoenberg's Second and Third String Quartets (Philharmonia Nos. 229 & 228) and Webern's String Trio (No. 175); for the descriptive type, Berg's *Lyric Suite* (No. 173).

18. Authentic versions in Zoltán Kodály, *Visszatekintés*, ed. F. Bónis, 2nd edn., Budapest, 1974.

19. *Bartók Essays*, p. 331.

20. Ibid., p. 354.

21. Reich, *Alban Berg*, p. 113.

22. For the letter, in English translation, see Columbia's *Music of Arnold Schoenberg*, vol. iii (M2S 709).

23. In English translation in *The Music of Arnold Schoenberg*, vol. ii (M2S 694).

24. All three reprinted in White, *Stravinsky*, pp. 528 ff.

25. Ed. John Kirkpatrick, New York, 1972.

26. 'Alban Bergs Kammerkonzert', *Pult und Taktstock*, February–March 1925, p.23.

27. See Rauchhaupt, op. cit., p. 131.

28. Ibid. This Webern issue is one of the most instructive cases in the field of self-analysis. Shortly after his letter to Kolisch, with the three movements now in their definitive order, Webern described the structure again in letters of 8 and 31 May 1939 to Erwin Stein. Both Kolisch and Stein allowed the texts of their letters to be published, the latter in English translation. Then a third friend of Webern, Willi Reich, fashioned a new version (in German) on the basis of Stein's. See Rauchhaupt, op. cit.

29. Transcribed by Anne Chenée and published in B. Suchoff, *Guide to Bartók's Mikrokosmos*, 2nd edn., London, 1971.

30. In the revised 1948 score (Edition Schott 2026).

Chapter 10

G. B. DONI, MUSICOLOGICAL ACTIVIST, AND HIS 'LYRA BARBERINA'

Claude V. Palisca

IT IS FITTING in a symposium on the traditions and present state of musical scholarship to ask the question: why has musicology in the past so rarely been a field of pure research, unlike other fields of the humanities? Why has it tended, rather, to be directed — some might say corrupted — by practical goals? In Britain, in particular, the study of early music has often been the servant of the performer and composer. 'Modal' counterpoint was for a long time studied as a tool for the composer, organist and choir director rather than as a means to knowing how music was composed in the past. Editions of early music, such as those of Edmund Fellowes, were published to serve as vehicles for choirs and to permit the music to be heard as living art, not as documents of an otherwise distantly dim culture.

This tendency has been characteristic of musicology from its very first practitioners. I shall cite two scholars whom I have come to know intimately over the years. The first is Girolamo Mei. As a member of a scholarly team around Piero Vettori in Florence in the 1540s he worked toward the establishment and reconstruction of the texts of several of the Greek tragedies. The object was not to perform them, though some were eventually translated or adapted and performed, but to reclaim them from the ravages and accretions of the centuries. Similarly in assisting Vettori to understand the musical references in Aristotle's *Poetics* towards the preparation of Vettori's *Commentarii in primum librum Aristotelis de arte poetarum*,[1] Mei was engaged in a disinterested search for an understanding of the Greek past. This was also his object in preparing the four books on the history of the Greek tonal system, *De modis musicis antiquorum*.[2] But these were barely finished in 1573, when Mei, who had never studied music and could not play or sing, became a musical reformer, urging his musical associates through essays and letters to reshape the music of their time in the image of ancient Greek music.

My second and central case history is that of Giovanni Battista Doni, who was inspired by reading one of Mei's crusading letters to embark on a similar programme of research, the focus of which also soon converged on the so-called Greek 'modes'. Mei had pointed to the 'modes' — or more properly *tonoi* — as the key to the power that ancient music had to communicate human emotions. If one wanted to regain this power, Doni became convinced, the ancient system of *tonoi* needed to be revived. As a Classical scholar, which he was by profession if not always occupation (like so many humanists he made his living as a secretary), Doni seemed content to pursue Greek letters and antiquities quite apart from any practical application. For example, he compiled 6,000 ancient inscriptions for publication (they were eventually published posthumously), for no other purpose than to make them available to antiquarians. He also collected drawings of lyres and kitharas, but these he set out to collect not out of a pure desire for knowledge but because he was searching for a model for a modern instrument that could be a medium for restoring the Greek tonal system. In the course of this campaign he became so interested in the ancient instruments themselves that he decided to write a history of the ancient lyre and kithara.

Thus Doni's motivation for research into the Greek lyre was deeper than an antiquarian curiosity. To be sure, he was fascinated by antiquity in general and Greek music in particular. But curiosity alone would not have led him down the thorny path of investigating instruments of which only iconographic and literary evidence remained. Like humanists in the previous century, he wanted musicians to revive certain qualities of ancient Greek music that he felt the modern lacked. The aura that surrounded the ancient 'modes' had cast its spell over musicians from Boethius to Glareanus, But now there was a further reason to try to revive these 'modes'. It had been definitively established by Mei, Galilei and Bardi that the system of the Greeks was altogether different from the church modes. Therefore the modes to which Glareanus gave the ancient Greek names could not be expected to work the marvellous effects that the ancient authors attributed to Greek music. If the real Greek system could be brought to life again, perhaps music could get a brave new start. Doni was the first to try to realize a revival of the Greek *tonoi* through practical strategies.

Doni recognized that modern musical instruments were incompatible with the ancient *tonoi,* because they could not accommodate the ancient system's unlimited possibilities of transposition and modulation. Moreover within each *tonos* there were — besides the diatonic — the chromatic and enharmonic genera. Instruments that were capable of performing in multiple keys and in the three genera needed to be developed. Doni designed among other instruments diharmonic viols and violins, triharmonic harpsichords, a theorbo with three fingerboards, a panharmonic viol, and — the most famous — the amphichordal lyre or lyra Barberina, named after Maffeo Barberini, whom Doni briefly served before Maffeo in 1623 became Pope Urban VIII. The investigation of ancient string instruments was thus an essential part of the project of reviving the ancient tonal systems, for Doni expected to find in lyres and kitharas models for new string instruments on which one might play all the ancient modes and genera.

Until now it has not been possible to retrace Doni's search for exemplars of the old Greek and Roman instruments, because the only existing edition of his essay 'Lyra Barberina', in which he reported his findings, lacked his iconographical documentation. Thus the route to the Barberini lyre and certain details of the instrument itself have been obscured. And what in retrospect is even more important, Doni's contribution to musical iconography and organology has been altogether lost from sight. If we are to evaluate his dual role of scholar and reformer, it is essential to consider the essay 'Lyra Barberina' in the state in which Doni left it for publication.

In 1763 Giovanni Battista Passeri published an edition prepared by Antonio Francesco Gori of the writings on music of Giovanni Battista Doni.[3] The opening essay, 'Lyra Barberina', was probably Doni's major scholarly work, left in manuscript when he died at the age of 53 in 1647. The title of the first volume is misleading, because the essay 'Lyra Barberina' occupies only the first 70 pages, while the remaining 354 contain other works of Doni, some previously published, such as *De praestantia musicae veteris*, but also many shorter essays not before printed. And what has been the bane of librarians and cataloguers is that the second volume has a totally different title: *De' Trattati di musica di Gio. Batista Doni Patrizio fiorentino, Tomo secondo.*[4]

Deceptive also is 'Lyra Barberina' as the title of the lead essay. It is not simply a description and presentation of Doni's new instrument: rather, it is a history of the Greek lyre, kithara and similar instruments, to which Doni tacked on a too brief description of his novel hybrid lute-lyre. It is the most ambitious history of the Greek lyre ever written; yet it is practically unknown to historians of instruments or of Greek music, who have omitted it from all their bibliographies.

The greatest deception of all in this publication is that the many representations of lyres, kitharas, psalteries and elegantly robed and unrobed men and women playing them were, with few exceptions, not at all the illustrations prepared and intended by Doni but drawings compiled and commissioned by the eighteenth-century editors, when, after exhaustive efforts — or so they claimed — to find the authentic illustrations, they gave them up as lost.[5] Even before Gori's edition was out Angelo Maria Bandini, Doni's biographer, complained that it was incomplete, lacking an *onomasticon*, or lexicon of Greek and Latin musical terms, and some poems that Bandini knew belonged to the book from a letter which Doni had written to Gaspar Scioppius.[6] Bandini in his biography of 1755 speculated that the complete autograph must have remained with Doni's friend Gabriel Naudé in Paris or with Cardinal Francesco Barberini in Rome.[7]

Both of Bandini's guesses were good. The Barberini collection in the Vatican Library possesses what must have been the presentation copy to Pope Urban VIII (Maffeo Barberini). This elegantly copied manuscript, Barberinus latinus 1897, must represent the earliest version of the treatise, as it stood around 1632. It is illustrated with ink-drawings of lyres and kitharas (Plate I) sketched by an artist from frescoes, bas-reliefs, coins, gems, and other art objects. Unfortunately the writing shows through from the reverse side (see Plate IVb).

Gori eventually located this manuscript, but only after the volume containing 'Lyra Barberina' was in print, though not yet published. As an addendum on the last pages of the first volume (pp. 414–24) he reported the variants from his printed version as reported by Abbot Simone Ballerini, Prefect of the Barberini Library, who collated the codex with the printed text. In listing the variants Gori noted that the Barberini manuscript had some pictures of lyres not unlike those in Johannes Bottari's *Roma sotterranea*,[8] to which Gori referred the reader.

The other possibility Bandini mentioned, that Doni's manuscript had remained with Naudé in France, was the better hunch, for a manuscript written partly in Doni's hand, with instructions for the printer, did remain in Paris and is now at the Bibliothèque Nationale. Doni had sent it to Gabriel Naudé, who was to have found a French publisher for the essay, and it was still in France when Doni suddenly died of a fever in Florence on 1 December 1647. This manuscript (shelf-mark latin 10274) presents a version that, compared to the Barberini manuscript, is much enlarged and revised. It is approximately equivalent to the draft published by Gori–Passeri, which was

PLATE I

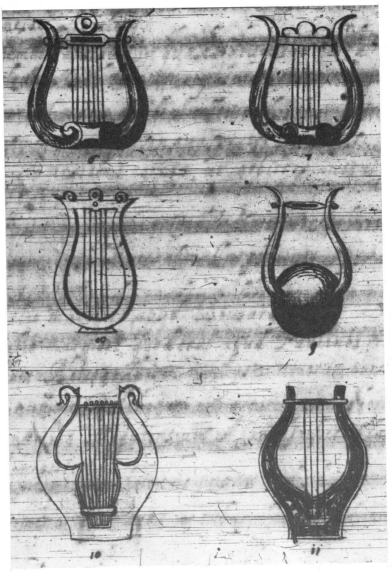

Illustrations for 'Lyra Barberina'
Rome, Vatican Libarary, MS Barberini 1897, f.17

184

copied from Doni's working duplicate of the Paris manuscript now in Pesaro.[9] The Paris manuscript contains, however, a few later revisions and additions. More importantly, it has the full complement of pictures that Doni intended for publication.

How Doni's definitive manuscript happened to remain unpublished in Paris in 1647, fifteen years after the dedication to Pope Urban VIII was signed ('Anno 1632' in the printed edition; 'Rome 9 August 1632' with autograph signature in the Paris manuscript) is a fascinating story in itself, of which I shall give here only the briefest outline. The sequence of events can be reconstructed from Doni's correspondence with Marin Mersenne, Gabriel Naudé, Nicolas-Claude Peiresc and the brothers Dupuy, among others. On 15 October 1633 Doni announced to Mersenne that he had just finished the essay. A month later he told Peiresc that he hoped 'to bring to light in this discipline [of music] many recondite and notably useful things: starting with the work on the lyra Barberina, which in a few weeks will begin to be printed'.[10] But then he became engrossed in other matters, and, he confessed to Mersenne in April 1634, the book had not begun to be printed.[11] In September 1635 he doubted that publishers in Rome would undertake it because of the many illustrations.[12] He decided in 1638 to try to get it printed in France.[13] Gabriel Naudé promised to find a publisher there through Jacques and Pierre Dupy (the Signori Puteani, as he often referred to them).[14]

In July 1645 the Dupuys still hoped to find a printer, but Doni, getting impatient, asked to have the manuscript returned, because he was angling to get Cardinal Francesco Barberini to sponsor its publication in Italy.[15] He hoped that when the Cardinal saw the *De praestantia musicae veteris libri tres*, which came out in 1647, he would be eager to have also the 'Lyra' essay see the light under his patronage.[16] In one of his last letters Doni urged Dupuy to consign the essay to Naudé, who would have it returned to Doni in Florence.[17] Doni died in December of that year, and nothing more was done to see 'Lyra Barberina' to press until, a hundred years later, Antonio Francesco Gori embarked on the project of publishing Doni's complete works.

Although the motive for writing 'Lyra Barberina' must originally have been to describe the new instrument, only the last six chapters pertain to the lyra specifically. The first eight report the fruit of research undertaken to find ancient models for modern instruments. Doni set out in the first chapter to distinguish among the numerous terms used to designate ancient plucked string instruments, for example *kithara, chelys, testudo, phorminx, kitharis, psalterium, magadis* and *sambuca*. While the first chapter deals with literary evidence, the second presents iconographic evidence. In the third chapter Doni dealt specifically with the psaltery, magadis and sambuca. Doni devoted Chapter 4 to distinguishing the lyre from the kithara and to enumerating different types of each, while in the following chapter he detailed their parts. The plectrum receives special attention in the sixth chapter, and in the seventh Doni tried to solve the mystery of the pecten, which he believed was a comb-like device used to pluck more than one string at a time. Doni's final chapter on the history of the lyre and kithara concerned the manner of holding and playing the instruments.

Throughout these chapters the text contains references to illustrations. Most of these references are retained in the text of the printed edition, but the figures supplied by the editors rarely illuminate the text, and, what is worse, the references in the text are not correctly coordinated with the plate numbers. In a few cases, though, thanks to Doni's identification of his sources, Passeri was able to track down Doni's intended illustration, and he included two figures of which Doni spoke that are not found in any of the manuscripts, namely the representation of Orpheus playing the magadis from a Vatican manuscript of Virgil and a detail from the Sarcophagus of the Muses.[18]

In the Paris manuscript Doni gave the source, whether an engraving in a printed book or a collection of antiquities, from which each figure was drawn. A variety of monuments are represented; for example on the two sides of folio 90 (see Plates II and III) there are gems (Nos. 1, 3, 28), coins (2, 4, 5, 6, 12, 13, 16–27 and 30–35), marble bas-reliefs (7, 8, 10, 11 and 36) and illuminations from a Bible (37 and 38). The greater part of the monuments are of Roman origin. From Greece there are a number of coins: No. 12, from Perinthus; 13, from Chalcidice; 16, from Mytilene; 18 and 19, from Delphi; 20, from Cranii; 23, from Chersonesus; 30, from Megara; 31, from Centuripae in Sicily; 34, from Lappa in Crete.

Justifiably, Doni applied a good measure of scepticism to the analysis of available representations of the lyre and kithara and its associated forms. He warned the reader to bear in mind that instruments portrayed on coins and astronomical charts served a symbolic function and often had little to do with instruments actually used by Greeks and Romans. As an example of the difficulties and contradictions that iconographic evidence posed, Doni scrutinized the lyre in the fresco known as the 'Aldobrandini Wedding' (Plate IVa):[19]

186

PLATE II

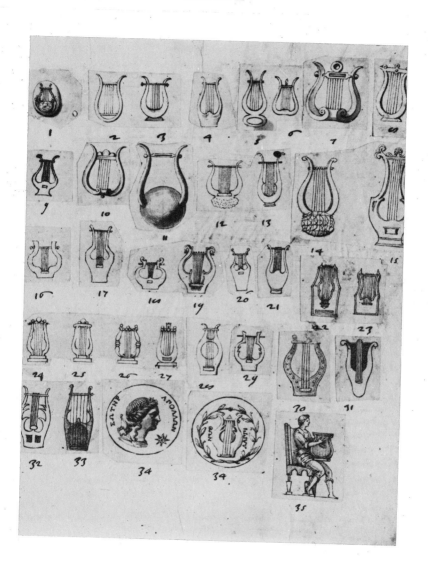

Illustrations for 'Lyra Barberina'
Paris, Bibliothèque Nationale, MS lat. 10274, f.90

187

PLATE III

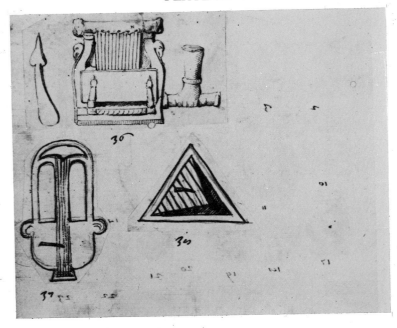

Illustrations for 'Lyra Barberina'
Paris, Bibliothèque Nationale, MS lat. 10274, f.90ᵛ

But it is important to present [for consideration] yet another form of kithara, from a very ancient picture, which, cut from the wall of a certain crypt, we find transferred to the Quirinal villa of the Aldobrandini. In it an ancient celebration of a wedding is graphically represented. The most noble Cassiano dal Pozzo engraved it in bronze,[20] and it was commented upon with erudite observations by Pignorio.[21] There, among other [human] figures is seen one of a girl holding a kithara suspended by a strap [*balteus*] and striking the strings with the right and left hands. This is the figure: [Plate IVb]

It is true that the painter portrayed few strings in the kithara of the Aldobrandinian player, and the rings around the yoke by means of which the strings are tied seem somewhat thick. On this account such a one is not to be considered truly a species of it exactly but rather

PLATE IV

(a) Fresco, 'Aldobrandini
Wedding', detail
Rome, Vatican Museum

(b) Drawing of lyre player from
'Aldobrandini Wedding'
Rome, Vatican Library. MS Barberini 1897, f.18ᵛ

something conjured up by some fertile Minerva. Where are the pegs [*claviculi*] or κόλλαβοι [*kollaboi*], which, the grammarians teach, were provided in kitharas and lyres and without which the strings cannot easily be tightened? Or are we to believe that they are lower, where the *echeum* appears. But, on the other hand, they can hardly be comfortably placed there, for they clearly tell us that they were above the yoke. Then, where are the 24 strings, which the author of the letter to Dardanus attributed to St. Jerome assigns to the kithara? Nor ought we conclude that when this picture was made the kithara had not yet reached that number of strings. The times of Epigonius and Simicius, whose [instruments] consisted of 40 and 35 strings, according to Atheneus, were much more ancient. Besides, music did not significantly develop beyond this point, so far as we know, under the Roman Caesars.[22]

Bolstered by the study of perhaps hundreds of representations of lyres and kitharas, and informed by reading the Greek and Latin sources, Doni was able to apply a critical eye to the Aldobrandini lyre-player's instrument. He returned to it repeatedly in his study, resolving some of the questions just posed.

The instrument that most fascinated Doni and to which he returned most often is that in the Sarcophagus of the Muses, then in the Villa Mattei and now in the Museo delle Terme in Rome. Strangely, it is not represented among the figures in the manuscripts, but Doni must have intended to illustrate it, as he spoke of details that would have been meaningless without a picture. He deplored the mutilated state of the bas-relief, but he probably knew it in much better preservation than it is now. Plate Va shows the detail in question as drawn by a contemporary of Doni for the collection of Cassiano dal Pozzo. As Emanuel Winternitz has shown,[23] this kithara was copied by Raphael in his *Parnassus* in the Stanza della Segnatura in the Vatican.

Doni speculated on the function of what appeared to be tables above and below, but he had no conclusive answer as to how they were used. He also wondered about the simultaneous use of the plectrum in the right hand and the fingers of the left hand on the strings such as may be seen in the figure from the Sacchetti Palace (Plate Vb). What does the right hand do with the plectrum? In 1924 Curt Sachs proposed that the lyre and kithara were tuned pentatonically, for example e–g–a–b–d'–e'; the missing notes f and c', semitones above the lower boundary notes e and b of each tetrachord, would be produced through stopping with the finger.[24] In 1939 Otto Gombosi modified this theory, suggesting that the stopping was done between the bridge and the string fastener (*chordotonos*) by the plectrum, held by the right hand, and he pointed to several representations as evidence.[25]

PLATE V

(b) Drawing of a marble sculpture formerly in the Sacchetti
Palace, Rome

Three hundred years earlier Doni had proposed a similar theory in a passage not in the early Barberini version, therefore dating from around 1640. The passage is in the Gori–Passeri edition but in a slightly earlier version from that of the Paris manuscript.[26] Little rounded blocks, Doni explained, are placed on the surface of the table (*tabula*) or magas to mark the place where the plectrum will depress the string to stop it, one for the semitone, point e, and one for the diesis, point f (see Fig. 1). In this way it was possible with a four-string lyre to obtain a descending scale such as *e′–c′–b–a–f–e* or an enharmonic variant of this. Doni admitted that this interpretation of the iconographic evidence was conjectural, but it was the best explanation he could offer.

Fig. 1

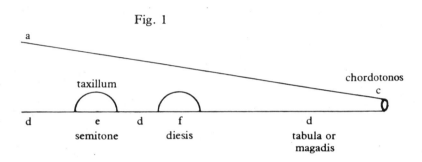

The sceptical modern scholar naturally asks: are Doni's monuments themselves authentic, and how well do the drawings represent them? The drawing of the lyre player from the Aldobrandini wedding in the Barberini manuscript can be compared to the photograph of the existing fresco (Plate IV). Doni's artist endowed the figure of the girl and her dress with a certain seventeenth-century elegance, but the lyre itself is quite faithfully rendered, with perhaps excessive reconstruction of the circular resonating chamber. The instrument held by the girl in the tomb of Atilia Urbica in Brescia, which Doni called the 'lyra posterior' or 'later lyre', is not rendered at all faithfully by Doni's artist, who transformed it into a lute (Plate VIa). A truer likeness must be that of the engraving published by Ottavio Rossi, on which Doni's was based (Plate VIb).

A number of other illustrations of coins and gems may be compared to the printed sources from which they were copied. The coins

PLATE VI

(a) Drawing of a detail from the
tomb of Atilia Urbica
Paris, Bibliothèque Nationale, MS lat. 10274,
f.14ᵛ

(b) Engraving, Tomb of Atilia
Urbica, detail
From Ottavio Rossi,
Le Memorie bresciane, opera istorica et simbolica,
Brescia, n.d., p.38

numbered 22 and 23 in the Paris manuscript (Plate II), the first a
Neapolitan coin, the second from Chersonesus, may be compared to
the representation in Agostini's *Dialoghi intorno alle medaglie* (Rome,
1592. Similarly the lyre that Doni identified as 'from an ancient gem,
in which is carved the contest between Apollo and Marsyas, with the
inscription "Neronis Caesar", after Simeonius' (Plate II, No. 28),
may be compared to the representation of the medal in Gabriele
Simeoni's *Discorso della religione antica de' Romani* (Lyon, 1559),
which in turn is translated from Choul's *Discours de la religion des
anciens Romains* (Lyon, 1556).[27] In all of these Doni's artist scrupulously followed the traits of the originals. Some of the instruments
were extracted from engravings of marbles represented in Jean Jacques Boissard's *Antiquitates romanae*.[28] Here too Doni's artist followed
his models punctiliously.

A number of Doni's figures were copied from the drawings made of Classical antiquities by artists employed by Cassiano dal Pozzo, secretary and librarian to Cardinal Francesco Barberini, for his *Museum chartaceum*. Ten volumes of the collection are now in the Royal Library at Windsor Castle, and a smaller group of 500 drawings are in the British Museum.[29] Doni had at least six of these copied. Comparison of the illustrations that Doni ascribed to the dal Pozzo collection reveal that they were copied accurately. For example, the kithara from what Doni described as a 'round base in which the figures of the ancient gods are represented in the gardens of the Farnesi Palace,' (Plate VII, lower left) may be compared to the drawing in the dal Pozzo collection of a puteal now in the Naples Museo Nazionale (Plate VIIIa). Similarly the kithara from 'a marble of the Farnesi Palace in which bacchanales are carved' (Plate VII, upper right) may be verified through the dal Pozzo drawing in Windsor (Plate VIIIb).

Whether, apart from iconography, Doni's scholarship on the ancient instruments will stand the test of deeper research remains to be seen. The history of the lyre and kithara still awaits definitive work. The publications of Theodore Reinach,[30] Hermann Abert,[31] and Tobias Norling,[32] the most recent of which are more than 40 years old, do not contradict Doni's basic information, though they do introduce some chronological order into the history of the instruments. The pictorial anthologies of Max Wegner[33] have extended the iconographic repertory back to more remote periods of Greek history, thanks to the many vases excavated since the seventeenth century going back to the archaic geometric period of the seventh century and the black-figured and red-figured vases of the sixth and fifth centuries B.C.

Doni's 'Lyra Barberina' must be assessed as a conscientious product of one of the earliest musicologists and iconographers, one who based his conclusions on hard facts and documents. Once the illustrations are joined to the text, the essay can be read with profit by anyone interested in the state of musical scholarship in Doni's age or in the history of ancient string instruments.

Turning now to Doni's activist side, it must be said that his amphichordal lyre (Plate IX) is very much a compromise between an ancient lyre and a large lute or chitarrone. Its ample, almost human torso, is fundamentally modelled on the ancient lyre of the type represented in No. 4 of the Paris manuscript (Plate II), drawn from a coin from the reign of Emperor Antoninus Pius (A.D. 138–161). Its archaic features may be identified by reference to the sketch in the Paris manuscript (Plate IX; the labelling of parts and the inventory are faulty in the Gori–Passeri edition): the *ancones* or arms (D), the *iugum* or yoke (G), the *cornua* or hollow horns, here built into the body as resonating cavities, and the *chordotoni* (T,S,V), through which strings are attached to the table. Perhaps also, the two-faced lyra Barberina was inspired by the three-faced *trigonon,* which could be pivoted to change *tonos.*

The construction of the instrument appears to have preceded the completion of the essay, for in a letter to Mersenne of 15 October 1633 Doni remarked: 'In general the instrument is successful; it has a very sweet tone, so that it surpasses the lute and the harp, while partaking of both'.[34] Six months later he wrote: ' . . . my amphichord turns out to have a sweeter tone every day, such that it surpasses by far the lute'.[35]

The amphichordal lyre was one of several instruments Doni devised to play the ancient tonoi. Among others were the diharmonic viols and violins, triharmonic harpsichords, a theorbo with three fingerboards, and a panharmonic viol.[36] Doni persuaded several composers to experiment with his instruments and in the ancient modes, notably Girolamo Frescobaldi,[37] Domenico Mazzocchi, Pietro Eredia, Gino Capponi, Ottaviano Castelli, Luigi Rossi, and Pietro della Valle.

Doni was disappointed that a truly first-rate composer had not taken up his system. He tried to interest Monteverdi in his ideas in 1633,[38] describing to him his new instrument, and in 1634 even sent him a sketch of the lyra Barberina, which Monteverdi acknowledged in a letter of 2 February 1634.[39] Probably piqued at not receiving acknowledgment from Monteverdi for a copy of the *Compendio del Trattato de' generi e de' modi della musica* (Rome, 1635), Doni in a letter to Mersenne coupled praise for Monteverdi's lament of Ariadne with the remark that the composer was, 'after all, like almost all of them, of little understanding, which is precisely the opposite of the ancient [musicians], who were generally persons of distinction and the most beautiful spirits and the most polished of those times'.[40]

Of the experiments made by various composers with Doni's restored ancient tonalities, the most extensive were those of Pietro della Valle. A manuscript survives of his [*Dialogo*] *per la festa della Santissima Purificazione a cinque voci con varietà di cinque tuoni diversi, cioé Dorio, Frigio, Eolio, Lidio, et Hipolidio.*[41] Here della Valle utilized two instruments that were built for him to accommodate the rapid changes of tonality, a cembalo triarmonico and a viola panarmonica. The cembalo triarmonico (Plate X) was built by Giovanni Pietro Polizzino for della Valle. It consisted of three keyboards. The middle

PLATE VII

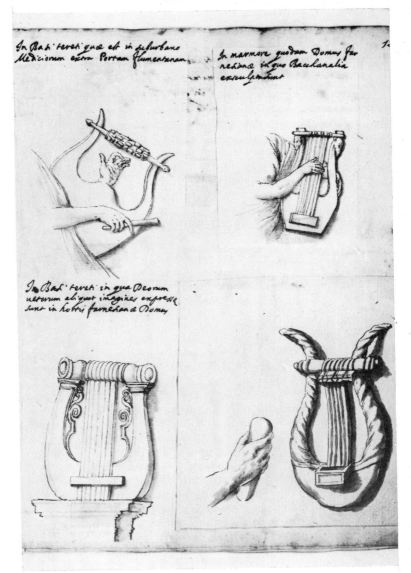

Four instruments copied from drawings in the collection of Cassiano dal Pozzo
Paris, Bibliothèque Nationale, MS lat. 10274, f.13

PLATE VIII

(a) Drawing of the Puteal Farnese in the dal Pozzo collection
Windsor, The Royal Library, No. 8302.

(b) Drawing of a bacchanale in the dal Pozzo collection
Windsor, The Royal Library, No. 7673

PLATE IX

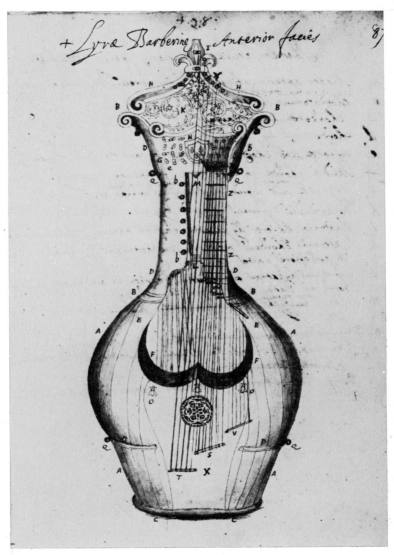

Sketch of Lyra Barberina, front view
Paris, Bibliothèque Nationale, MS lat. 10274, f.87

PLATE X

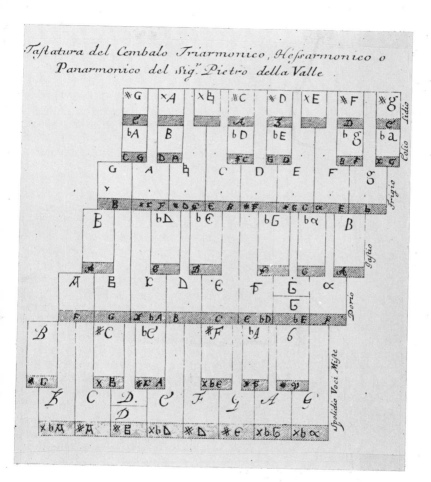

Cembalo triarmonico
Illustrated in Doni, 'Trattato secondo sopra gl'instrumenti di tasti', in *Lyra Barberina*,
ed. A. F. Gori and G. B. Passeri,
Florence 1763, p. 330

one played the Dorian tonality, and its black keys were suited to the Iastian; the top keyboard, which sounded a third higher than written, accommodated the Phrygian, with split keys permitting Aeolian and Lydian. The lowest keyboard supplied the Hypolydian and sounded a tone lower than written. Just tuning prevailed throughout.

The notation and tonal system used in della Valle's *Dialogo* were devised by Doni to restore to use the ancient *harmoniae* and tonoi, in which he believed resided the expressive vigour of ancient Greek music. Doni derived his understanding of the ancient system mainly from Ptolemy, according to whom there were two types of mutation possible in melody writing, one of mode or *harmonia*, the other of key or tonos. In the first — of octave species or mode — the melodic intervals and their order and relationships changed, in the second — modulation of key — only the pitch level changed.

In the *Compendio del Trattato de' generi e de' modi della musica*,[42] Doni gave a chart of modulations for two of the modes and tonoi, the Dorian and Phrygian (Exx. 1–4). The Dorian mode has the rising melodic form mi, fa, sol, la, mi, fa, sol, la. In the second staff Doni showed how it may be transposed to the Phrygian tonos, a whole tone higher. The melody remains the same, while the pitch rises by a whole tone. (We would say that it has been transposed from its natural key to the higher key of two sharps.) If one wished to sing a Phrygian mode in the Dorian tonos, one would remain in the *e–e'* octave but use the necessary accidentals to produce the succession characteristic of the Phrygian mode: re, mi, fa, sol, re, mi, fa, sol (Ex. 1b). In going from Ex. 1a to 1b a mutation of mode occurs, the melody remaining on the pitch level of the Dorian tonos. Supposing instead that one wished to sing the Phrygian mode in the Phrygian tonos; then the same syllables, re, mi, fa, sol, re, mi, fa, sol, would be sung starting on *f♯*, because the Phrygian tonos is a whole tone higher than the Dorian. This is represented in Ex. 3b. The Phrygian melody is now at its normal Phrygian pitch level.

Doni devised a simplified notation that eliminated the multitude of sharps in the transpositions. Ex. 4 shows how the modulation from Dorian tonos and mode to Phrygian tonos and mode would be notated. The initial *f♯* would indicate the modulation to the Phrygian tonos; then the Phrygian mode would be given in its natural notes, as we would today indicate an instrument in E. This is demonstrated in Ex. 4b.

Pietro della Valle modified Doni's notation in that he provided a key to the transposition just before the shift of tonality, the change of pitch being signalled by a *custos*. Della Valle thus realized the variety

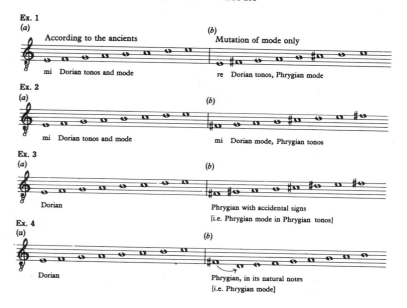

Ex. 1
(a) According to the ancients
mi   Dorian tonos and mode

(b) Mutation of mode only
re   Dorian tonos, Phrygian mode

Ex. 2
(a)
mi   Dorian tonos and mode

(b)
mi   Dorian mode, Phrygian tonos

Ex. 3
(a)
Dorian

(b)
Phrygian with accidental signs
[i.e. Phrygian mode in Phrygian tonos]

Ex. 4
(a)
Dorian

(b)
Phrygian, in its natural notes
[i.e. Phrygian mode]

of tonality that Doni felt was missing from the music of their time, while preserving the pure intonation of intervals. One passage in the *Dialogo* reaches F♯ minor from the original D major, then, shifting from Phrygian to Hypolydian, makes an enharmonic change to E♭ major (notated as D♯ major). Then through a C♯ major chord it leads back to the starting point, D major.[43] The panharmonic instruments assure just intonation throughout the rather strained chordal juxtapositions.

The starting point of Doni's research on ancient instruments was the conviction that a medium had to be found for performing the ancient tonalities. An observer and critic of the contemporary musical scene, he responded to what he perceived as a deficiency of the music of his time. He had welcomed the new dramatic style of monody; indeed he was one of the most intelligent and articulate critics of this new music. But by the 1630s the novelty of recitative had worn off, and composers were turning toward more lyric styles, which Doni also applauded. He deplored, however, the lack of tonal and harmonic and therefore expressive variety in this music, which tended to stay within a narrow range of keys. On the one hand, he wanted to see more modal variety and more liberal use of modulation; on the other, he realized that the tuning systems in use did not permit them. This led him to the search for instruments that in his time could expand the range of tonalities and modes and bring to life the ancient effects.

The mingling of practical goals and scholarly research exemplified in Doni's work has been a source of strength and vitality in the discipline of musicology. The stimulus that scholarship and practice have exerted on each other are not unique to music but it has decisively affected the directions of musical scholarship since its earliest practitioners. Doni's work illustrates both the enthusiastic creativity and the methodological immaturity that this alliance bred.

NOTES

1. Florence, 1573.
2. Rome, Vatican Library, MS Vat. Lat. 5323. For other copies see C. V. Palisca, *Girolamo Mei: Letters on Ancient and Modern Music to Vincenzo Galilei and Giovanni Bardi*, American Institute of Musicology, 1960.
3. *Io. Baptistae Doni Patrici Florentini Lyra Barberina* ΑΜΦΙΧΟΡΔΟΣ *accedvnt eivsdem opera pleraqve nondvm edita, ex avtographis collegit, et in lvcem proferri cvravit Antonivs Franciscvs Gorivs Basilic. Bapt. Flor. olim Praep. distribvta in tomos ii. Absolvta vero stvdio et opera Io. Baptistae Passeri Pisavrensis cvm praefationibvs eivsdem.* Florentiae Typis Caesareis Anno M. D. CC. LXIII.
4. I have prepared for the series 'Antiquae musicae italicae studiosi' of the University of Bologna, edited by Giuseppe Vecchi, a more extensive study of the essay than the present one, accompanied by a facsimile edition of the 1763 edition, with corrections, all of Doni's illustrations, together with their sources, and the glossary of Greek and Latin terms that Doni intended to publish with the essay.
5. Passeri wrote from Bologna to Abbot Annibale Camillo Olivieri in Pesaro on 26 September 1761 that Gori had printed two volumes in folio of Doni's works after working on the project for 30 years, but a number of lacunae had still to be filled. Now he was almost finished. 'But I cannot find anywhere the engravings of antiquities that Doni cites, and I see that Gori had the idea of putting others in their place. I have written to Florence about these apprehensions, but if they do not satisfy me, it would be proper that I derive the plates from the relics that he cites according to his intention' (quoted in Francesco Vatielli, *La 'Lyra Barberina' di G. B. Doni*, Pesaro. 1908, p. 23).
6. Angelo Maria Bandini, *Commentariorum de vita et scriptis Joannis Baptistae Doni*, Florence, 1755, p. lxix n.6. Doni's letter to Scioppius is in Doni, *Commercium litterarium*, ed. Antonio F. Gori, Florence, 1754, cols. 156–8.
7. *Commentariorum*, p. lxix.

8.   Giovanni Gaetano Bottari, *Sculture e pitture sagre estratte dai cimiteri di Roma; pubblicate gia dagli autori della Roma sotterranea*, Rome, 1737–54, ii. 55–61. Doni cites this on p. 415 of the Gori–Passeri edition.

9.   The manuscript on which the Gori–Passeri edition was based, according to Vatielli (*La 'Lyra . . .*', p. 20), was an autograph later acquired by the Biblioteca Oliveriana in Pesaro, where he saw it. Actually this codex, Bibl. Oliveriana, MS 68, is written by a scribe with corrections in Doni's hand. It once belonged to Antonio Francesco Gori, whose brother continued to claim it even after Passeri had donated it to the Olivieri collection. It must have been the prototype for the fair copy written by Gori that served the printer of the Gori–Passeri edition: Florence, Biblioteca Marucelliana, MS A294. This, which contains marks for paragraphing, italics, and decorated capitals, was followed by the printer in every detail, including some misspellings.

10.   Richard Schaal, 'Ein unbekannter Brief von G. B. Doni', *Acta musicologica*, xxv (1953), 88–91. The letter to Mersenne is in *Correspondance du P. Marin Mersenne*, ed. Paul Tannery & Cornelius De Waard, iii (Paris, 1946), 497 ff.

11.   Mersenne, *Correspondance*, iv (1955), 90.

12.   Ibid., v (1959), 391–2.

13.   Ibid., vi (1960), 384.

14.   Naudé had already intervened to arrange for the publication of Doni's two French treatises, and while reporting that they were still with Doni's cousin, Bishop of Riez, to whom they were dedicated, he urged Doni to send the manuscript of the 'Lyra'. Naudé's letter to Doni, of 18 April 1642, is in Mersenne, *Correspondance*, ix (1970), 123. Naudé had reported on 16 February 1641 to Doni (ibid., x (1967), 509) that Robert Ballard was ready in January to take something else off the press and to put Doni's two treatises on, but he still lacked the manuscript.

15.   Doni was already trying to get the manuscript back in 1644, for Naudé wrote to him on 15 December 1644 from Paris assuring him he was trying to retrieve the book from the Dupuys, 'who esteem it very much' (Paris, Bibliothèque Nationale, Ms. ital. 1671, ff. 24–25). On 29 July 1645 Naudé, now in Rome, wrote that before leaving Paris he urged the Dupuys to let him have the 'Lyra' manuscript, but they still were optimistic about getting it printed.

16.   In an undated letter, but obviously of 1647, Doni sent to an assistant of Cardinal Mazarin, to whom the book is dedicated, copies of *De praestantia musicae veteris libri tres*, intimating that Cardinal Francesco, who was now in exile in France, might support the publication of the 'Lyra' essay (Doni, *Commercium litterarium*, cols. 239–40).

17.   Florence, Bibl. Marucelliana, MS. A290, f. 92^V (Doni's draft of the letter). However, so far as getting anything printed in Florence, Doni was extremely disappointed with the work of the printer Amator Massa, who did the *De praestantia*. See *Commercium litterarium*, col. 231.

18.   'Orpheus in pictura antiquissimi Codicis Virgiliani in Bibl. Vaticana' is Tab. III, N:II, a plate prepared by Passeri. Tabula V, Nos. I, II, IV, V and VII, prepared by Gori, are drawn from the figure of the Mattei Sarcophagus of the Muses in Rudolfus Venuti, *Monumenta Matthaeiana*, Augsburg, 1778, Tab. xvi.

19.   This fresco was excavated in 1604 or 1605 near the Arch of Gallieno in the Esquiline Hill in Rome. It was purchased by Cardinal Pietro Aldobrandini for the villa given to him by Pope Clement VIII in 1601. In 1818 Pius VIII gained possession of the fresco, and in 1838 Gregory XVI had it placed in the public gallery of the Vatican Library, where it may be seen today. See Leonard von Matt, *The Art Treasures of the Vatican Library*, New York, 1974, pp. 19–20, including a colour reproduction. The work dates from the beginning of the Christian era.

20.   A drawing showing the wedding in reverse as if it were a sketch for an engraving is in the collection of the British Library, London, that contains many drawings formerly owned by Cassiano dal Pozzo. It is illustrated in Cornelius C. Vermeule, 'The Dal Pozzo-Albani drawings of Classical Antiquities in the British Museum', *Transactions of the American Philosophical Society*, n.s. 1/5 (1960), 77, Fig. 97. The drawing is in vol. 2, f. 79, No. 414 of the collection.

21.   Lorenzo Pignoria, *Antiquissimae picturae quae Romae visitur typus . . . accuratè explicatus*, Padua, 1630, contains a commentary and a folding engraving of the fresco. A copy is in Florence, Biblioteca Nazionale Centrale, Palat. Misc. 2.G.16.4.

22.   Translated by the author from Doni's Latin in 'Lyra Barberina,' Gori–Passeri edn., i. 12–13, as corrected through the Paris manuscript, f. 11. Folio 11^V, which once contained a pasted drawing of the Aldobrandini lyre player, is now blank.

23.   'Musical Archaeology of the Renaissance in Raphael's *Parnassus*', *Musical Instruments and their Symbolism in Western Art*, New York, 1967, pp. 185 ff. and Plates 78, 79, 85 and 88.

24.   'Die griechische Instrumentalnotenschrift', *Zeitschrift für Musikwissenschaft*, vi (1924), 289–301.

25.   *Tonarten und Stimmungen der antiken Musik*, Copenhagen, 1939.

26.   Gori–Passeri edn., p. 42; Paris MS, f. 50^V.

27.   I am indebted to Mark Lindley for locating the Choul and Simeoni volumes in the British Library.

28.   *Romanae vrbis topographiae & antiquitatum . . . iiii*, Frankfurt, 1597–1602. The lyre numbered 6 in the Barberini MS (Plate I, top left), equivalent to Paris MS No. 7, identified by Doni as 'from a marble that was in the Villa of the Carpi, after Boissard', is from Boissard, Pars IV, p. 82. Barberini No. 9 (Paris No. 11), 'from another marble with the inscription, IOVI SANCTO BRONTONTI . . . at the Paulini according to the same Boissard', is from Boissard, Pars IV, p. 137.

29.   The figures that were copied directly for Doni from the Cassiano dal Pozzo collection in Windsor are in the Paris MS, f. 9^V, No. 36, and ff. 12^V–13^r. They correspond to the following volumes and numbers in the Windsor Royal Library, MSS A40 to A52, as catalogued in Cornelius C. Vermeule, III, 'The Dal Pozzo-Albani Drawings of Classical Antiquities in the Royal Library at Windsor Castle', *Transactions of the American Philosophical Society*, n.s. lvi/2 (1966): vol.i, f. 17, Cat. No. 8417; vol. vi, f. 32, Cat. No. 8584; vol. iv, f. 15, Cat. No. 8415; vol. ii, f. 49, Cat. No. 8304; vol. ii, f. 47, Cat. No. 8302; vol. vii, f. 45, Cat. No. 8673.

30.   'Lyra', *Dictionnaire des antiquités grecques et romaines*, Paris, 1904, iii. 1437–51.

31.   'Lyra', *Real Encyclopädie der classischen Altertumswissenschaft*, xiii/2 (1927), 2479–89.

32.   'Lyra und Kithara in der Antike', *Svensk Tijdskrift för Musikforskning*, xvi (1934), 77–98.

33.   *Das Musikleben der Griechen*, Berlin, 1949; *Griechenland* ('Musikgeschichte in Bildern', ii/4), Leipzig, 1963.

34.   Mersenne, *Correspondance*, iii (2nd edn., 1969), 508–9.

35.   8 April 1634; ibid., iv (1955), 90.

36.   Sketches for a number of other instruments, some of them prototypes for the Barberini lyre, are in Florence, Biblioteca Nazionale Centrale, MS Palatino 959, fasc. 3. In a letter to Mersenne of 27 March 1640 Doni apologized for not being able to invite Mersenne to hear the lyra Barberina or the diharmonic viols, not having anyone at the moment who played them. However Doni promised that if Mersenne were to come to Rome he could hear the diharmonic and triharmonic harpsichords, the big panharmonic viol, and the diharmonic violin *(Correspondance, ix. 218–19)*.

37. Doni reported to Mersenne in a letter of 22 July 1640 that Frescobaldi had obtained permission from Cardinal Barberini to have an organ built to play the various tonoi on the model of the triharmonic harpsichord. Still, Doni did not have much faith in him as an exponent of the new music: 'As for Frescobaldi, he is the least well bred of all, seeing that he is a very coarse man, although he plays the organ most perfectly and is an excellent composer of fantasies, dance pieces and similar things, but as for setting the words, he is very ignorant and devoid of judgement. You might say that he has all his erudition on the tips of his fingers. And I do not doubt that he is esteemed more far from here than where he is!' (translated from Mersenne, *Correspondance*, ix (1965), 287).

38. Monteverdi's reply of 22 October 1633 is in G. F. Malipiero, *Claudio Monteverdi*, Milan, 1929, pp. 291–4, translated in *The Monteverdi Companion,* ed. Denis Arnold and Nigel Fortune, London, 1968, pp. 83–85.

39. Malipiero, op. cit., p. 296; *The Monteverdi Companion,* p. 87. Doni had sent similar sketches to others, for example to Mersenne with a letter of 15 October 1633 (*Correspondance*, iii (2nd edn., 1969), 509) and to Michelangelo Buonarroti, Junior, with a letter of 23 December 1633 in Florence, Bibl. Medicea-Laurenziana, Archivio Buonarroti, MS 46, f. 822.

40. Mersenne, *Correspondance,* vi (1960), 30.

41. Rome, Biblioteca Nazionale, MSS musicali 123. I am indebted to Professor Howard Smither for a copy of this score.

42. Rome, 1635, pp. 33–34.

43. See Agostino Ziino, 'Pietro della Valle e la "musica erudita", nuovi documenti', *Analecta musicologica,* iv (1967), 97–111 (including facsimile of the original notation and transcription of passage in question).

Chapter 11

THE VALUE OF ICONOGRAPHICAL SOURCES IN MUSICAL RESEARCH

Walter Salmen

MUSICOLOGY is concerned with all musical sound, past and present, both with the musicians and instruments that produced that sound and with those who heard it. This being so — so that the object of research is not only musical compositions, to be analyzed in the abstract, divorced from their realization in performance — then it necessarily follows that music that has survived in notated form or in recordings cannot be the only source for musicological research. In order to include the whole of what we term musical life or musical culture other evidence must be taken into account: written testimony, surviving instruments and pictures. Depending on the problem in question and its chronological period and geographical locality, one or other of these source-groups will be of primary importance. For example, in the case of dance, one is completely reliant on notated music for the music itself; for the musicians who performed it and for the choreography, however, one must turn to verbal and visual evidence, while for the location and graphic reconstruction of what took place, one is reliant almost entirely on pictorial evidence. Pictorial works, in particular, provide evidence towards the solution of complex problems for which there is no adequate substitute. Iconography and, proceeding from that, iconology, are indispensable components of modern musicology, in as far as this aims to encompass the full reality of *musica* in human life, so as to present as vividly as possible a picture of life and art as they really were. To re-create a picture of the past is certainly a principal aim of historical research. And a reconstruction of any specific musical occasion is all the more convincing if it can be related directly to surviving pictorial material, whether in the form of sculpture, paintings, photographs or film.

Iconography and iconology are indispensable in musicology especially with respect to questions which otherwise, for want of sources, would be investigated either superficially or not at all. These include the whole complex of pre- and early history of music, that is, the whole period (in some places reaching well into the Middle Ages), from which there is no notated music. To learn anything of the music of the Vikings, the Illyrians, the Celts and other tribes, there are, apart from archaeological discoveries of instruments that are now mostly unusable, only pictures, which do give at least a vague impression of the role of music in ritual, war, or at *symposia*.[1]

The same applies to dance, whether it be alone, in pairs, in threes or in a group. For lack of treatises or detailed descriptions, the history of dance could only be written from around 1450, were it not for pictures representing figures, positions, steps, holds, dance accessories and other choreographic details from early times onwards.[2] I want to consider a few relatively early examples; but they could be extended up to the most recent times with just the same source value. A dissertation published in 1976 on the beginnings of the waltz and the Ländler in Vienna during the eighteenth century showed that without pictorial sources even this theme could not have been adequately elucidated.[3] Two pictures of eleventh and fourteenth century Serbian and Bulgarian origin show in default of other sources the great age and the continuing tradition of single-sex round dances in Bulgaria, which survive to the present day as *Kolo*. The use of the pointed toe and the bending of the arms are especially noteworthy.[4] Very different is the feudal bearing (emphasizing their social standing) of the dancers from the nobility of South Tirol in the fourteenth century (Plate Ia) or the way the sixteenth century peasants run in an open chain in Bavaria[5] or in Sweden (Plate Ib) — this woodcut dating from 1555 shows in addition the re-formation of the circle into an arch. The other important figure of the bridge — formed with swords — is shown in a drawing from Zurich, although there are no descriptions of this as early as the sixteenth century.[6] Thus the picture is in fact the only source for this feature of the dance. The figure of the rose is shown in a picture from Nuremberg which also allows one to see a sequence of steps in successive stages.[7] The various types of hold are never described in the Middle Ages, so that details of, for example, the hand-hold or the hold using a kerchief (Plate II) can again only be deduced from pictures. The adornment of the dancer according to rank is shown in the representation of a middle-class woman by Albrecht Dürer.[8] There are as yet no specialized studies of the manner of instrumental accompaniment for dancing, whether simply by pipe and tabor, as shown in Plate II, or the prerogative of the nobililty,

207

PLATE I

(a) Fresco in Schloss Runkelstein near Bolzano, *c.* 1390–1400

(b) Woodcut in Olaus Magnus, *Historia de gentibus septentrionalibus*, 1555

PLATE II

Miniature, Paris, Bibliothèque Nationale, MS Arsenal 601, f.2^V, 15th century

straight trumpets (Plate III). But studies of this sort will only be achieved through a sufficiently extensive collection of pictures — although naturally verbal quotations from medieval poetry will also need to be taken into account, cliché-ridden though most of them are. The social status of the musicians taking part can again be most surely deduced from pictorial evidence. If they wear so-called *Spiel-mannsschilde* ('minstrel's badges'), for example, they can be identified as town waits.[9]

To demonstrate the need for this branch of research in the area of organology, I should like to refer merely to three specific instances. At a recent conference on the organ and organ playing in the sixteenth

PLATE III

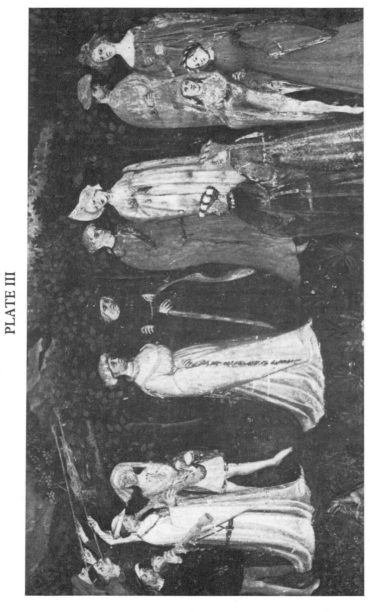

Fresco in the Adler Tower at Trento, 15th century

century, art historians, curators and organ experts disputed the question as to whether the organ with a closable frontal case stood mostly with the wings open or whether these were closed when the organ was not in use. The pictures collected to date show a majority with open wings. Iconography can also contribute more than it has hitherto to our knowledge of the technical development of instrument building. Thus an engraving from 1615 shows that the method of making sheet tin for organ pipes has remained unchanged up to the present day.[10] Organology is especially reliant on pictorial sources in the consideration of the instruments that were disparagingly called 'amusa' in the sixteenth century and 'lumpen instrumenta' in the seventeenth and therefore discounted in the usual classifications. Seventeenth-century crib figures, hitherto unconsidered as sources of musical information, have recently proved to be a rich fund of evidence in the continuing task of cataloguing and classifying the diversity of straight horns, trumpet-like instruments, peasant harps and other instruments in frequent use.[11] Even in the history of keyboard instruments, for example in the case of the vertically strung *clavicymbel* of the fifteenth century, and the method of playing instruments there are still many details to be found out.

The systematic collection and evaluation of pictorial evidence is quite indispensable in questions concerning the uses of music in society, including 'pre-musical' phenomena such as military signals and watchmen's calls. The preparation of my book *Musikleben im 16. Jahrhundert*, published in 1976, was sufficient to convince me that a comprehensive picture of musical life in town and country can never be gained simply from the music that was written down. In a city like Florence musical sounds of one sort or another were to be heard almost uninterruptedly, day and night, and more than ninety per cent of this daily music-making occurred without any written record — or indeed any formal process of composition. There were the various distinctive and sophisticated chimes of the bellringers,[12] the signals of the tower musicians, the calls of the constabulary during the arrest and torture of criminals, the work songs, the playing of the street musicians, the ceremonial escort of mounted trumpeters for high-ranking travellers — all this has disappeared and its sounds cannot be recaptured. Pictures provide momentary glimpses of all this in more or less specific situations; though they cannot re-create the aural experience, they can at least clarify the social circumstances of this activity.

Recent publications such as the lavishly illustrated journal *Early Music* show how reliant research in music-making and performance-practice is on pictorial sources. Here it is not only a question of where and by whom music was made in church, palace or at home and what instruments took part; the grouping of instruments in ensembles is also of interest. The assumption that the *ad lib.* instrumentation of music around 1600 allowed limitless freedom of choice is shown to be highly questionable if a sufficient number of pictures are compared. These show certain standardized groupings, which ought to serve as models for modern performances. For example several pictures show that flautists always play from the soprano parts. This custom is evident even from caricatures, such as the one of an animal orchestra from 1610 at the Hirschenhaus in Berchtesgaden, Upper Bavaria.[13]

So far we have discussed the possibility of gleaning information from pictures that reflect aspects of practical musical life and can therefore be taken to represent real situations. But we should also consider the significance for musical scholarship of pictures that are to be understood in a symbolic sense. They provide a 'Musikanschauung' in the real sense of the word. This sort of pictorial evidence provides men's visual realization of what lies beyond musical practice — of the ideas and the essence of music that verbally are expressed in conceptual terms. This is not only a question of the great symbolic personifications of music such as Apollo, Orpheus, David and St. Cecilia on the one hand, and devils, witches, Bacchus and Pan on the other; there are also pictures that offer supplementary interpretation to such basic concepts as 'symphony', 'tragic opera', 'dance' of men and gods, 'domestic music' or *musica* pure and simple. The collection and evaluation of this abundant material are at present in their infancy. Particularly in the nineteenth century this was an important theme for many artists, but from earlier centuries too there is a quantity of documentary evidence that has not been recognized as such. Perhaps I might give one example: the reign of Emperor Maximilian I (1493–1519) is celebrated in writings on musical history as a cultural peak in the South German/Austrian region. Hitherto a sequence of four sandstone reliefs on a house in Innsbruck (Plate IV) has gone unnoticed. The house stands near the famous 'Golden Roof', and the reliefs, from the studio of Georg Türing, represent more than just the loose association of four musical scenes. It seems rather that here the sculptor was attempting to depict symbolically a total view of *musica practica* before 1520, in the form in which it was prized by the emperor and his followers. In simplified form this in my opinion comprises: (a) military music represented by drummer and piper; (b) 'soft' music, with lute, cornett and fiddle; (c) dance, with shawn and bagpipe; and (d) 'strong' music, with long trumpet (with a single

PLATE IV

Sandstone relief in Herzog-Friedrich-Strasse, Innsbruck, before 1520, studio of Georg Türing

loop), metal horn (semi-circular in shape) and cornett. This embraces a comprehensive depiction of secular music in an age before a rift had yet developed between lowly folk music on the one hand and elite 'art' music on the other. On one of the most noble houses of the early sixteenth century, the piping soldier, the dancing peasant, the proud court trumpeter and the refined playing of the lutenist depict realistically in a single frieze the *musica profana* of the time.

I hope that this very brief survey of a greatly expanding field of study may provide some stimulus for looking at pictures afresh and examining them for their possible value as musical sources. Iconographical evidence can be found almost everywhere in Europe and is only waiting to be used in the service of musical scholarship.

213

NOTES

1. See the chapter 'Vorgeschichte' in *Musikgeschichte Österreichs*, ed. Rudolf Flotzinger & Gernot Gruber, Graz, 1977, p. 29. For reasons of space the present paper restricts itself to European questions.

2. W. Salmen, 'Ikonographie und Choreographie des Reigens im Mittelalter', *RIDIM Newsletter*, ii/2 (1977), 18.

3. R. Witzmann, *Der Ländler in Wien*, Vienna, 1976.

4. See for example *Musica antiqua europea orientalis, Bydgoszcz 1966 Polska: Acta scientifica congressus*, i (Warsaw, 1966), 127.

5. W. Salmen, *Musikleben im 16. Jahrhundert* ('Musikgeschichte in Bildern', iii/9), Leipzig, 1976, Plate 15.

6. Ibid., Plate 26.

7. *Musik und Bild: Festschrift Max Seiffert*, ed. H. Besseler, Kassel, 1938, Plate 7.

8. See W. Salmen, 'Vom Musizieren in der spätmittelalterlichen Stadt', *Das Leben in der Stadt des Spätmittelalters* ('Veröffentlichungen des Instituts für mittelalterliche Realienkunde Österreichs', ii), Vienna, 1977, Pl. 61.

9. R. Nissen, 'Silberne Boten- und Spielmannsabzeichen und ihre Träger', *Westfalen*, xlvii (1969), 1.

10. Salmen, *Musikleben*, Plate 89.

11. See G. Busch, 'Die Musikinstrumente in Tiroler Krippen', *Beiträge zur Volksmusik in Tirol*, Innsbruck, 1978, p. 153.

12. W. Salmen, *Musikgeschichte Schleswig-Holsteins von der Frühzeit bis zur Reformation*, Neumünster, 1972, Pl. 7; W. Salmen, *Bilder zur Geschichte de Musik in Österreich*, Innsbruck, 1979.

13. W. Salmen, 'Die Musizierbilder von 1610 am Hirschenhaus zu Berchtesgaden', *Schönere Heimat*, lxv (Munich, 1976), 172.

Chapter 12

MARTINI, ROUSSEAU, BURNEY AND FORKEL IN TWENTIETH-CENTURY PERSPECTIVES

William W. Austin

MUSIC SCHOLARS can trace continuous strands in their discipline back from the present into antiquity, if they think of the discipline of musicology as more comprehensive than the history of music. Are we not all disciples of the theorist Aristoxenus and his master Aristotle, even though the master maligned the 'father of history' Herodotus? Such long, tenuous continuities are attractive, in promising to help us cope with the accelerating ramifications of scholarship and the multiplying contacts across our unstable national and cultural frontiers. Some of us, indeed, seek to press the search farther back, as Walter Wiora[1] and Othmar Wessely[2] do, to rediscover roots of thinking about song and dance that antedate Greek distinctions between theory and practice, between myth and history, between the nature of things and their human uses and abuses. For our urgent questions about musical activities in a crowded noisy world, we need such long perspectives.

A firmer continuous twisted rope within the enterprise of music history goes back to the eighteenth century. Then music theory (for craftsmen) and aesthetics (for philosophers, connoisseurs, and amateurs) began to unravel, while critical historical thinking in all fields grew thicker, tougher, more intense, ambitious and influential. Music history was not yet so big and institutional as it was to be with Mocquereau, Riemann, and Adler, but it was on the way.

The multi-volume histories of music by Giambattista Martini (1757–81), John Hawkins (1776), Charles Burney (1776–89) and Johann Nikolaus Forkel (1788–1801) are familiar enough. We may remember less vividly some French contributions such as Jean Benjamin de Laborde's four-volume *Essai* (1780),[3] an unprecedented critical assemblage of materials for music history in French and Latin, with no pretence at a coherent narrative. The writings on music of

Jean-Jacques Rousseau cannot rank so near as Laborde's to those of Martini, Burney, and Forkel. But Rousseau's contain ideas more stimulating, comprehensive and memorable than any of Laborde's. Rousseau can be studied usefully in connection and contrast with Forkel, as Wulf Arlt has shown.[4] Both may well be juxtaposed with Martini and Burney to provoke discussion of our own various perspectives on persistent eighteenth-century trends, methods and presuppositions. Martini, Burney and Forkel all acknowledged Rousseau's brilliance, though they may have agreed with Laborde that he was 'seductive to read, dangerous to believe'.[5] Burney was proud of especially close connections with Rousseau and his music. The conscientious Hawkins must have resisted Rousseau's lure, for, as Forkel marvels in his review of Hawkins,[6] his book does not mention Rousseau. Yet even Hawkins, in a posthumous footnote,[7] credits Rousseau with a valid insight about the history of chant.

Forkel is closest to us of the four authors. Not only is he the youngest — too young to have caught the attention of Martini or Rousseau, or to have vexed Burney with his critical citations or his unacknowledged borrowing;[8] he is also the only one of the four to have bridged the gulf of discontinuity between earlier and later eighteenth-century styles and tastes that separated J. S. Bach from his sons, whose friendship Forkel enjoyed and profited from. Forkel's study of Bach (1802), more than his unfinished history or his peerless bibliography (1792), keeps his fame alive. The most advanced twentieth-century Bach studies build on his foundations, with the help of technological devices that he would have envied, such as photography, electronic computers and jet travel for scholars subsidized by governments. Currently advancing studies of Byrd and Josquin and many more emulate Forkel, particularly in source-criticism, in archival research for biographical fact, in editing and in emphasis on forms and styles; these are central in music history as we know it, while subordinate places are assigned to musical grammar or theory on one side and on the other to criticism or aesthetics and declamation or performance-practice. Forkel showed the path of systematic collective advance, in which merely competent workers can collaborate with outstanding scholars. We not only use Forkel's methods but also, to a great extent, we confirm his argument that Bach's works transcend his time and endure into times more enlightened, more romantic or more chaotic. Few people would challenge this argument, though many of us regard Forkel's motivations, religious and patriotic, as less enlightened than he supposed. Moreover, just as some of us, like old Hawkins, find transcendant values in Byrd and Josquin, so most of us think we learn from Beethoven and Debussy how to hear and play Bach in ways that no historian can teach. Some would extend this list to include Stravinsky, Schoenberg, and Bartók. Some would include that great pupil of Guido Adler, Anton Webern. Maybe a few would add Aro Pyart or another still younger composer. Forkel, with reasons that seemed convincing to him, viewed Byrd and Josquin as stepping-stones to Bach, and he saw Gluck, Haydn and Mozart as misguided geniuses, decadents, not classics. Have we agreed on reasons to disagree with him? Or do many of us, disclaiming any responsibility for 'general history' simply let each other locate the peaks between historical growth and decay according to our various tastes?

Burney appeals to us as more enlightened than Forkel about Haydn and other contemporary composers, but in his treatment of Bach and most earlier music he repels us as shallow, smug, pseudo-scientific and unromantic. Exceptional passages, like the long one on Purcell, enable a reader like Lawrence Lipking[9] to defend Burney from glib critics. But Lipking agrees with most modern historians that Burney's eruditon is not so critical or logical as Hawkins's or Forkel's.[10] Burney's energetic and tactful journalistic methods of inquiry may affect us, whether we like them or not, whether we develop them with video-tape or deny them the dignity of scholarship. If modern historians of antiquity have succeeded in teaching us respect for Herodotus,[11] we may give new consideration to Burney. His emphasis on biography, stronger than Forkel's, might suggest some new sorts of coordination between musical journalism and scholarship, comparable to twentieth-century developments in political and literary history and criticism. Burney's demonstration that music history can be an attractive art in itself will continue to inspire. His most recent biographer, Roger Lonsdale,[12] helps us to see his unique achievement in its immediate context, or to mine his journals for vivid observations left out of his general history.

Some presuppositions that Burney and Forkel share may affect us too. Both linked music with painting and sculpture and the history of these arts, at the expense of dance and sometimes even of poetry. Burney was soaring above the status of his dancing-master father; Forkel was climbing above that of his dancing-master colleague at the University of Göttingen. Neither appreciated the contributions of the dancers Hilferding, Angiolini and Noverre to the music of Jomelli, Traetta, Gluck and younger composers. Though Burney lacked much knowledge of the exemplary historical scholarship of Johann Winckelmann, important for Forkel, he knew Winckelmann's translator

217

Henry Fuseli and was swayed by the vast authority of his friend Joshua Reynolds; he emulated Reynold's extraordinary breadth of taste, which could relax his own theoretical authority. All these authors assume that customers for their books, for objects of art and for tickets to operas and concerts matter more to the hopes of mankind as a whole than most people matter. Burney and Forkel expect to see the class of public art-consumers prosper and expand so as to outvote any hereditary privileged oligarchy or any mob that might reduce civilization to a new Dark Age. They aim to guide readers to the good taste in music that the growing public should uphold. This aim is what gives history its right to more publicity than most music theory. In accordance with this aim, history can neglect the varied hopes and fears of musical employees of the old churches and states or the newer theatres and publishing industries; it can ignore the songs of new sects like the Methodists and the Hasidim; it can pass lightly over the majority of men, women and children throughout the ages who feed the race and make their own songs and dances.

Among twentieth-century musicologists, how many dislike these bourgeois assumptions and neglects? Of those who do, can any claim that the enterprise of musicology has yet made great progress in overcoming them? Ethnomusicology, jazz research, music sociology and psychology and a vast array of new music theories or methods of analysis all struggle to coordinate valiant scattered inquiries; but the history of works of art and their composers, their styles and forms, holds a central position in musicology because this history can boast of a steady advance, despite internal problems. Rousseau anticipated our discontents. 'It was not in a theory of progress', as Jean Starobinski has observed, 'but by his horrified awareness of danger and at the same time of fecundity in temporal existence, that Rousseau is the most important witness in his age to the discovery of history.'[13] This awareness of danger and fecundity depends partly on an older, broader concept of music than that of most historians. Rousseau's interests in ancient theory and contemporary refined practice he kept always in the perspective of wretched masses and apocalyptic hopes. He could love an illiterate singer's crude ballads or a village choir's droning chants as much as any aria or symphony. He could propose an edition of songs from the thirteenth and fourteenth centuries, and he could see many of the problems facing editors. He could follow the changes of fashion represented by Rameau, Pergolesi and Gluck. He could reasonably claim to have participated in these changes, without supposing that his compositions ranked either with the masters' or with the old songs closer to nature than theirs. He had learned, partly from Voltaire, to despise all warring states and Churches and to subordinate their histories to those of the arts and sciences, but he put no great trust in the families of tradesmen, bankers, lawyers, administrators or academic types who formed the growing audience and market for art. The possibility of a whole human society was his greatest concern; its unlikelihood was his despair. Music fed him and motivated him and consoled him. He theorized about it, as he theorized about liberty, equality and fraternity, without beginning to legislate or to recommend any political party. His theorizing in all fields depended, as Lionel Gossman puts it, on his 'discovery and application of an historical method of analysis'.[14] Moreover, he showed, as Gossman says again, that 'historiography is itself a vital part of history'. He challenged the doctrine of the gradual perfection of the art of music because he questioned the purposes of the art. His challenge disturbed Forkel and others, who could not grasp its motive. When Rousseau wrote questions to Burney, the reply contained no answers; can we yet answer Rousseau's questions about world-wide music? In his *Dictionnaire de musique* (1767) Rousseau contributed to scholarship in ways that may repay a more thorough study than this book has yet received, even in the sympathetic and critical survey of Rousseau as musician by Julien Tiersot[15] or the detailed accounts of Rousseau's earlier musical writings by Marie-Elisabeth Duchez and Robert Wokler, who each independently in 1974 published the manuscript 'Du principe de la mélodie''.[16] Wolker suspects that 'in the next decade or so, the *Dictionnaire de musique* may become as much a focus of Rousseau studies as are the *Contrat social* and the *Emile* today'. The Dictionary, with only a little study, nourishes brave thinkers like Jacques Attali, who cites it more than once in his book with the Rousseauesque subtitle 'Essay on the political economy of music', along with his accusation that today's musicological and historical tradition is trying to preserve a scheme of linear progress outgrown by all the human sciences.[17] Did Rousseau believe, as Attali does, that music prophesies social change? Scholarship is needed to answer such a question — music scholarship coordinated with philosophical and literary Rousseau scholarship. Rousseau's own music scholarship, as he acknowledged, was incomplete and even amateurish, whereas Forkel established — or reformed — a university profession, and Burney proved that scholarship could compete commercially with fiction. But Rousseau's biases and inconsistencies about harmony and counterpoint need not spoil his insights into the theory and practice of rhythm and melody, into poetics, or into history.

The revolutionary Rousseau and the Franciscan Father Martini may seem closer to each other in twentieth-century perspectives than they could have seemed to Burney or Forkel. Martini's famous scholarship was more than the diligent and judicious learning of a conservative specialist: it was an integral part of a long-established vocation in which the miseries and hopes of all people could never be forgotten. He addressed fellow musicians and their ecclesiastical and civic patrons, trusting their devotion to justice and truth[18] and caring little for the market-place of connoisseurs and amateurs. His scholarship included active speculative theory. It included more history and more systematic bibliography than did any earlier music scholar's because he felt the need for history to guide theory toward more nearly perfect conformity with natural law. His vocation included persistent musical practice; his compositions, not yet so famous as Rousseau's, were more profound and poetic. The coordination of Martini's history, theory and practice has been expounded by Bernard Wiechens in a book on all Martini's church music.[19] Howard Brofsky's articles [20] on the instrumental music whet an appetite to hear good performances. Martini's keyboard sonastas are not merely interesting — they are both challenging and consoling. His happy coordination must have informed his famous lessons to J. C. Bach and Mozart and his generous help to Burney. It would perhaps be not quite accurate to say that for Martini history was subordinate to living music and musicians. For besides his sense of musicians' need for history, he meant to coordinate music history with broader histories like those of Lodovico Antonio Muratori and Francesco Saverio Quadrio, where music had already taken a more prominent place than it was to find with Voltaire, Hume, Gibbon, or Hegel. History was a tireless critical inquiry. While the world's complexities could never be transparent, yet some obstacles could be moved so as to let the light of truth penetrate into ever more of the dark folds. Martini's history was critical of myths old and new about the relations between nature and culture. Yet it claimed no utter autonomy or hegemony, no status as a science superior to that of music theory, no gift of revelation or prophecy. Martini's three volumes are not enough to serve as a model. (His fourth was to begin with the Etruscans — wonderful eighteenth-century topic!) But if we regard his view of history in the context of his theory and practice and his whole life, we may learn something from it. When his vast correspondence and miscellaneous manuscripts are eventually published, we may learn much.

Modern musicology can well pursue further the kind of historical scholarship established by Forkel. Our primary sources are not so nearly exploited as those of political or literary history. Editorial methods are still being improved. Our products interest a growing number of amateurs, scattered all around the globe in the age of high-fidelity recording; though not a growing proportion of mankind or any coherent group, these amateurs include some great scholars and thinkers in neighbouring disciplines, like Henri Marrou, Karl Popper and Northrop Frye. The application of our discoveries in musical practice, dubious as this may be, expands at a rate unimagined by Forkel and his contemporaries. If, to support the continuance of Forkelish work, some of us cling to what I should call a myth of progress or a myth of scientific history, such myths are tolerable; their devotees can tolerate historical criticism of them too. But we need also the journalistic energy and tact and flexible taste of Burney. In our crowded world of mobile peoples we need much more of his gifts. We need all we can find of brilliant thinking and seductive writing like Rousseau's and devoted persistence and comprehensiveness like Martini's. While we may wish also for untraditional things that none of the four provides, we can still use these four sources to refresh the historical tradition that flows through us to another generation. Even if we merely use a knowledge of Martini, Rousseau, and Burney to help us restrain any boasting about progress on the path of Forkel, we may hope to multiply our contributions to the world's enlightenment.

NOTES

1. 'Musikwissenschaft und Universalgeschichte', *Acta musicologica*, xxxiii (1961), 84–104; 'Musikgeschichte und Urgeschichte', *Svensk Tidskrift för Musikforskning*, xliii (1961), 375–96; *Historische und systematische Musikwissenschaft: ausgewählte Aufsätze*, Tutzing, 1972; 'Zur Vor- und Frühgeschichte der musikalischen Grundbegriffe', *Acta musicologica*, xlvi (1974), 125–52.
2. *Musik*, Darmstadt, 1972.
3. *Essai sur la musique ancienne et moderne*, Paris, 1780.

4. 'Natur und Geschichte der Musik in der Auffassung des 18. Jahrhunderts: J.–J. Rousseau und J. N. Forkel', *Melos / Neue Zeitschrift für Musik*, ii (1976), 351–6.

5. *Essai*, iv.364.

6. In *Musikalisch-kritische Bibliothek*, ii (1778), 166 ff.; reprinted in Hawkins, *A General History of the Science and Practice of Music*, ed. O. Wessely ('Die grossen Darstellungen der Musik in Barock und Aufklärung', v), Graz, 1969, pp. xv–xxxviii.

7. *History*, 2nd edn. London, 1875, i.278.

8. *A General History of Music*, London, 1776–89, iv.603.

9. *The Ordering of the Arts in 18th-Century England*, Princeton, 1970, pp. 269–324.

10. See H. Edelhoff, *Johann Nikolaus Forkel: ein Beitrag zur Geschichte der Musikwissenschaft*, Göttingen, 1935; W. Franck, 'Musicology and its Founder, Johann Nicolaus Forkel', *The Musical Quarterly*, xxxv (1949), 599–601; R. Stevenson, ' "The Rivals" — Hawkins, Burney, and Boswell', ibid., xxxvi (1950), 67–82; T. Kneif, 'Forkel und die Geschichtsphilosophie des ausgehenden 18. Jahrhunderts', *Die Musikforschung*, xvi (1963), 224–37; V. Duckles, 'Johann Nicolaus Forkel: the Beginnings of Music Historiography', *Eighteenth-century Studies*, i (1967), 277–90; W. F. Kümmel, *Geschichte und Musikgeschichte . . . von der Aufklärung bis zu J. G. Droysen und Jacob Burckhardt*, Marburg, 1967.

11. See A. Momigliano, *Studies in Historiography*, London, 1966.

12. *Dr. Charles Burney: a Literary Biography*, Oxford, 1967.

13. Introduction to Rousseau, *Discours sur l'inégalité*, in *Oeuvres complètes*, iii (1964); reprinted in Starobinski, *Jean-Jacques Rousseau: la transparence et l'obstacle*, 2nd edn., Paris, 1971, p. 354.

14. 'Time and History in Rousseau', *Studies on Voltaire and the 18th Century*, xxx (1964), 311–40.

15. *Jean-Jacques Rousseau*, Paris, 1920.

16. Duchez, '*Principe de la mélodie* et *Origine des langues:* Un brouillon inédit de Jean-Jacques Rousseau', *Revue de musicologie*, lx (1974), 33–86; Wokler, 'Rameau, Rousseau and the Essai sur l'origine des langues', *Studies on Voltaire and the 18th Century*, cxxvii (1974), 179–238.

17. *Bruits: essai sur l'économie politique de la musique*, Paris, 1977, pp. 14, 121–2, 20.

18. *Storia della musica*, Bologna, 1757–81, i.5.

19. *Die Kompositionstheorie und das kirchenmusikalische Schaffen Padre Martinis*, Regensburg, 1968.

20. 'The Symphonies of Padre Martini', *The Musical Quarterly*, li (1965), 649–73; 'The Keyboard Sonatas of Padre Martini', *Quadrivium*, viii (1967), 63–74.

Chapter 13

A FRENCH CRITIC'S VIEWS ON
THE STATE OF MUSIC IN LONDON (1829)

Vincent Duckles

ARTICLES on the state of music in some particular place, city or country acquired almost the status of a literary genre in the early nineteenth century. They were a familiar journalistic device common to most of the music periodicals of the time. Sometimes these 'state-of-music' accounts took the form of reports from a correspondent writing from abroad; or they might be utilized as a means of commenting on musical trends or events at home. A few representative titles from *The Harmonicon*, one of the two leading British music journals of the first quarter of the century, will recall this practice to mind: 'The State of Music in Vienna', 'The State of Music in Sicily', 'On the Present State of Music in the Netherlands', 'On the Present State of Music in Rome' and so on. The last-named account was the work of Franz Sales Kandler, a Viennese dilettante whose descriptions of musical life in Italy were translated and widely circulated within the international network of periodical publications. Richard Mackenzie Bacon, editor of *The Quarterly Musical Magazine and Review*, the first English journal devoted solely to music, found the 'state-of-music' device particularly congenial. Each of the ten annual volumes that made up the life of this quarterly carried an article covering the progress of events, institutions, and personalities active in London for the year under review. Articles of this nature functioned as a kind of annual report to the public informing all those interested in new devolopments in the art. Most of these reports were anonymous, that is, they took the form of 'Letters to the Editor' from such correspondents as 'An Amateur, or 'An Observer', but there is reason to believe that they were commissioned, if not actually written by Bacon himself.

Sometimes his judgements were severely critical, but on the whole there is a feeling of satisfaction with the condition of music, a conviction that in spite of certain defects the health of London's musical life was basically sound. This is the impression conveyed by the concluding paragraph of the 'Sketch of the State of Music in London' as reported in the *Quarterly Musical Magazine* for May 1823:

> Here then our sketch is finished. All the particulars decidedly prove that science is extending its influence every hour over a wider space. There is no indifference to art — no lack of patronage. On the contrary, the liberality of the British public is found sufficiently vast to embrace the talent, we may say, of the world, for an asylum and a support are rendered to genius come from where it may. And so we would have it.

Where could one find a more disarming expression of faith in England's power to sustain the musical world through the liberality of its music lovers? Here was a nation prepared to accept its role as the universal patron of genius, come from where it may. Yet beneath this euphoria there lurked a persistent element of doubt. Too many critics had expressed the view that the English were basically an unmusical people. Could England produce genius as well as nurture it? Could English musicians function as creators as well as consumers of musical value? These were troublesome questions and a good deal of ink was wasted in an attempt to answer them. One such attempt was made by the Rev. John Edmund Cox (1812–90) who wrote anonymously a book called *Musical Recollections of the Last Half-Century* (London, 1872). Although Cox did not choose to identify himself, he was clearly an informed member of the inner circle of English musical society. His explanation of the supposed deficiences of English music was based on two observations: first, the absence of an indigenous body of English folk music; and, second, the English habit of self-depreciation in matters related to culture and the arts.

> Whence, then, arises the idea that we are not a musical people? It may, perhaps, have its origin in the fact of our having fewer national melodies than almost any other nation on the face of the globe. Do we not hear daily of the Scotch, the Irish, and especially the Welsh — of the French, the Italian, the Spanish, the American, and even 'nigger' melodies? But where are we to look for the English? The fact is, that, of all the world we exhibit perhaps the most curious picture of pride and discontent. Absent from his country, an Englishman sees united in her all beauty and perfection, thinks of her with enthusiasm, and speaks of her as the mistress of his soul. Returned, the scene is totally changed: every country he has visited has something to recommend it above his own.

Doubts about the scope of England's folk music were certainly not justified, at least after the publication in 1838 of William Chappell's *Collection of National English Airs*, the object of which was 'to give practical refutation to the popular fallacy that England has no national music'. As for the Englishman's tendency to praise other cultures at the expense of his own, that is an explanation more whimsical than sound. Yet it cannot be denied that some English musicians suffered a sense of inferiority as they compared their art with current developments on the Continent. Not only did the Italian and German styles seem more advanced than their own, but there was an unexpected challenge from France, England's long-time rival.

One man responsible for this confrontation of cultures was the noted French music critic and historian, François-Joseph Fétis. In the spring of ·1829 Fétis paid an extended visit to London. His purpose was two-fold: he expected to serve as accompanist for Madame Malibran on her second English tour; and he intended to read a series of public lectures on the history and theory of music. For one reason or another, these plans did not materialize. Malibran's concerts were curtailed because of her excessively high fees, and the lecture series did not attract the expected response. In fact, only one lecture was given, at the home of Sir George Warrender. The remainder of the series was cancelled, according to *Grove's Dictionary*, because of the lateness of the season. But one suspects that there was a more compelling reason for this lack of interest; namely, that Dr. Crotch, Professor of Music at Oxford, was at that very moment delivering a similar series at the Royal Institution, where he had, in fact, been enlightening the minds of the public for a period of 30 years or more.

Never a man to retreat in the face of adverse circumstances, Fétis diverted his energies into the writing of a series of eight letters to his son, Eduard, in Paris, voicing his impressions 'sur l'état actuel de la musique à Londres'. The letters were printed initially in Fétis's journal, the *Revue musicale*, between 24 April and 2 July 1829. He regarded them as important enough to reprint them as a chapter in his *Curiosités historiques de la musique* (1830). By this time they had been translated into English and serialized in *The Harmonicon*, whose editor, William Ayrton, was one of the most enterprising journalists of his time. He provided a platform for Fétis's controversial views, but did not let the Frenchman's critique go unanswered. He responded to each of the letters with vigorous annotations, correcting, disputing, denying Fétis's observations point for point. The argument soon spilled over into the pages of the *Quarterly Musical Magazine*, where its editor, Richard Mackenzie Bacon, printed two long responses attributed to 'An Amateur' defending British musicianship and the institutions that supported it. Another comment came from the composer Henry Rowley Bishop, who found it necessary to contradict some unflattering remarks made about his work. His letter was duly published in *The Hamonicon*. The complete documentation of this correspondence is given in the Appendix, p. 237 below.

As is the case with most polemics, it is difficult to separate the issues from the personalities involved. Fétis's reputation as an uncompromising critic was well established. History has underlined the fact that he was dogmatic in the extreme, opinionated, intolerant, egocentric, and without doubt one of the most stimulating musical minds of the nineteenth century. In 1829 he was a vigorous 45 years of age and at the height of his powers. These attributes can be witnessed in the lithograph portrait made by J. B. Madou in 1831 and now in the Bibliothèque Royale in Brussels (see Plate I).

In his first letter to Eduard, dated 24 April 1829, Fétis foreshadows the outlines of his critical method. It is a sociological approach centred in the view that man is the product of his social environment, a concept that can be traced directly to Rousseau and the Encyclopedists. In Fétis's own words (as translated in *The Harmonicon*):

> It is on institutions, on the constitution of society considered in a musical point of view, on the habits of a people, and the influence of their language, that I ground the principle both of my praise and my critique.

Within this framework of ideas, Fétis formulates his own answer to that far-reaching question: are the English an unmusical people? In his considered opinion, English music did indeed occupy the lowest rung on the ladder of musical accomplishment. It suffered a serious handicap in receiving little or no support from the state. Granted, English mercantile society fostered the development of an admirable type of individual, but the kind of political freedom offered the individual in England's *laissez-faire* society had proved a mixed blessing as far as the arts were concerned. The artist, and particularly the musician, was forced to work out his salvation in an unsympathetic, even hostile world.

> The individual when left to himself, . . . isolated in the midst of society, is a feeble being, whose efforts are every moment liable to be paralysed . . .

PLATE I

F.-J. Fétis: lithograph by J. B. Madou
Brussels, Bibliothèque Royale

The traditional English view of music, even at this late date, remained within the orbit of Charles Burney's famous dictum to the effect that 'Music is an innocent luxury, unnecessary, indeed, to our existence, but a great improvement and gratification of the sense of hearing'. In other words, music played a peripheral role to the serious business of living.

Fétis attempts to defend his views on the basis of historical evidence. He cites the vitality of English music during the reigns of Henry VIII and Elizabeth I and claims it was due to the direct intervention of these monarchs in the musical affairs of the nation, plus the fact that they imported many celebrated Franch and Gallo-Belgian musicains into their courts. Nevertheless, English music from the late sixteenth century onwards entered into a decline from which it could be rescued only by the genius of Handel. Here is his version of that familiar *excuse*:

> Handel, with his lofty genius, his profound science, and his prodigious fecundity, came, at the commencement of the eighteenth century, to console England for the deplorable state of its music, by naturalizing himself an Englishman, by setting all his admirable works to English words, and bestowing every care in bringing their execution to perfection. Then commenced the reign of foreign musicians in London; all the great singers of Italy were successively invited to visit this capital, and were soon followed by instrumentalists of note.

The editor of *The Harmonicon* took sharp issue with this reading of history. He saw no significant influx of foreign musicians in the sixteenth century, and he found the condition of music at the commencement of the eighteenth as anything but deplorable if one took into account the surviving madrigal tradition and the vitality of English church music as represented by Farrant, Byrd, Gibbons, Child, Clarke and Croft — to say nothing of Purcell. He reminds Fétis that during the comparable period in France only one musician commanded the attention of the public — Lully, an Italian!

In his second letter, of 1 May 1829, Fétis directs his attention to the London orchestras of the period, particularly the Philharmonic Society. The spring of 1829 was not a very opportune time to pursue such an investigation. Several of the most important musicians of the King's Theatre were on strike beacause of a threatened reduction in their wages, and in protest to the high-handed methods of Nicholas Charles Bochsa, harp virtuoso and current Director of the King's Theatre. But the Philharmonic Concert, founded in 1813, was in reasonable good health. Fétis was struck by the energy of the ensemble, and did not hesitate to rank it as one of the two leading orchestras in Europe. Its only near rival, as might be expected, was the orchestra of the Ecole Royale (the Paris Conservatoire). The French orchestra excelled in its youthful vigour and flexibility. It displayed a superior sensitivity to graduations of light and shade, possessing that subtle quality of *chaleur*, or warmth of execution. In general, he felt that the strings of the London orchestra were surpassed by their Parisian counterparts, with the exception of the double bass section which was ruled over by the famous bass virtuoso, Dominico Dragonetti.

> These artists [the double basses] allow everything to be heard, mark distinctly every part of their bowing, as well in legato as in detached passages; preserve all the shades of expression; strike the note with unerring precision, and seem to use no greater effort than if they were playing the violin or viola.

One interesting sidelight to this discussion was a consideration of the respective roles of the leader and the conductor in French and English orchestras. The French ensemble customarily took its cues from a violinist-leader situated among the strings. In the course of time this musician moved to the rostrum at the front of the orchestra where he conducted with a bow or baton in the modern fashion. At the same time English orchestras still favoured the archaic arrangement in which the conductor was seated at a piano reading and occasionally playing from the full score. The worst result of this procedure was that the instrument could sometimes be heard and its timbre destroyed the effect intended by the composer.

The third letter, 10 May 1829, brings Fétis into vivid contact with one of the most characteristic of British musical institutions, the London musical club. He was invited to be a guest at a meeting of the Society of Melodists, one of the more recently established clubs, but one that conducted its meetings along the lines established by the Catch Club, founded in 1761, and the Glee Club, in 1783. The evening's programme was organized according to the traditional pattern. 'During dinner toasts were drunk to the king, to the glory of the British navy, to the prosperity of English melody, and to some of the most distinguished members of the society.' Needless to say, Fétis found the experience refreshing and original. It caused him to remark on the Englishman's steadfast adherence to his native traditions, a loyalty that extended to the favourite song forms, the catch and the glee.

229

> The English are devoted to their institutions; they carry their conviction in this regard to such a degree that nothing can shake it . . . Were the whole of Europe to raise its voice against catches and glees, these pieces of national music would not be admired a whit the less by every true-born Englishman.

One is tempted to dwell on that intriguing prospect of 'the whole of Europe' raising its voice against catches and glees, but Fétis does not elaborate on the point.

In the second part of his third letter, he makes a digression into the nature and history of Welsh music based on his own experience as a spectator at the Eisteddfod that took place on 6 May 1829. Here we find him in his element as a keen observer of musical phenomena, with an intense curiosity about unfamiliar styles. Not without reason has Fétis been called one of the founders of ethnomusicology. He is fascinated by the artistry of Richard Roberts, 'the blind bard of Caernavon', and by the intricate improvisations in a *pennillion* executed by three natives of Wales. William Ayrton, our critic's critic, reacted with some dismay to Fétis's enthusiasm for these primitive spectacles. He held that the Welsh in preserving a barbarous language and music were retarding the progress of civilization in a part of the island that still stood much in need of it. Fétis himself had arrived at a similar conclusion. He held that the 'wild airs' of the Welsh musicians served to confirm an impression he had already formed; namely, that in no part of the world, save perhaps in England, where barbarism is found so close by the side of civilization, could a similar spectacle have been witnessed.

In his fourth letter, dated 21 May 1829, Fétis directs his attention to the institution he regards as crucial to the development and survival of English music — the Royal Academy of Music. This is the point at which his inherent chauvinism comes to the surface. He cannot resist the temptation to deal in personalities rather than principles. He is particularly virulent in his treatment of Dr. Crotch, Director of the Royal Academy. Crotch was no mental giant but he exemplified more convincingly that any of his colleagues the ideal of the scientific musician in England. He also served as spokesman for the art to the general public through his *Specimens of Various Styles of Music* (London, *c.* 1807–22), a collection of musical examples used to illustrate his lectures. As mentioned above, he was engaged in giving a lecture series at precisely the time when Fétis arrived in London. If Fétis heard any of his rival's productions — and he undoubtedly did — he was not impressed.

> The lectures which the Doctor is this moment reading at the *Institute of Sciences* are not of a nature to excite a more exalted idea of his ideas or of his knowledge; for all he does is to give over and over again the specimens of different styles which he published in three volumes several years ago. In these lectures, each of which lasts an hour, the professor speaks for ten minutes without saying anything, and during the remainder of the time plays the compositions of different masters.

Fétis goes out of his way to cast aspersions on Crotch's reputation as a child prodigy. 'Dr. Crotch', he says, 'is an instance of the little dependence that is to be placed on precocity of talent, and how rarely the future of such prodigies corresponds to the expectation of the past.'

Another victim of Fétis's acid pen was the violinist Franz Cramer (1772–1848): 'the only reputation he enjoys is in the reminiscences of his father, a distinguished violinist who lived for many years in London'. The Professor of Cello, Robert Lindley, one of the most admired musicians of his time, was accused of having a 'vulgar style', while the theory department was in such a sad state that 'with the exception of a Frenchman named Jousse, there [did] not exist in London a single professor who [had] just notions of counterpoint, fugue, or the other parts of the art of writing'. Naturally, the two editors, Ayrton and Bacon, were quick to rise to the defence of their maligned colleagues. Poor Mr. Jousse, a modest instructor in the rudiments of music, and author of an elementary violin method, was caught in the cross-fire of these warring factions. Bacon, in the *Quarterly Musical Magazine*, is particulary scathing in his commentary.

> Hear this ye Clementis, ye Crotchs, ye Attwoods, ye Horsleys, ye Wesleys, ye Worgans, and ye Adams, and ye Bishops! Hear and hide your diminished heads!! But who is this erudite and elevated professor. (of musical science)? Ye will never guess, except his country discovers him to your sight. It is no less a person than M<small>R.</small> J<small>OUSSE</small>!!! Tremble therefore and abscond.

In all fairness it should be noted that Fétis gives high marks to several of the departments within the Academy, notably the piano section presided over by Cipriani Potter, the clarinets under Thomas Lindsay Willman and the flutes under Charles Nicholson. The principal composer was Thomas Attwood, whose compositions Fétis admires, but whose genius is blunted by the necessity of giving continual and fatiguing lessons. Thus the teaching staff of the Royal

Academy is not different from that of other music schools. Some instruction is good, some is unsatisfactory, but the chief weakness of the institution in Fétis's eyes resided in the fact that it did not have sufficient financial support from the government. Consequently it had to select its scholars from among those young musicians who came from affluent families, not necessarily those with the most talent.

In his fifth letter, dated 5 June 1829, Fétis addresses his son with some observations on the state of sacred music in England. He regards a flourishing condition in church music as prerequisite to the health of a nation's music in general. With this premise in mind, he sees little hope for England, 'where there is, properly speaking, no real church music, though occasionally music is performed in the churches'. Fétis admits that he is baffled by the nature of Anglican chant, attributing its lack of rhythmic definition to a fault originating in 'certain difficulties in pronunciation which I am not in a condition to estimate'. He also finds himself at a loss to understand the appeal of Henry Purcell, whose Te Deum and Jubilate he heard at a benefit service held in St. Paul's for the Sons of the Clergy.

> I must confess that my curiosity was considerable to hear the music of Purcell, whom the English proudly cite as worthy of being placed in the same rank with the greatest composers of Germany and Italy . . . I was in a perfectly admiring disposition of mind when the *Te Deum* of this giant began; but what was my disappointment upon hearing, instead of the masterpiece which they had promised me, a long succession of insignificant phrases, ill-connected modulations, and incorrect, albeit pretending, harmonies.

But he notes with admiration the great provincial music festivals, organized for charitable purposes, where complete oratorios were performed employing expensive soloists and massed choirs. At the same time he deplores the increasing commercialism of these events. His most memorable musical experience took place on 2 June, when he heard a chorus of between 6,000 and 7,000 children from the charity schools sing at a benefit concert given in their behalf at St. Paul's Cathedral.

> At the appointed signal, Mr. Attwood, the organist, sounded the key-note and seven thousand children's voices sang in unison the 100th Psalm: *All people that on earth do dwell*. To have any idea of the power of such an unison you must hear it. The organ, majestic as it is , is but an accessory to an effect like this.

232

The sixth and seventh letters, 12 and 22 June, are devoted to the lyric theatre. The first treats of Italian opera as performed in the King's Theatre, while the second is concerned with problems related to the maintenance of a national opera. What emerges from these letters is not so much a discussion of style or repertoire as a rehearsal of the trials and tribulations of the opera producer, beset by bankruptcy, menaced by financial scandals, threatened by fires and riots. In Fétis's view all of these conditions stem from one basic cause; namely, the fact that cultural institutions cannot be left at the mercy of private enterprise. They are not self-supporting. 'It is necessary that the government either should charge itself with them, or it should indemnify those who run the risk.'

Fétis begins his discussion of national opera with the somewhat paradoxical statement to the effect that the growth of a national school of opera presupposes a thorough acquaintance with Italian models. 'These models, whether as regards singing or composition, are more necessary to the English than to any other people, because their habitual calm renders them less disposed to the cultivation of music.' But economic factors rather than psychological ones provide the greatest deterrent to the development of a national operatic style in England. There is very little incentive to encourage English composers to work in the field of opera. There is no market for the publication of opera scores, only for 'favourite song' collections, pasticcios, and the like. Publishers such as Mazzinghi and Reeves issued quantities of these pseudo-operas consisting 'solely of shreds, snatched from the genuine Italian, French, or German operas, to which they have tacked airs of their own fashion, with some Scotch and Irish melodies; a sort of seasoning which is here indispensable'. In short, Fétis finds English opera suffers from a forced compromise between economic expediency and artistic integrity. The situation is summed up in the figure of the impresario Thomas Cooke.

> He was at once musical director, leader of the orchestra, and actor for the part of the second tenor, when the opera requires it. If the character has not to appear before the second act, this gentleman directs during the first, then yields his post to some miserable fiddler; returns afterwards, enveloped in a cloak, to beat the great drum in an *obligato* passage, because there is no one to fulfill this duty, or lends his assistance to the contrabasses, who are not sufficiently numerous. In this manner is music treated in the English opera.

The eighth and final letter, dated 2 July 1829, is in many respects a recapitulation of ideas previously expressed. Here, however, his principal target is the British aristocracy on whom he blames everything that is superficial or fashionable in the London musical scene. 'In England everyone learns music, not in order to know it, but because it is fashionable to expend money on this art.' Fashion also dictates attendance at private concerts as well as at public lectures.

> Become fashionable, and your reputation will be assured as well as your fortune. A man wishes to give a course of history, literature, or music, and knows nothing about the matter; yet this is of no consequence, for if it be fashionable to attend his lectures, all the world will flock thither. [The reference is obviously to Dr. Crotch.]

Thus, what began as an honest effort to understand and evaluate the state of London's music as seen through the eyes of a disinterested foreign visitor, has deteriorated into a sustained tirade against all English musical practices and institutions. As his hostility mounts Fétis loses all claims to objectivity, although in his final remarks there is, perhaps, some acknowledgment that his picture of England's musical life is more than slightly overdrawn.

> It was necessary that I should enter into these details, in order to shew the truth of the proposition which I have several times advanced, namely, that if music makes no progress in England, the want of institutions and the defective manner in which society is constituted, are the causes; for, I repeat, I do not believe the English are absolutely destitute of musical faculties. The English aristocracy, which injures every thing . . . does more harm to music than to any thing else.

It is clear that Fétis's letters are not models of social criticism. He may mave hit the mark on one or two occasions, but the bias of his position is too obvious for one to accept without reservations. But in spite of their superficial character, these letters offer some useful suggestions with respect to musicological method. For one thing they can lead us to a renewed appreciation of the resources to be found in the nineteenth-century music journals. Imogen Fellinger has provided us with a comprehensive bibliography of nineteenth-century periodicals (*Verzeichnis der Musikzeitschriften des 19. Jahrhunderts*, Regensburg, 1968), but a detailed investigation of their contents will be a job for generations of future scholars. Beginning with Rochlitz's *Allgemeine musikalische Zeitung*, founded in 1798, one can trace their influence through *Cäcilia* (edited by Gottfried Weber and Siegfried Dehn in Mainz), the *Berliner allgemeine musikalische Zeitung* (edited by A. B. Marx), *Iris im Gebiete der Tonkunst* (Rellstab), *Eutonia* (by

Johann Gottfried Hientzsch), to mention only a few. France entered the picture early with Fétis's *Revue musicale* (1827) which merged with the *Revue et Gazette musicale de Paris* in 1834. England was well represented, not only in the two journals treated in this paper, but in *The Musical World* (1836) and *The Musical Times*, the latter running uninterruptedly from 1844 to the present day. These periodicals were not isolated or circumscribed by national boundaries; they harboured an international community of critics and journalists who played no small part in the shaping of ideas and opinions which made musicology in the modern sense possible. What they printed can be taken as a guide to the musical mentality of their time, and a foundation on which future scholarship can be based. Examine, if you will, the table of contents of almost any of the journals mentioned above. It will present a profile of pre-musicological activity that is surprisingly comprehensive.

Here is a sampling of topics taken from the pages of *The Harmonicon*:

ETHNIC AND FOLK MUSIC
On the origin of music
The state of music in Calcutta
On the chorusses of the Persian Dervishes, with six specimens of
    Persian melodies
Capt. Parry on the music of the Exquimaux
State of music among the Turks
On the music of the Hindoos
Music of the Siamese
Bermese musical instruments

HISTORICAL STUDIES
An essay on the Gregorian Chant
Historical sketch of music in Germany
On the Semiography, or musical notation, of the Greeks
Origin and history of the organ
The *Miserere* of Allegri
Remarks on music of the 15th, 16th, and 17th centuries
History of the Conservatories of Italy

ACOUSTICS
Rev. C. Smith on the vibrations of a tuning-fork
On musical calculations
On the velocity of sound
Curious experiment relative to sound
On the ratios of the diatonic and chromatic intervals.
On the vibrations of air in cylindrical and conical tubes

THEORY AND AESTHETICS
On unity and variety in music
Letter on the character of keys
On the national characteristics of music
On the term 'imitation' as applied to music
Outline of a system of modern harmony
A treatise on melody

There is another aspect of Fétis's thought that is worth noting. He was one of the first to apply the methods of sociology to the study of music, that is, to recognize the importance of sociological explanations of musical behaviour. It was a method used increasingly throughout the nineteenth century, if not always with valid results. At worst it resulted in feeble generalizations about the nature of art in society. At best, however, it could supply a rich background of facts to cover the bare bones of history.

APPENDIX

DOCUMENTATION

(a) Eight letters from Fétis to his son, published in *La Revue musicale*, v (1829), and in English translation in *The Harmonicon* of the same year, with commentary by the editor of that journal

I (24 April 1829): *Revue musicale*, pp. 313–19; *Harmonicon*, pp. 181–4.

II (1 May 1829): *Revue musicale*, pp. 361–9; **Harmonicon*, pp. 214–17.

III (10 May 1829): *Revue musicale*, pp. 385–92; **Harmonicon*, pp. 184–6.

IV (21 May 1829): *Revue musicale*, pp. 409–17; *Harmonicon*, pp. 217–20.

V (5 June 1829): *Revue musicale*, pp. 457–64; *Harmonicon*, pp. 241–3.

VI (12 June 1829): *Revue musicale*, pp. 481–8; *Harmonicon*, pp. 244–6.

VII (22 June 1829): *Revue musicale*, pp. 529–36; *Harmonicon*, pp. 275–8.

VIII (2 July 1829): *Revue musicale*, pp. 560–67; *Harmonicon*, pp. 278–81.

* Letters II and III are inverted in the *Harmonicon* printing.

(b) Additional material

'Grande Rumeur musicale', *Revue musicale*, vi (1830), 82–89.
'The *Revue musicale* and The Harmonicon', *Harmonicon*, 1830, pp. 154–6.
'Dernier Mot: Sur les diatribes dirigées contre le rédacteur de la *Revue musicale*, à l'occasion de ses Lettres sur l'état actuel de la musique en Angleterre', *Revue musicale*, vi (1830), 553–63.
'Reply to M. Fétis, Editor of the *Revue Musicale*. By Henry R. Bishop, Esq.', *Harmonicon*, 1829, pp. 299–300.
'To the Editor', *The Quarterly Musical Magazine and Review*, x (1829), 311–22, 411–35.

Chapter 14

OPERA RESEARCH: TRADITION AND PROGRESS

Anna Amalie Abert

SOME 50 years ago Hermann Abert began a discussion of fundamental problems of operatic history with the words:

> Anyone concerned with operatic matters will do well to keep constantly in mind the fact that there is no absolute yardstick that can serve for all the various historical aspects of the subject; the question, 'What is an opera?' has to be answered afresh for each new generation at least.[1]

The methods, tasks and aims of opera research will naturally differ from generation to generation, depending on the particular manner in which a specific age views the phenomenon of opera. Indeed, the diversity of interpretations and viewpoints is especially noticeable because of the many-sidedness of the subject matter. It remains the perfect right of every young generation to believe it has found the philosophers' stone and to depreciate the work and achievements of its predecessors; though all progress must build on the past, each new age, through a broader perspective and greater fund of sources, really does revitalize opera research, allowing new aspects to be explored and, accordingly, new results obtained — and any member of an older generation who wishes to hold his own is forced to come to terms with fresh developments and to re-examine his own position. But this process must never be allowed to degenerate into an opposition of conservative and progressive attitudes. For though old notions must be abandoned, misconceptions resolved, and though historical personalities, events and developments constantly appear in new perspectives, the material to be researched itself remains the same. Even supposedly outdated opinions not infrequently resurface, and on closer examination the seemingly enormous differences between the old and the new often shrink to a mere shift in emphasis.

The purpose of this paper is not to discuss what modern opera research should be according to the opinion of ultra-progressives, but rather to show how it really is. It is especially important to realize that musicological interest has only recently turned towards opera on a larger and more intensive scale. Beginning in the mid-1950s and gaining momentum since the sixties, this tendency can be seen clearly by comparing conference programmes of the last twenty years. Since the 1958 Congress in Cologne opera has steadily increased its share of attention, whether in formal papers (for example four in Cologne, five in Ljubljana in 1967, eight in Copenhagen in 1972) or in round-table discussions and symposia (one in New York in 1961, four in Salzburg in 1964, three in Bonn in 1970). Previously, and in the period between the Wars, opera played at best a very subordinate role at musicological congresses — or none at all. In contrast, at the Vienna Congress in 1909 an entire section, with no less than nine papers, was devoted to opera. And at the preceding Basle Congress in 1906 Ludwig Schiedermair could begin his paper on the state of opera history:

> The flowering of the music drama in the second half of the nineteenth century is surely the reason why music historians again turned more of their attention to the history of opera. The painstaking scholarly treatment it is now accorded must be attributed to the development of a genuine discipline of musical scholarship in the last decades of the nineteenth century.[2]

It is true that the fruits of opera history in the decades around the turn of the century were modest in quantity; but in quality they were sometimes highly significant, with results that are in many ways still indicative. It must be remembered that this generation of researchers, unlike those of today, had no adequate earlier work on which they could build, by way of either reliable editions or scholarly literature. At least at the outset, therefore, it was not possible for them to engage in the critical re-examination of earlier views — an activity that is often so fruitful in any area of research and which in fact provides continuity from one generation of scholars to the next. Instead, theirs were the joys of discovery; yet even here the lack of suitable material for comparison frequently left them somewhat helpless. As true scholars, however, these men sought to find reference points against which to order, evaluate and bring into a broader continuity the findings of their individual researches. But here, once again, their limited source knowledge meant that they lacked the necessary material. Moreover, the new historical approach that sought to understand every work of art in the context of its own time was only beginning to emerge, and a tendency towards hero-worship still survived as a legacy of the Romantic era. All these factors worked together with the development of the music drama in the second half of the nineteenth century, referred to by Schiedermair, to determine the character of opera research during this initial period. It was clearly a reflection of its time. With the exception of the very beginnings of opera, whose relatively circumscribed history had already allowed consideration in some detail by Winterfeld and especially by Vogel and Goldschmidt,[3] the overall development, because of the shortage of source-material, was portrayed through a few outstanding composers, and the whole was then set in the context, not of its own time, but of the turn of the century — that is, of its hero, Richard Wagner.

Wagner's influence, in fact, positive or negative, can be felt strongly not only in the operatic works composed around the turn of the century, but also in the opera research of that time. In this respect a comment by Romain Rolland is particularly indicative:[4]

> During the course of this study I shall frequently refer to the name, example and reflections of Wagner. This in no way prevents me from reserving my total independence of mind and feeling. But one is constantly obliged to revert to him, not only because he is the termination of our musical evolution and, as it were, the synthesis of all progress accomplished before him, but particularly also because he is almost the only musician of the century to have pondered at length on music and on the art of drama.

After this profession of faith it is not surprising to find Wagner applied as the object of comparison in the most diverse contexts. In Rolland's view, for example, the scenic ostentation in Michelangelo Rossi's opera *Erminia sul Giordano* destroys the equilibrium between the arts; only in Wagner, with the help of the modern orchestra, did something of the sort become feasible, since only his dominating artistic understanding had the power to forge together the mass of different elements into a single unified art-work.

Alongside Wagner, Gluck also appears as both hero-figure and model in this early period of operatic research. Rolland, for example, in relating Monteverdi to Gluck, found that the former had not yet realized his ideal of the *Tragédie humaine* in his own century, and that only Gluck's genius at the end of the eighteenth century had made it possible. The two German scholars Heinrich Bulthaupt and C. H. Bitter both compared Gluck and Wagner, Bulthaupt favouring

Wagner over Gluck, Bitter praising Gluck over Wagner.[5] Both display the typical subjective verve of this pioneer generation that now strikes us as strange and occasionally comic, but also as fascinating. Surveys of operatic history written about the turn of the century are generally built around the great masters, Monteverdi-Gluck- Mozart-Wagner, regarding other composers more or less as forerunners of imitators. Thus in Bulthaupt, Cherubini and Méhul become imitators of Mozart. Even Oscar Bie's book written as late as 1913 follows this general scheme.[6]

More important for operatic research than Wagner's role as hero-figure, however, was the enormous influence exercised by his works, and by the views expressed in his writings, on the historical approach of the music historians of that time. This becomes particularly noticeable in the case of critical musicologists, who while striving for objectivity unconsciously submitted to this historical consciousness. Thus Rolland, for example, saw operatic decadence already setting in with Scarlatti. Perhaps the most characteristic example of this mode of thought can be found in the writings of Hermann Kretzschmar, who can be regarded as one of the leading opera researchers of the period. It is true that in his essay 'Aus Deutschlands italienischer Zeit' he strongly challenged the contemptuous rejection of eighteenth-century Neapolitan opera by such contemporary music historians as Bulthaupt and Bitter, as well as their naive belief in the evolutionary progress of music, and with justification accused them of making judgements on the basis of a much too limited amount of source-material.[7] Yet when he writes of the 'vapid display of coloratura' in many arias and describes Metastasio's dramas as being 'inimical to music' it becomes apparent that in reality he too rejects the very essence of Neapolitan opera. He acknowledges only the aspect of it that relates to the 'music drama', namely the large-scale *accompagnati*. These conclusions, however, did not prevent Kretzschmar from appealing for more intensive study of the works of these composers. Edward Dent, in his biography of Scarlatti (1905), was one of the first to follow this summons.

Even Kretzschmar's essay 'Die venetianische Oper und die Werke Cavallis und Cestis',[8] which was of fundamental importance during his time, exhibits the same mixture of scholarly objectivity and time-bound subjectivity when, for instance, he sees as the cardinal error of Venetian librettos 'the total incapacity to think in terms of antiquity, grandeur or ethics'. The Wagnerian influence is most pronounced, however, in his portrayal of nineteenth-century opera as a whole in his *Geschichte der Oper*, published only in 1919 but written over a period of many years. In it, such passages as the enraptured description of *Der Freischütz*, the rejection of Meyerbeer and many other examples give one the impression of hearing Wagner himself, although here too there is often an unmistakable striving for objectivity.

The first major distinction, then, between past and present opera research is the difference in criteria by which historical phenomena are evaluated, caused in turn by the difference in the available quantity of source-material. A second, no less important, is the different significance accorded by music historians then and now to the individual artist in relationship to society as a whole. Here again Romain Rolland serves as a particularly characteristic example. Drawing a parallel between Alessandro Scarlatti's role in Italian opera and Reinhard Keiser's in German, he sees Scarlatti as signifying the end of a magnificent era within a decadent environment, Keiser as representing a new beginning for a culturally awakening people. If this finds expression in their works, Rolland stresses, it is not the fault of the respective social conditions, but rather the fault or to the credit of the artist himself: Scarlatti had been satisfied with reflecting the taste of his environment without attempting to improve it, whereas Keiser had endeavoured to raise German art to a higher level of perfection. The vulnerability in fact of Rolland's thesis is not the point here; important in our context is only the conclusion Rolland draws from it: 'As Schiller said, it is for the artist to command the people, not the people the artist!'. This emphasis on the importance of genius runs through all the writings of the period. With Kretzschmar it is apparent when he repeatedly attributes changes within the genre to a lack of suitable talent: in his *Geschichte der Oper*, for instance, the rapid rise of *opera buffa* is credited to the deficiency of outstanding composers within the realm of *opera seria*.

In this we can also see the third and most important difference between tradition and progress in opera research: the different roles assigned to society and the environment. It is not at all the case, as is often supposed, that the earlier historians totally disregarded these matters. Kretzschmar, for example, in the introduction to his *Geschichte der Oper*, stresses the necessity of referring to theatre and stage statistics and to contemporary memoirs in order to establish the position of individual works in the repertoire, their reception by the audience and the public's general preferences, and he calls for a thorough examination of librettos, which he considers to mirror better than any other source the cultural and moral life of a time and its people. What can this mean except a conception of opera as a

242

reflection of the social and intellectual life of a given period? The older generation was fully aware of the strong links between the genre of opera and society, although this was viewed as only a peripheral matter and did not affect the actual creation and character of a work of art. In general it was sufficient to establish the social conditions in question and then to transfer one's full attention to the works themselves, without worrying too much about the connection between the two. Romain Rolland goes so far as to deny any such link when, discussing the transition to Venetian opera, he writes that the *opéra populaire* had effectively nothing in common with the *opéra public*, concluding: 'It is not the accidental circumstances of a production that determine the character of a work but its animating spirit, its inner purpose'. This attitude can be seen particularly clearly in the writings on comic opera. Rolland and Kretzschmar present *The Beggar's Opera*, for example, purely as a primitive opera parody, without the slightest acknowledgement of its important and powerful social criticism. The *opéra comique* is described by Rolland as a 'joli monstre', a pastime that is not to be taken quite seriously, though Kretzschmar does allude to the political undertones found even at the earliest period of the genre.

Overall, the writings of this period give the impression that the neglect of social considerations was not solely a matter of basic attitudes, but also simply the result of a lack of relevant information. These early researchers, after all, were pioneers, confronted with an abundance of unknown material. They had enough to do merely in taking stock of the available scores and libretti and attempting some degree of analysis and stylistic classification. However outdated and even comical their views may be at times, condescension is quite out of place: the younger generation stands on their shoulders.

The music historians who began their work after the turn of the century, such as Abert, Dent, Prunières, Solerti and others, consistently continued the tradition established by their predecessors. But they were no longer under the shadow of Wagner and the subjective attitudes of their time; they worked in the historical awareness of objective modern scholarship. Thus, despite their proximity to the older generation, they stand, in the terms of our present title, on the side not of tradition but of progress. On the other hand, they did maintain the traditional approach in regarding environmental conditions as being subordinate in importance to the work itself. Their main emphasis was still on the music, to which the text assumed only a supporting role; the scenic aspect, as before, was only of peripheral interest. Only in the period between the wars did opera research begin gradually to branch out into literary and purely theatrical questions and into art history. The interdisciplinary character of the subject-area became more and more apparent.

With these developments the ground was gradually laid upon which the most recent progress in opera research could be carried out. The gulf that separates this youngest generation from the oldest was bridged by the timely progressive work of two further generations. This continuity can no more be doubted than the genuine progressiveness of the modern working methods. On the basis of the achievements of the past, the present generation is now in a position, on the one hand, to view the material in a new light and to classify it in new and broader contexts. The old hero-worship of the individual has been replaced by the veneration of society as the hero figure. On the other hand, modern scholars have become acutely aware of the gaps left, through insufficient source-material, by the older generation, and are endeavouring to fill them. Their methods, however, are fundamentally unchanged from those of their predecessors.

In contrast, the methods employed in the first current are extensively new. The centre of attention is not the individual work of art but its social environment. Above all, the work of art is no longer seen as a unique creation, but as something changeable, dependent for its spiritual genesis, practical realization and continued existence on social, economic and political conditions. It is not only classified stylistically into a given time period, as was previously the case, but is also interpreted out of that period as a product of the above mentioned environmental conditions. These new assessments carry modern opera research far beyond all previous endeavours. They open a new and wider field of activity, whether purely musicological in nature, involving questions of transmission, revision and authenticity, or whether interdisciplinary in character, probing into the various different art forms and organisations that determine the shape of an opera, as well as into its practical regulation and the public for which it was written.

It was particularly in this first direction that modern opera research took on a new appearance; but that does not mean that it has dominated recent work in terms of quantity. On the contrary, a large number of young scholars are occupied with filling in gaps, as mentioned above — that is, with the collection and analysis of hitherto unexplored material. In doing so they are in general continuing the